THE CRISIS OF LITERATURE
IN THE 1790s

This book offers an original study of the debates which arose in the 1790s about the nature and social role of literature. Paul Keen shows how these debates were situated at the intersection of the French Revolution and a more gradual revolution in information and literacy reflecting the aspirations of the professional classes in eighteenth-century England. He shows these movements converging in hostility to a new class of readers, whom critics saw as dangerously subject to the effects of seditious writings or the vagaries of literary fashion. The first part of the book concentrates on the dominant arguments about the role of literature and the status of the author; the second shifts its focus to the debates about working-class activists, radical women authors and the Orientalists and examines the growth of a Romantic ideology within this context of political and cultural turmoil.

PAUL KEEN is Assistant Professor in the English Department at Simon Fraser University, British Columbia. His articles and reviews have appeared in *Mosaic*, *Irish University Review*, *British Journal of Eighteenth-Century Studies*, *The Wordsworth Circle*, *English Studies in Canada* and *Critical Mass*.

CAMBRIDGE STUDIES IN ROMANTICISM 36

THE CRISIS OF LITERATURE IN THE 1790s

This series aims to foster the best new work in one of the most challenging fields within English literary studies. From the early 1780s to the early 1830s a formidable array of talented men and women took to literary composition, not just in poetry, which some of them famously transformed, but in many modes of writing. The expansion of publishing created new opportunities for writers, and the political stakes of what they wrote were raised again by what Wordsworth called those 'great national events' that were 'almost daily taking place': the French Revolution, the Napoleonic and American wars, urbanization, industrialization, religious revival, an expanded empire abroad and the reform movement at home. This was an enormous ambition, even when it pretended otherwise. The relations between science, philosophy, religion and literature were reworked in texts such as *Frankenstein* and *Biographia Literaria*; gender relations in *A Vindication of the Rights of Woman* and *Don Juan*; journalism by Cobbett and Hazlitt; peotic form, content and style by the Lake School and the Cockney School. Outside Shakespeare studies, probably no body of writing has produced such a wealth of response or done so much to shape the responses of modern criticism. This indeed is the period that saw the emergence of those notions of 'literature' and of literary history, especially national literary history, on which modern scholarship in English has been founded.

The categories produced by Romanticism have also been challenged by recent historicist arguments. The task of the series is to engage both with a challenging corpus of Romantic writings and with the changing field of criticism they have helped to shape. As with other literary series published by Cambridge, this one will represent the work of both younger and more established scholars, on either side of the Atlantic and elsewhere.

For a complete list of titles published see end of book

THE CRISIS OF
LITERATURE IN THE 1790s

Print Culture and the Public Sphere

PAUL KEEN

CAMBRIDGE
UNIVERSITY PRESS

CAMBRIDGE UNIVERSITY PRESS
Cambridge, New York, Melbourne, Madrid, Cape Town, Singapore, São Paulo

Cambridge University Press
The Edinburgh Building, Cambridge CB2 2RU, UK

Published in the United States of America by Cambridge University Press, New York

www.cambridge.org
Information on this title: www.cambridge.org/9780521653251

First published 1999
This digitally printed first paperback version 2006

A catalogue record for this publication is available from the British Library

Library of Congress Cataloguing in Publication data

Keen, Paul.
The crisis of literature in the 1790s: print culture and the public sphere / Paul Keen.
p.   cm.– (Cambridge studies in romanticism; 36)
Includes bibliographical references (p.).
ISBN 0-521-65325-8 (hardback)
1. English literature–18th century–History and criticism.
2. Literature–Public opinion–Great Britain–History–18th century.
3. Authorship–Public opinion–Great Britain–History–18th century.
4. Literature and society–Great Britain–History–18th century.
5. Books and reading–Great Britain–History–18th century.
6. Romanticism–Great Britain–History–18th century.
7. Printing–Great Britain–History–18th century. 8. Great Britain–History–1789–1820.
I. Title. II. Series.
PR448.S64K44 1999
820.9´006–dc21   99-11165   CIP

ISBN-13 978-0-521-65325-1 hardback
ISBN-10 0-521-65325-8 hardback

ISBN-13 978-0-521-02722-9 paperback
ISBN-10 0-521-02722-5 paperback

*For my father and mother, and for my wife,
Cynthia, with love.*

In my introduction to the Third Part, feeling the importance of my subject in its various branches, I asserted that, 'LITERATURE, *well or ill conducted*, IS THE GREAT ENGINE *by which*, I am fully persuaded, ALL CIVILIZED STATES *must ultimately be supported or overthrown*.' I am now more and more deeply impressed with this truth, if we consider the nature, variety and extent of the word, Literature.

T. J. Mathias, *The Pursuits of Literature*

I went out drinking with Thomas Paine,
He said all revolutions are not the same.

Billy Bragg, 'North Sea Bubble'

Contents

Acknowledgements

The idea that all texts bear the traces of many overlapping communities of readers and writers has become an article of faith in the academy today, but it is also an accurate description of the genesis of this book. I am extremely fortunate to have enjoyed the encouragement and insights of many friends in the Eighteenth-Century Studies Group at the University of York where I wrote this, and in the Politics of Print Culture MA. in the Department of English at Simon Fraser University where I revised it for publication. First thanks must go to John Barrell, whose influence has been challenging and liberating in equal measures. He performed the delicate task of encouraging me to confront my own unexamined assumptions in such a way that my gratitude, and my enthusiasm for the project, grew throughout the three and a half years that I worked with him on it. Marilyn Butler, Stephen Copley, Greg Dart, Leith Davis, Tom Furniss, Mary Ann Gillies, Ludmilla Jordanova, Jon Klancher, Emma Major, Margaret Linley, Betty Schellenburg, John Whatley and Jerry Zaslove all offered important suggestions along the way. Four close friends have influenced this book in less direct but more fundamental ways: Steve Boyd, Janice Fiamengo, Scott McFarlane and Tarik Kafala have all insisted on the larger contexts within which this sort of work is rooted. I hope that it has been faithful to their influence. The input and support of all of these people were matched by my mother's enthusiasm and insights, which made this project not only better but more rewarding than it would otherwise have been. I would like to thank Josie Dixon and my two readers from Cambridge University Press, who ensured that the process of seeing this book through to publication remained a learning process. Needless to say, all of the errors in this book are my own, but there would have been several more of them if not for the diligent attention and collegiality of Rachel Coldicutt during the copy-editing stage. I was fortunate to be able to rely on the support of the Social Sciences and Research Council of Canada. A President's Research Grant and a Publications Grant from Simon Fraser University helped enormously with the latter stages. Part of chapter 5 will appear in an article included in *English Literature and the Other Languages*, edited by Ton Hoenselaars and Marius Buning (Rodopi, 1999), and is reprinted here with their kind permission. Marx and Engels watched over every page, and were it not for their fervour for batting crumpled-up versions of it down the stairs, this project might not have gone through as many stages as it did.

Heartfelt thanks are due to the friends from outside the university who grew tired of hearing about the eighteenth century and who dragged me to Leeds matches (they never won!) and who helped to make my years in York as entertaining and, frequently, as distracting as they were: Terry and Olivia, Pete, Guy, Terry-Ball, James, Andy, Mick, Opera-John, Mark and Sabine, and Tim and Melinda. Tarik, Ben and Guy provided an unfailing supply of beds, couches, floors and backgammon within easy range of the British Library. Maggie let me pull pints for a year in the Golden Ball. Cycle Heaven kept me on two wheels. Jim and Eric proved to be ideal neighbours in the York Beer Shop. Finally, I am more grateful than I can say to have been blessed with the company of the ringleader of this crew, Cynth, who ensured that a project which might at times have felt like a burden always remained an adventure, and who during these years showed great wisdom in agreeing to become my permanent literary critic and partner.

Abbreviations

AR	*Analytical Review*
AAR	*Asiatic Annual Register*
BC	*British Critic*
ER	*Edinburgh Review*
GM	*Gentleman's Magazine*
MM	*Monthly Magazine*
MR	*Monthly Review*
RR	*Retrospective Review*

Problems now and then

Raymond Williams begins his foreword to *Languages of Nature* with William Hazlitt's report, in 1825, of a conversation about the dead. 'I suppose the two first persons you would choose to see', writes Hazlitt, 'would be the two greatest names in English literature, Sir Isaac Newton and Mr Locke.' Williams's point is that if 'the use of "literature" there is now surprising, where "science" or "natural philosophy" might be expected, the problem is as much ours as theirs'.[1] This book is rooted squarely within that problem. Its focus lies along the disputed border between 'the literary' and the merely 'textual', and in the gap between definitions of literature in our own age and in what is now known as the Romantic period, a time of social and technological transformation during which literature became a site of ideological contestation, generating a series of questions with far-reaching implications: what constituted 'literature'? What sort of truth claims or authority did it possess? What kind of community should it address?

If an important part of the recent rise of interdisciplinary approaches has been the exploration of the historical evolution of the academic disciplines themselves, then it may be of some help to our own debates to understand more about the theoretical tensions of this earlier age, not least because those struggles found their partial resolution in the development of the academic discipline of English Literature, which is today the subject of various theoretical challenges that aim at redrawing the boundaries between the disciplines.[2] The 'enlightened philosophers' of the late eighteenth century were chastised by critics such as Edmund Burke for arguments about the relationship between literature and political reformation that are both wholly different from, and strangely similar to, the claims advanced by the advocates of 'the new cultural politics of difference' who are dismissed just as sum-

1

marily today as the politically correct.[3] The same questions about
literature – what it is, what sort of truth claims or cultural authority it possesses, and what kind of community has access to that
authority – have resurfaced in new but equally powerful ways.[4]

Williams is correct in saying that 'the problem is as much ours
as theirs' because the definition of literature has *always* been a
problem: it has always been the focus of struggles between multiple overlapping social constituencies determined to assert contending definitions, or to appropriate similar definitions in sometimes radically opposed ways. And this struggle has always (though
not always explicitly) been political: a means of laying claim to
important forms of symbolic capital, of legitimating or contesting
social privileges by writing the myths of a national or regional
community, or by naturalizing or protesting against changing
relations of production. These struggles never take place in a
vacuum. They represent different forms and levels of engagement,
attempts to speak the most powerful existing languages of public
virtue, morality, and political and legal authority, in different ways
and for different reasons. Alluding to Paul De Man's comment
that audience is a mediated term, Jon Klancher argues that

the cultural critic or historian must multiply the mediators, not eliminate them. He or she must excavate the cultural institutions, the competitive readings, the social and political constraints, and above all, the
intense mutualities and struggles in social space that guide and block
the passage of signs among historical writers, readers and audiences.[5]

Offering a similar argument for a more socially grounded exploration of literary culture, Robert Darnton rejects 'the great-man,
great-book view of literary history' as a 'mystification' of literary
production which occults the important role of 'literary middlemen' such as publishers, printers, booksellers, editors, reviewers
and literary agents[6]. He suggests that widening our focus to
include the many texts which a 'canon of classics' approach has
encouraged us to ignore will 'open up the possibility of rereading
literary history. And if studied in connection with the system for
producing and diffusing the printed word, they could force us to
rethink our notion of literature itself.'[7]

My own critical project is driven by a similar interest in the
shifting cultural geography within which literary texts are
inscribed, and out of which their meanings are inevitably pro-

duced. Darnton pursues this aim by shifting his attention from the great men and books of canonical literature to the middlemen and supposedly lesser authors of the publishing industry, and by concentrating his focus on original editions, 'seizing them in all their physicality' in order to 'grasp something of the experience of literature two centuries ago'.[8] Klancher widens his focus by attending to a social category that poets such as William Wordsworth reduced into abstraction – the identity of reading audiences. This book seeks to recuperate as a lively area of critical debate another theoretical concern that was similarly effaced by Romantic poets: the meta-critical issue of the definition of literature. Rather than offering any stable definition of literature in the Romantic period, I treat the tensions between the various responses as a complex and shifting field of discursive conflict.[9]

In offering a few initial comments about the most general characteristics that were attributed to literature in the period, I am obviously implicating myself within the very struggles from which I want to preserve a critical distance. But given the historical confusion highlighted by Williams, it is probably worthwhile emphasizing that for most people who thought about it at all, and contrary to many of our inherited assumptions, literature referred not merely to works of imaginative expression but to works in *any* subject. The January 1795 edition of the highly conservative journal the *British Critic* listed 'the several articles of literature' that it covered, in order of importance, as: 'Divinity, Morality, History, Biography, Antiquities, Geography, Topography, Politics, Poetry, British Poets Republished, Translations of Classics, Natural Philosophy and History, Medicine, Transactions of Learned Societies, Law, General Literature' (*BC* (1795): i). In an account of the current state of literature, the *Monthly Magazine* similarly argued that

if former times have enjoyed works of more fancy, and sublimity of imagination, than are given to us, we, in return, possess more useful acquisitions. If they have had their Spencer, Tasso, and Shakespere, we boast Newton, Locke, and Johnson. – Science, taste, and correction, are indeed the characteristics of the present day (*MM* 7 (1799): 112).

The *Monthly Review* reflected this assessment in its celebration of the Dissenting theologian, political theorist, chemist, and educational pioneer Joseph Priestley (in July 1791, the same month that Priestley's house and library were destroyed by a Church-and-

King mob in Birmingham) as 'the literary wonder of the present times' (*MR* 5 (1791): 303).

This approach to literature was reflected not only in the wide range of subject matter that was attributed to it, but in assumptions about its social function. However differently they might interpret the claim, critics on both sides of the political divide could find some measure of common ground in the *Analytical Review*'s conviction, in its discussion of the Birmingham riots, 'that the diffusion of knowledge tends to the promotion of virtue; and that morals can form the only stable basis for civil liberty' (*AR* 11 (1791): 175). The *Times* would affirm this role in its response to the planned increase in stamp duties two decades later: 'such a measure would tend to the suppression of general information, and would thereby incalculably injure the great cause of order and liberty *which has been maintained no less by British literature than by British valour*, and to which the Press of this country may honestly boast that it has contributed no weak or inefficient support'.[10] Literature, or the republic of letters as it was often referred to, was celebrated by the advocates of this vision as the basis of a communicative process in which all rational individuals could have their say, and in which an increasingly enlightened reading public would be able to judge the merit of different arguments for themselves. It is in this sense of publicity, more than any idea of imaginative plentitude, that we must understand both the ideal of the universality of literature in the period *and* the exclusions which this ideal helped to legitimate.

The hopes and anxieties generated by this communicative ideal have strong parallels with responses to 'the information revolution' in our own age. Although rooted in the printing press rather than computers (the Internet or World-Wide Web, electronic publishing), it was similarly discussed in terms of empowerment, rationalization, and inevitably, alienation.[11] Commenting on the resemblance of the eighteenth-century revolution to our own, Clifford Siskin notes the ambivalence which the spectre of technological progress aroused:

Echoes of their mix of promise and threat, anticipation and dread, resound in the writings of the eighteenth and early nineteenth centuries in Britain – a time and a place when the newly disturbing technology was writing itself . . . Having lived so comfortably and so long with this now mundane technology, we must work to reconstruct the shock that accompanied its initial spread in Britain. Writing proliferated then as something new through, in large part, writing about writing – that is, writers through the eighteenth century were so astonished by the sheer volume of writing they began to encounter that they wrote about it – and thereby astonished themselves.[12]

This book is, in part, an exploration of those shockwaves; it focuses on many of the people who wrote about writing, but it also emphasizes that some people embraced writing's emancipatory promise – an enthusiasm which only heightened the discomfort of others. Focusing on the enthusiasts, Darnton suggests that the French 'revolutionaries knew what they were doing when they carried printing presses in their civic processions and when they set aside one day in the revolutionary calendar for the celebration of public opinion'.[13] The parallels between these epochs reverberate throughout this study. So too, I hope, do the many differences. Rather than insisting on a precise correlation, I am suggesting this analogical relationship in order to displace the loftier equation of literature with 'imaginative expression'.

In *The Function of Criticism*, Terry Eagleton describes the dominant eighteenth-century concept of literature in terms similar to my own emphasis on a communicative process between rational individuals:

Only in this ideal discursive sphere is exchange without domination possible; for to persuade is not to dominate, and to carry one's opinion is more an act of collaboration than of competition . . . What is at stake in the public sphere, according to its own ideological self-image, is not power but reason. Truth, not authority, is its ground, and rationality, not domination, its daily currency. (17)

There are few better descriptions of the appeal of this version of literature in the period. My quarrel with it, however, is precisely over the question of period. Eagleton's differentiation between this discourse and the dominant approach to literature in the age that followed conforms to a crude strategy of periodization which distinguishes between the Enlightenment and Romanticism.[14] His argument, of the latter period, that '[c]riticism in the conventional sense can no longer be a matter of delivering verifiable norms, for . . . normative assumptions are precisely what the negating force of art seeks to subvert', forgets that most reviewers continued to cover a far wider literary field than is suggested by the reference to 'art' (41). Nor was 'judgement' necessarily 'tainted with a deeply suspect rationality' (42). For many, the reviews were important precisely because of their ability to facilitate rational debates by exercising proper judgement at a time when the increasing levels of literary production threatened this communicative process.[15]

By reducing the scope of literature to aesthetic expression, and by assuming that criticism was felt to be incompatible with the exercise of reason, Eagleton tumbles down a slippery theoretical slope which equates a discussion of literature in what we now refer to as the Romantic period with 'Romantic literature' – a body of writings which is in turn equated with a set of master narratives that are widely known as 'the ideology of Romanticism'. Rather than reproducing this before-and-after scenario, I will argue that we need to rethink the relationship between Enlightenment and Romantic discourses in terms of the sort of historical interpenetration which emerges out of an analysis of the anxieties generated by the struggle to assert contending definitions of literature as a politically charged social phenomenon. The distinction between literature as aesthetic expression and this more broadly focused approach, in which the emphasis was more educational than spiritual, is exemplified in a passage from Leigh Hunt's journal, *The Reflector*: 'Pursue the course of poetry in England, and you will find it accompanied with literature . . . [England's poets] by their literature enriched their poetry; and what they borrowed from the public stock of art and science, they repaid with interest, by the pleasure and instruction which they afford mankind' (1 (1812): 358–9). Far from equating literature – 'the public stock of art and science' – with poetry, the passage reverses modern assumptions by suggesting that poetry is better when its author is well-acquainted with literature.

The ideal of the bourgeois public sphere was a dominant but highly contested position that was most closely associated with the reformist middle class. Conservative thinkers worried that literary freedom led to political unrest, that the universalist rhetoric of the public sphere reflected the particular interests of the professional classes, and that the legal distinction between speculative and seditious works could no longer be relied upon to regulate the free play of intellectual debate. Equally disconcerting was what seemed to be the overproduction and the increasingly fashionable status of literature, which unsettled its equation with the diffusion of knowledge and social progress. Reviews were hailed as a possible means of halting this sense of cultural decline, but critics were frequently denounced for acting as demagogues rather than 'sovereigns of reason'.[16] What was ultimately at stake in these debates was the proximity of the literary and political public spheres. The more reformist the critic, the more he or she tended to insist on their close connection, whereas conservative critics tended to think of them as distinct cultural domains.

Nor was there any consensus about the limits of the interpretation of this ideal of publicity amongst those who agreed with it in principle. Debates about the usefulness of literature as a public sphere were exacerbated by the growth of what Nancy Fraser has described as 'subaltern counterpublics', whose protests against the exclusionary nature of the republic of letters unsettled the social boundaries which made this vision possible.[17] Attempts by working-class and women activists to appropriate the Enlightenment belief in the reformist power of print culture were dismissed as evidence of the revolutionary agenda of people who could not appreciate the difference between ideas and actions. Equally troubling, however, was the hybridity of both groups – lying outside of the male learned classes but determined to claim an equal share in the blessings of the Enlightenment – at a time when the social authority of literature already seemed to have been eroded by its very popularity. Coleridge argued that 'among other odd burs and kecksies, the misgrowth of our luxuriant activity, we now have a READING PUBLIC – as strange a phrase, methinks, as ever forced a splenetic smile on the staid countenance of Meditation; and yet no fiction! For our Readers have, in good truth, multiplied exceedingly.' Critics worried that modern readers preferred stylish appearances over 'serious Books', that authors with more greed than talent had become successful by appeasing them, and that authors of real merit were being overshadowed.[18] In such an atmosphere, it was easier for critics to denounce those who asserted their rightful place in the expanded reading public as part of the problem rather than to welcome them as potentially serious writers and readers. Or, if these new readerships were allowed to be serious in their attitudes towards literature, this commitment was denounced as evidence of a politically radical spirit determined to subvert the established social order.

The political changes triggered by the French Revolution, which

I examine in chapter one, unfolded far more rapidly than did the history which I focus on in chapter two, which treats the dream of the republic of letters as an expression of the aspirations of the professional classes. But as debates arose about the relationship between literature and political authority, these apparently distinct histories became part of the same story of the fragmentation of the ideal of literature as a public sphere. The excesses generated by the French Revolution, on the one hand, and by the information revolution, on the other, converged in an antagonism towards those new readerships who, critics argued, could not be trusted to resist either the inflammatory effects of seditious writings or the vagaries of literary fashion. Ironically, however, if these emergent groups were denounced for their irrationality, it was partly because their appropriation of the Enlightenment emphasis on literature as a guarantee of rational liberty coincided with broader concerns about the sustained viability of precisely this equation.

The movement from chapter 1 to chapter 2 presupposes two critical transitions: a shift in focus from literature to authors, and a redefinition of politics as a struggle for professional distinction (the status of the author) rather than for national agency (revolution, government reform, the rights of man). As Nancy Fraser puts it:

[the] elaboration of a distinctive culture of civil society and of an associated public sphere was implicated in the process of bourgeois class formation; its practices and ethos were markers of 'distinction' in Pierre Bourdieu's sense, ways of defining the emergent elite, of setting it off from the older aristocratic elites it was intent on displacing on the one hand and from the various popular and plebeian strata it aspired to rule on the other.[19]

The first of these shifts, from a focus on a cultural product (literature) to a group of producers (authors), generates a correspondingly different matrix of social concerns, values, and tensions that found their most coherent articulation in terms of classical republicanism. Saying this, however, necessarily invokes an ongoing historical debate between critics who have identified two very different discourses – classical republicanism and bourgeois liberalism – as the dominant discourse of the age. Exploring the tensions between these different discourses in the late eighteenth century, Isaac Kramnick distinguishes between classical republicanism, which 'is historically an ideology of leisure', and bourgeois liberalism, which 'is an ideology of work'. Republicanism 'conceives of human beings as political animals who realize themselves only through participation in public life, through active citizenship in a republic. The virtuous citizen is concerned primarily with the public good, *res publica*, or commonweal, not with private or selfish ends'. Liberalism, on the other hand, is a 'modern self-interested, competitive, individualistic ideology emphasizing private rights'.[20]

Clearly, the location of professional authors within a thriving commercial sector fits more comfortably with Kramnick's definition of liberalism than with classical republicanism. This obviously creates problems for an account of late eighteenth-century literary production that stresses the latter discursive structure. Rather than evading this problem, chapter 2 foregrounds it by arguing that, far from being naive or misguided about their situation, authors evoked the spirit of classical republicanism because it enabled them (as members of the republic of letters) to mobilize a vocabulary of cultural value and a claim to symbolic authority that counterbalanced the extent to which their immersion within the social and economic practices of commercial individualism had eroded traditional bases of authorial distinction.

Romantic literature has almost always been read (as indeed many of the authors of the period viewed their own work) in relation to the turbulent political developments of the age: what William Wordsworth refers to 'the great national events which are daily taking place, and the encreasing accumulation of men in cities, where the uniformity of their occupations produces a craving for extraordinary incident, which the rapid communication of intelligence hourly gratifies'.[21] The attempts of authors (many of whom were involved in the 'great national events' of the day) to insist on the central importance of a particular type of knowledge means that we have to understand the pressures shaping literary production not only in relation to the struggle for reform, but in terms of this other field of politics as well – what Fraser describes as a politics of distinction. The critical challenge is less one of selecting an alternative definition of 'the political' than of synthesizing these domains (national agency and distinction) into a single field of contestation within which the struggle to define literature must be located. If Wordsworth's observation gathers together fears about the French Revolution, the Industrial Revolution, and the information revolution ('the rapid communication of intelligence'), his immediate connection of these developments to the shrinking readership for Milton and Shakespeare suggests that this interpenetration of different forms of struggle was never far from the surface. The attempt to assert different interpretations of authorial distinction based on different ideas about literature (and inevitably, different ideas about the identity of 'the reader') was played out in a volatile ideological terrain whose tensions were profoundly implicated in the more pressing conflicts of the age.

The complex intersection of these two histories – the political turmoil of the 1790s and the broader hegemonic shift towards the meritocratic bias of the professional classes – demands that reactions against subaltern counterpublics be read as the expression of anxieties about the state of literature generally. But it also forces us to recognize the extent to which the social formation within which these dynamics operated was characterized by overlapping points of consensus *and* difference. It was wholly possible for critics on either side of the political divide to share a common sense of the importance of professional authors as a group whose efforts were helping to reshape society in the industrious self-image of the middle classes. Journals such as the *British Critic* and the *Gentleman's Magazine*, both stridently opposed to the 1790s campaign for political reform, were none the less part of a more gradual reform movement which simultaneously rejected the political struggle for reform and valorized individual productivity in opposition to the perceived idleness of aristocratic privilege.

The object of this study is the long history of the changing status of literature as a public sphere, but its focus crystallizes in the 1790s when the contradictions inherent in this discourse were most dramatically foregrounded. This is partly because the events of this period helped generate a discursive shift in the dominant ideas about literature (the beginning of the end of the bourgeois ideal of publicity), and partly because the tensions which informed this shift helped to clarify what was always at stake in this ideal. As Paul Yachnin notes, 'contradiction opens up ideology to interrogation and manipulation because contradiction disturbs the placidity of discursive practices'.[22] Crisis may precipitate discursive change, but it also foregrounds the various beliefs which inhere in the discourse which is under pressure. The 1790s consti-

tuted the moment of greatest crisis in a larger cultural moment –
now known as the Romantic period – which was itself characterized by a crisis in the meaning of literature that 'forced writers
to see that the possibility of alternative readings merged with the
possibility of alternative social orders'.[23]

Whereas part 1 concentrates on the dominant arguments for
and against the idea of literature as a public sphere, part 2
shifts its focus to the margins. Chapters 3 and 4 explore the aspirations of working-class activists and 'masculine' (i.e., rational)
women, and the denunciations with which these aspirations were
met. In chapter 5, I switch from the national to the global context
in order to emphasize that this characterization of literature as a
public sphere was defined not only in terms of class and gender,
but in terms of race as well.

Some people, it is true, dismissed this debate about literature
as a public sphere altogether in favour of an equation of literature
with poetry. But these Romantics, as we now refer to them, none
the less sought to establish the importance of their vision of aesthetic expression in terms which recuperated, even if in an
inverted form, the central points of this prior debate. They
invented none of the tropes which are today most closely – and
often most negatively – associated with them: transcendence, the
universality of truth, the autonomous self. Instead, as I will show
in my conclusion which focuses on William Wordsworth's 1802
Preface to *The Lyrical Ballads* they reinterpreted existing ideas
about literature in private rather than public terms, relating them
to the play of the imagination rather than the exercise of reason.
But these shifts cannot erase the important continuities that
existed between the lyrical ideals of the poets and the more secular ambitions of other authors. It is impossible to understand the
poets' reinterpretation of these ideas except by situating their
efforts within the existing debates whose central assumptions and
values they inflected in startlingly new ways. To forget this is to
make the mistake of simply reproducing the Romantic myth of
the originality of the creative act. The point of concluding with
one of the most established Romantic poets is to dispel an either/
or approach that simply inverts those selective processes which
underlie our inherited canonical assumptions in favour of a more
socially grounded version of print culture. More important than
performing this reversal is the challenge of recognizing the dial-

ogic nature of all texts in a period of acute discursive friction. If poetic inspiration was frequently imaged as an aeolian harp, then we must recognize the winds that tickled the creative strings in a more worldly way than the poems themselves might suggest.

This study intersects with three different debates that are ongoing within the academy today: the discussions generated by Jurgen Habermas's work on the bourgeois public sphere, the continuing struggle to wrestle with the distorting effects of the master narratives of 'Romanticism', and the growing effort to come to terms with the wider implications of the institutional history of English literature. I want to outline my points of intersection with each of these debates, but I also want to emphasize that their ongoing separation reproduces certain refusals which have their roots in this period. It is not only by understanding more about each of them, but also by trying to think through their points of interconnection, that we can better recognize our own implication within some of the cultural developments whose history we are trying to understand.

THE BOURGEOIS PUBLIC SPHERE

My interest in the republic of letters coincides with the historical issues raised by Habermas's *The Structural Transformation of the Public Sphere* and participates in the debates that have developed since its translation into English in 1989. I found my way into these issues, however, from the opposite direction from Habermas. Rather than beginning with a set of political and philosophical concerns that focused on print culture as the most important means for their realization, I began by asking what literature meant to people in the period, and only then realized that the assumptions that I was encountering were bound up with these political and philosophical ideas. I have tried to contribute to the exploration of the ways that ideas about the public sphere were shaped by changing patterns of readership and literary production by maintaining a double focus: on the dominant arguments for and against this ideal, on the one hand, and on subaltern counterpublics – women, the working class, and in a different way, constructions of Oriental literature – on the other. These multiple, overlapping, and frequently conflicting counterpublics were simultaneously assimilationist, since they employed the Enlightenment emphasis on the social importance of rational enquiry, and anti-systemic, since they challenged the universally inclusive self-representations of the bourgeois public sphere. Habermas stresses that the public sphere was generally seen as a space of rational contestation, but as the debate initiated by his work has also clarified, the cultural geography of that space was itself an important focus of contestation. The limits, within which any issue could be laid open to question, were themselves increasingly questioned.

The reaction against these subaltern counterpublics during the Romantic period suggests that the social limitations of the bourgeois public sphere were not accidentally imposed historical contingencies which prevented the full realization of its democratic ethos; rather the ethos was itself a new means of class and gender domination which expressed itself in terms of accessibility, the social neutrality of reason, and the ever-expanding diffusion of knowledge. Saying this, however, should not prevent us from recognizing those genuinely emancipatory effects which are also associated with the bourgeois public sphere.

What has not been theorized explicitly enough are the ways that reason played a mediating role in the reproduction of these asymmetries of power. The extent to which class and gender differences, or the power relations underpinning imperialism, could ever be bracketed by participants in the exchanges which characterized the public sphere depended wholly on the supposedly neutral status of reason. Within rational debate, it was widely held, individuals succeeded according to the force of their ideas alone. Social rank could be of no importance. This belief underpins Habermas's claim that 'rational discourses' are 'self-corrective in terms of being sensitive to a critique of systematic exclusionary mechanisms built into them ... Once an observer's information enters that same and so far unchanged discourse, it is implied that participants cannot go on, in light of their self-understanding, without identifying the rules of the games they have been playing as being selective and revising them.'[24]

This approach is markedly different from the position of someone like Michel Foucault, for whom this construction of reason is merely one of the ways that power perpetuates itself. Habermas's is in many ways a more attractive model because it allows for the possibility of meaningful interventions into existing debates

by previously excluded voices. But the reaction to the claims of
women and working-class activists in the late eighteenth century
highlights the limitations of this more optimistic approach. It is
important to recognize not only the extent to which ideas about
universality were differentially produced, but the ways that these
dynamics were mediated rather than eliminated by contested
notions of the social identity of reason. Ideas about the capacity
of different social groups for rational enquiry provided the ammunition for the reinforcement, rather than the correction, of structural exclusions. As Geoff Eley puts it, 'who is to say that the
discourse of the London Corresponding Society was any less
rational than that of, say, the Birmingham Lunar Society?'.[25] What
was at stake was a struggle over the availability of a foundational
value system within which the democratic potential of the
intersubjective communicative process (rational enquiry), which
was itself supposed to generate these values, could be contained.

The emotional intensity of the backlash against the intrusions
of these subaltern groups suggests the importance of reading
these developments in ways which interfuse social and psychoana-
lytical theory. Prior anxieties about the state of literature must be
factored into any account of the bitterness of the reaction against
those potential entrants whose aspirations threatened to erode the
already blurred boundaries of the republic of letters. This reading
does not eliminate or even contest the political worries which
manifestly characterized these objections to the radicalized claims
of new entrants in a politically turbulent age, but it does demand
that we understand these responses as having been intensified by
other, often seemingly unrelated, factors. Pursuing this line of
enquiry means tracing the ways that non-political frustrations
about the state of literature helped to generate more explicitly
political reactions to the question of who could lay claim to literary
authority.

Central to these revisions of Habermas's account of eighteenth-
century print culture is the question of his sense of the cultural
location of the literary public sphere. Habermas's distinction
between the literary and public spheres in the eighteenth century
is based on his relatively narrow definition of 'literary', by which
he refers primarily to epistolary novels – a genre which combines
the private world of the imagination with the social activity of
letter-writing. Reading these sorts of texts enabled people to
recognize their own subjectivity. This process of identity formation

was crucial because it allowed people to understand themselves as a 'public', a conceptual achievement that made it possible to conduct those critical transactions which Habermas assigns to the political sphere. This is fine as far as it goes, but by failing to appreciate the considerably broader and highly contested definition of literature in the period, Habermas underestimates the complexity of the relation between the political and literary public spheres. For reformers, for whom literature functioned as an 'engine' of social progress by facilitating debate on all issues of public interest, the literary and political spheres were profoundly interrelated. Conservatives tended to be more supportive of the separate-spheres model described by Habermas which restricted the literary sphere to private concerns. Rather than imposing either view on the period, it is important to recognize the struggle to assert these contending definitions as an expression of the wider political tensions of the time.

Considering these issues, which collectively foreground the extent to which the public sphere was always already felt to have declined, helps us to resist Habermas's account of the more recent decline of communicative processes from a critical role into the passive one of producing consent. This theory of historical decline, which has been attributed to Habermas's uncritical acceptance of the Frankfurt School's (and particularly Adorno's and Horkheimer's) post-war pessimism about popular culture, reproduces rather than establishes a critical distance from those late eighteenth-century attitudes towards the ideal of the bourgeois public sphere which it aims at studying. It has been challenged by critics who argue that current communications systems also empower marginal voices, providing new opportunities for various interventions into decision-making processes.[26] I want to complement these studies by pointing out the extent to which fears about the decline of literature as a means for developing dissenting responses to public authority already characterized late eighteenth-century constructions of the public sphere, which, it seems, could only be celebrated on the condition that it had already degenerated.

ROMANTICISM

Virtually every new anthology of Romantic literature or criticism is prefaced with a statement of the editor's commitment to the broader project of rethinking the exclusionary effects of the master narratives of Romanticism.[27] This revisionary challenge has taken several important and often theoretically sophisticated forms, from the deconstruction of Romantic poetry's meditations on self-presence, to the recuperation of non-canonical authors and genres, to the attempt to historicize the Romantic poets' insistence on a spiritual focus that transcends the particularities of history. None of these strategies is unimportant, but neither are they without their own risks. The effort to recuperate 'new' authors supplements rather than undermines the notion of a Romantic canon. Deconstructive and New Historicist approaches to canonical texts inevitably monumentalize the very 'Romantic ideology' they are attempting to displace.

As Jon Klancher, Steven Cole, and Robert Young have pointed out,[28] Renaissance critics such as Stephen Greenblatt tend to explore literary texts as heterogeneous sites of cultural negotiations which must themselves be understood as the effects of power. Much of the New Historicism produced in the 1980s by Romantic critics, on the other hand, tended to offer ideological critiques of the ways that poems deflect attention away from unsettling social realities.[29] The former approach concentrates on recovering the dialogical nature of texts; the latter highlights the ways that texts resist any adequate recognition of these complexities. Reflecting on the New Historicism, Robert Young argues that the task of 'charting ... the circulating relations between aesthetic and other forms of production works best in those historical periods, such as the Renaissance, where there was no modern concept of literature, thus allowing literary texts to be mapped against the political and other discourses of which they formed a part'.[30] My point is that Young's observation ought to apply to the late eighteenth and early nineteenth centuries, though Romantic New Historicists frequently approach the period as though this 'modern concept of literature' were already in place.

Jerome McGann's *The Romantic Ideology* is perhaps the most influential example of this critical strategy. In it, McGann proposes a two-pronged critique of 'these dramas of displacement and idealization' which characterize both Romantic poetry and modern critics who remain trapped within the theoretical limits of Romanticism (1). The key to escaping this hermeneutical circle, McGann argues, is to preserve a respect for the historical difference between our own age and the period that we are studying. Only by doing this are we able to escape 'cooptation [which] must always be a process intolerable to a critical consciousness, whose first obligation is to resist incorporation' (2). Despite this respect for the importance of maintaining a sense of historical difference, though, McGann reproduces the very assumptions whose discursive force he would oppose, by slipping between references to 'works of literature' and 'poetry' in a way that suggests their equation (3, 14). In doing so, McGann erases a sense of historical difference by imposing our own institutionally sanctioned ideas about literature onto the Romantic period. Like the critics whose practices he would question, McGann's critique falls prey to an 'uncritical absorption in Romanticism's own self-representations' (1). The formal issue of McGann's ahistorical equation of literature with aesthetic expression is important because it coincides with the overwhelmingly canonical focus of Romantic New Historicists throughout the 1980s. This dynamic inadvertently reinforced those historical distortions which find expression in the Romantic canon even as critics attempted to rewrite the historical distortions practised by the authors within this canon. However valuable each of these studies have been in themselves, collectively they reflected and reinforced a particular view of late eighteenth-century literary culture which has its origins in the selective processes of that period.

This does not mean that these interventions are not valuable. New Historicist critics' emphasis on the necessity for a return to historically grounded approaches, and their speculations about what this might entail, may have tended to focus on 'the Big Six' poets (and overwhelmingly, on William Wordsworth), but their interrogation of the ontological claims of Romantic poetry helped to move Romantic studies beyond investigations which connect an inherited canon of poetry with a wide range of historical influences, to approaches that concentrate on literature as a heterogeneous field of cultural production in itself. In the introduction to his *New Oxford Book of Romantic Period Verse*, McGann emphasizes the importance of this second wave of Romantic New Historicism which subordinates a critique of historical displacements in canonical poetry to a more positive analysis of various oppositional forms of cultural representation (xix–xx). These latter approaches are informed by a mediated conception of agency in which the self (understood individually and collectively) both shapes, and is shaped by, the dominant discourses of the period. Individuals may still not be able to transcend history, but as a growing body of recent work demonstrates, they are none the less able to inscribe themselves within it, and in doing so, to gain a limited measure of autonomy without necessarily reproducing the myth of the self-determining subject.[31]

Having stressed the ongoing centrality of Enlightenment thought in the 1790s, I want to insist that I am *not* interested in rethinking our critical relationship to the narratives of Romanticism by deploying an Enlightenment/Romantic binary which reads 'reason' as the basis for radical engagement and 'imagination' as a justification for a retreat from politics into a Burkean conservatism. Both approaches (Romantic and Enlightenment) can be either progressive or reactionary (or, more likely, simultaneously both) depending on how they are deployed. Both also tend to contain greater aspects of the other than this sort of binary suggests. And as I argue in my conclusion, assessments of the political dynamics inherent in these alternative strategies frequently say as much about critics' relation to our cultural and political moment as they do about the writers that we would pass judgement on. Rather than trying to adjudicate in either direction, I am interested in approaching the Romantics from a different angle altogether by asking questions that are related to an alternative politics of authorial distinction. In other words, I am interested in the ways that these poets mobilized existing cultural assumptions in order to highlight the importance of the poet rather than in exploring their changing relation to the reform movement as an end in itself.

This book is an attempt to reinforce the multiplication of literatures that are studied within the Romantic period, not by exploring a particular field of neglected writing but by focusing on the meaning of the word literature itself (though in doing so I have drawn on several different types of literature which are deservedly becoming a focus of critical attention in their own right). Incorporating an adequate recognition of the contested nature of literature into the historical analysis of particular texts and genres highlights the fact that what texts say is inevitably shaped by the often embattled discursive position out of which these communicative acts are produced. As James Raven has argued, the 'circumstances of literary production and the methods of literary circulation influence not only the form but also the content of texts' (5). We can only begin to understand the meaning of particular poems (and novels and plays, but also essays, histories, travel narratives, scientific treatises, and so on) once we have suspended the historically erroneous equation of literature with aesthetic expression in favour of an approach which situates the origins of this equation within the period's 'huge, still largely unknown world of text-making'.[32] Adopting such an approach encourages us to extend the range of our critical focus to include 'non-literary' genres. But it also makes the study of aesthetic texts (i.e. canonical poetry) more interesting because it invites an approach which focuses our attention on self-representational strategies whose polemical force the texts themselves might encourage us to overlook.

THE MAKING OF ENGLISH STUDIES

An important part of the current challenge to entrenched assumptions about the study of English Literature necessarily involves addressing the question of the nature of the social spaces that we occupy as we engage with these issues. As Susan Stewart has suggested, 'it is impossible to separate the epistemological imperative . . . from the ethical imperative of a reexamination of the relations between power and knowledge'.[33] There are an increasing number of accounts of the history of 'English Studies' which trace the growing importance of university programmes dedicated to the study of 'valuable works' written in the vernacular, isolated from the social conditions of their production, and fused into a cohesive tradition that could be studied wholly in relation to itself.[34] Exposure to this body of writing was thought to have all of the improving effects that were assumed to characterize any encounter with great art, and the more particular benefit of being steeped in a tradition which could be said to characterize the glory of England's national identity.

This ideal of the literary tradition as a cultural domain free from social contradictions recuperated the universalist assumptions of the public sphere, but only to the extent that it remained securely within the cultural, rather than the political, domain. It was guided less by a reformist spirit of futurity than by a Burkean emphasis on tradition as a bulwark against unsettling social developments, but this conservatism did not deprive it of an active cultural role. Advocates of programmes of English Studies frequently displayed a spirit of moral evangelism which manifested itself in the desire to promote the 'improvement' of growing sectors of the population, both within England and throughout the empire, by developing programmes of English Studies that would impress upon people the values which this corpus of great works were felt to evoke. I want to reinforce these histories of English Studies (which frequently begin in the 1830s with the founding of King's College, London, or with Macaulay's *Minute on Indian Education*) by exploring the complex discursive shifts that prefigure its institutional history.

Focusing on William Godwin's political thought in the various editions of his *Enquiry Concerning Political Justice* (1793), Mark Philp identifies 'the end of the eighteenth century' as the historical moment when 'literature and radicalism parted company':

With the radicals' objectives blocked by government action and conservative propaganda, and with the break up of the radical associations and the consequent erosion of the links between these organisations and other intellectual currents and circles, the conditions for a continuing literary radicalism were destroyed. The torch of literary progress and innovation passed to new groups – more inward-looking, more conservative in their judgements, and more divorced from political questions and movements.[35]

In her introduction to *Burke, Paine, Godwin, and the Revolution Controversy*, Marilyn Butler offers a similar account. She argues that one of the victims of the political backlash of the middle and later 1790s was the idea that the arts were 'impregnated with politics' (12). Disoriented by the violence of the French Revolution and by a state campaign to suppress seditious writing, radical literary figures increasingly focused on 'personal experience' rather than 'public problems'. This is a well-known story, but as Butler also notes, these developments affect us as literary critics today in ways which too often undermine our sensitivity to the cultural complexities of the period:

our approach to political prose is bedeviled because we are ourselves Romantics or post-Romantics; we have been taught the primary aesthetic values adopted by literary men after their political defeat. So we tend to ask questions which already pre-judge the issue, by smuggling in aesthetic and individualistic values – such as 'who wrote the best prose?' or 'which are the masterpieces?' If these are really the right questions, the answers follow without much room for dispute. (16)

More important than posing answers to these questions, perhaps, is the task of interrogating the nature of the questions we feel compelled to ask in the first place, recognizing as we do so that they are never without their own selective implications and institutional histories. The seemingly expansive equation of literature with a profound depth of meaning – an assumption which is itself bound up with the humanist ideal of subjective plentitude – is premised on an ironically narrow set of assumptions about what this phenomenon 'literature' is, that can be so endlessly interpreted once we have learned to recognize it. In *The Anatomy of Criticism*, for instance, Northrop Frye refers to 'a feeling we have all had: that the study of mediocre works of art remains a random and peripheral form of critical experience, whereas the profound masterpiece draws us to a point at which we seem to see an enormous number of converging patterns' (17). Frye's argument for a form of criticism which avoids value-judgements (28) is belied not only by his confidence in the unproblematic availability of this distinction, but by his more basic equation of 'the masterpieces of literature', which constitute the focus of 'literary criticism', with aesthetic expression (15). However sophisticated and even politicized our theoretical frameworks might be, the overwhelming tendency to bring them to bear on aesthetic texts is itself the product of particular historical processes that are deeply at odds with the emancipatory spirit which underpins many of these theories.

Registering our institutional complicity with the political dynamics of the period reveals still-existing continuities that shape our approach to reading literary texts but, crucially, it also explains the continuing resistance to various critical approaches. The emphasis of 'theory' on the nature of those questions which we as literary critics feel licensed to ask has concentrated our attention on the ways that the perpetuation of certain types of questions reinforces existing asymmetries of power. It has also highlighted the institutional norms and practices through which these biases are (often unconsciously) perpetuated. This book is intended, more than anything else, to be a genealogy of an historical shift in the sorts of questions that were, and are today, associated with the study of literature – a transformation which Philp and Butler associate with the political conflicts of the late eighteenth century. Recognizing the nature of these developments enables us to sustain the effort of disentangling our own critical position from the cultural assumptions we inherit from the period.

This critical challenge begins with establishing a more interdisciplinary approach to the questions of what literature *meant*, and *to whom*. By posing these questions we highlight our own inscription within academic disciplines which, however implicitly, continue to shape our readings of the past. It enshrines the concept of literature not as a foundational category which accurately describes our own critical commitments, but as one of many versions of literature whose interrelations can in themselves constitute the object of our study. This book, like Siskin's *The Work of Writing*, registers the productive potential inherent in our own institutional crisis – the fact that our ways of knowing (disciplinarity) and working (professionalism) as members of English departments have become 'disturbed and disturbing' (8) – by seeking to reverse 'the standard displacement of writing by Literature – opening both, perhaps to new ways of knowing' (227). By recognizing more clearly the nature of the influence which past events continue to exert, we can better understand the cultural predicament of our own age, in which attempts to foreground questions about the range of questions that we as 'literary critics' feel licensed to ask, are still frequently rejected as a political intrusion into a territory that ought to transcend the narrowness of what are denounced as mandate-driven approaches. Tracing both the lines of intersection between these three debates – the bourgeois public sphere, the cultural legacy of Romanticism, and the evolution of English Studies – and the sorts of historical refusals which help to explain their frequent isolation from each other, will help us to facilitate a more truly historical analysis of literature in what we call the Romantic period, and to develop a clearer sense of what is at stake in the current debates about the character and content of English Studies.

PART ONE

Enlightenment

CHAPTER ONE

The republic of letters

Never was a republic greater, better peopled, more free, or more glorious: it is spread on the face of the earth, and is composed of persons of every nation, of every rank, of every age, and of both sexes. They are intimately acquainted with every language, the dead as well as the living. To the cultivation of letters they join that of the arts; and the mechanics are also permitted to occupy a place. But their religion cannot boast of uniformity; and their manners, like those of every other republic, form a mixture of good and evil: they are sometimes enthusiastically pious, and sometimes insanely impious.

Isaac D'Israeli, 'The Republic Of Letters'

SPARKS OF TRUTH

In a review of Jean d'Alembert's *History of the French Academy*, in October 1789, the *Analytical Review* acknowledged the intellectual preeminence of the author, but rejected his arguments in favour of such academies. D'Alembert was, the review allowed,

a man distinguished in the most learned society in Europe by the universality and depth of his knowledge; by his proficiency in grammar, particular and universal, philology, metaphysics, history, the fine arts, and, above all, geometry. (5 (1789): 161)

D'Alembert's *History of the French Academy*, though, was written 'rather in the character of an apologist than that of a philosopher', biased by his personal position as the historian to the institution. In fact, the review suggests, the social advantages that d'Alembert attributes to 'academies, or literary societies, will be found, on reflection, to be the very strongest argument that can be brought against them' (163). Such societies may well act as a safeguard against 'licentiousness and extravagance', but at the price of deterring 'genius and invention' (ibid.). Only in the absence of so venerable an institution could intellectuals be expected to retain an integrity in their work that would have otherwise been constrained by the temptation to conformity that the presence of such an institution would inevitably exert. Indeed, one implication of the *Analytical Review's* suggestion that d'Alembert wrote in the character of an 'apologist' rather than that of a 'philosopher', that he was committed to defending something rather than discovering the truth about it, was that his *History* was evidence of this very point; d'Alembert's critical abilities had been influenced by his private connections with the Academy, his perceptions swayed by his personal obligations. Free of the influence of such an institution, the *Analytical Review* suggested, 'the *solitary student* . . . views things on a grander scale, and addresses his sentiments to a wider theatre: to all civilized and refined nations! To nations that are yet to rise, perhaps in endless succession, out of rudeness into refinement' (ibid.).[1]

Not everyone shared this opinion. Isaac D'Israeli suggested that 'it is much to the dishonour of the national character' that 'no Academy, dedicated to the BELLES LETTRES, has ever been established'.[2] Those who agreed with D'Israeli insisted that such an academy would stand as a monument to the advanced state of British civilization, and would encourage the exertions of authors by the powers of public recognition which it would be able to bestow upon them. Nor, many implied, was the regulating effect of such an institution wholly undesirable; literature, like any human activity, was prone to excesses which detracted from its greater glory. The disciplinary function of such an institution, where it was properly exercised, would help to foster, rather than impede, the literary efforts of the nation. None the less, despite the enthusiasm of advocates such as D'Israeli, the *Analytical Review's* scepticism about the usefulness of academies was widely shared. It was informed by a belief in the different national spirit of Catholic France and Protestant England: the former characterized by too unquestioning a respect for dogmatic power, the latter blessed with a love of liberty. Linda Colley notes that these perceptions were strengthened by the long series of wars fought between England and France throughout the century. The British 'defined themselves as Protestants struggling for survival against . . . the

French as they imagined them to be, superstitious, militarist, decadent and unfree.'[3]

Because of the perceived connection between liberty and knowledge, the debate about academies reflected a series of distinct but overlapping views about what the *Monthly Review* described as 'that grand palladium of British liberty, THE FREEDOM OF THE PRESS' (17 (1791): 121). Print was for many both an index and a guarantee of freedom – one of the glories of an advanced civilization and an important means of opposing arbitrary authority. Arthur O'Connor insisted that the invention of the compass and the printing press had determined the course of history in a direction which Pitt's repressive measures were powerless to halt unless he was prepared to 'consign every book to the flames' and 'obliterate the press'.[4] An anonymous pamphlet entitled *TEN MINUTES ADVICE TO THE PEOPLE OF ENGLAND, On the two Slavery-Bills Intended to be brought into Parliament the Present Session* (1795), agreed that 'whenever a tyrant wishes to abandon himself to the lust of dominion, his first step is to reduce and degrade his subjects to a state of ignorance . . . by cutting off that social intercourse, and unrestrained exchange of opinions, from which all knowledge, all information is derived, and from whence flows the consciousness of dignity, and the rank of human nature' (6).

As the political divide widened at the end of the century, a belief in the centrality of print culture to British liberty remained one point on which – however differently they might interpret it – opposed critics could still find some measure of common ground. The unparalleled social, economic, and political advantages which were seen to be enjoyed by the current generation, and the unprecedented productivity of authors in all fields of literary endeavour, were hailed by critics from various political perspectives as proof of the equation between print and the public good.

Janet Todd is right in noting the extent to which celebrations of the quasi-political authority of the reading public anticipate Percy Shelley's emphasis on poets as unacknowledged legislators.[5] Marilyn Butler similarly describes this growing interest in current issues as an 'informal Congress of the educated classes' – a shadow government of enlightened public opinion which would have no formal role within the political process, and no direct influence, but which no responsible government would wish to, or could even

hope to, oppose.[6] In his unsuccessful but highly publicized defence
of Thomas Paine for *Rights of Man*, part 2, Thomas Erskine offered
a stridently reformist version of precisely this proposal: 'government, in *its own estimation*, has been *at all times* a system of perfection; but a free press has examined and detected its errors, and
the people have from time to time reformed them. – This freedom
has alone made our government what it is; this freedom alone can
preserve it'. 'Other liberties', he continued later in the same trial,
'are held *under* governments, but the liberty of opinion keeps
GOVERNMENTS THEMSELVES in due subjection to their duties'.[7] The
Analytical Review insisted in similar terms that '[l]iterature, by
enlightening the understanding, and uniting the sentiments and
views of men and of nations, forms a concert of wills, and a concur-
rence of action too powerful for the armies of tyrants' (2 (1788):
324–5). As Thomas Holcroft more succinctly put it in his novel
Hugh Trevor (1797), the 'nation that remarks, discusses, and com-
plains of its wrongs, will finally have them redressed' (364).[8]

   William Godwin presented a classic version of this reformist
argument in a section entitled 'Literature' in his *Enquiry Concerning
Political Justice* (1793):

> Few engines can be more powerful, and at the same time more salutary
> in their tendency, than literature. Without enquiring for the present into
> the cause of this phenomenon, it is sufficiently evident in fact, that the
> human mind is strongly infected with prejudice and mistake. The various
> opinions prevailing in different countries and among different classes of
> men upon the same subject, are almost innumerable; and yet of all these
> opinions only one can be true. Now the effectual way for extirpating
> these prejudices and mistakes seems to be literature.[9]

Godwin's description of literature as an engine may sit a bit
uncomfortably with our own age's more aesthetically based
assumptions, but it reflects the practical side of late eighteenth-
century middle-class culture. For many authors, but for political
dissenters especially, the question of what you could do with literature was more important than the question of what belonged to
it. Literature was valuable because, as an engine, it was both a
means of facilitating debate between an unlimited number of participants, and a vehicle for spreading the lessons which emerged
from those debates throughout a growing reading public. What
was vital was that literature remain characterized by a wide-range
of exchanges *between* different authors, rather than merely

a means of reporting the isolated discoveries of unconnected individuals:

[I]f there be such a thing as truth, it must infallibly be struck out by the collision of mind with mind. The restless activity of intellect will for a time be fertile in paradox and error; but these will be only diurnals, while the truths that occasionally spring up, like sturdy plants, will defy the rigour of season and climate. In proportion as one reasoner compares his deductions with those of another, the weak places of his argument will be detected, the principles he too hastily adopted will be overthrown, and the judgements, in which his mind was exposed to no sinister influence, will be confirmed. All that is requisite in these discussions is unlimited speculation, and a sufficient variety of systems and opinions. (15)

Such a vision synthesized a recognition of the paramount importance of private judgement with the Humean ideal of sociability. People would decide their opinions for themselves, but they would do so as members of a community dedicated to intellectual exchange. In *Godwin's Political Justice,* Mark Philp suggests that this perspective emerged out of Godwin's own immersion within a literary community that 'lived in a round of debate and discussion, in clubs, associations, debating societies, salons, taverns, coffee houses, bookshops, publishing houses and in the street ... conversation ranged through philosophy, morality, religion, literature, and poetry, to the political events of the day' (127). Our impressions of the period may have traditionally focused on the charismatic image of the Romantic outcast, but as Philp notes, '[t]hese men and women' who dominated the late eighteenth-century literary scene 'were not the isolated heroes and heroines of Romanticism pursuing a lonely course of discovery; they were people who worked out their ideas in company and who articulated the aspirations and fears of their social group' (127).

Godwin's position may have balanced the energies of private judgement against the constraints of social exchange, but it remained a potentially anarchical vision, as we will see below. It licensed an endless number of authors to engage in an endless series of debates on every imaginable subject, including politics, guided only by the decisive force of something known as reason. But Godwin insisted that unchecked debate ultimately led to social cohesion rather than dissension by developing widely shared standards of opinion amongst the reading public:

Literature has reconciled the whole thinking world respecting the great principles of the system of the universe, and extirpated upon this subject the dreams of romance and the dogmas of superstition. Literature has unfolded the nature of the human mind, and Locke and others have established certain maxims respecting man, as Newton has done respecting matter, that are generally admitted for unquestionable. (III, 15)

Behind the anarchic spectre of apparently random intellectual collisions lay the reassuring teleology of the gradual progress of truth – a force which, because it was both unifying and liberating, was ultimately the strongest ally of sound government.

Godwin's ideas about literature as an overtly political communicative domain represented an extreme version of a set of beliefs that had been evolving over the previous centuries. In her study of the republic of letters in the late seventeenth and early eighteenth centuries, Anne Goldgar notes that the 'term first appeared in its Latin form in the fifteenth century and was used increasingly in the sixteenth and seventeenth, so that by the end of that century it featured in the titles of several important literary journals'.[10] Lacking any official regulations or geographic territory, the identity of this community was consolidated by those modes of affiliation – exchanges of books, visits, and letters of introduction – which evoked an ethos of cooperation between its members. Their goal may have been the pursuit of knowledge, but scholars were expected to pursue this ambition in a virtuous and disinterested manner guided by a paramount concern for the republic of letters itself.

The late seventeenth- and early eighteenth-century republic of letters was always implicitly political because it was part of a broader hegemonic shift toward the middle class. But Goldgar distinguishes between the literary republics at the end of the seventeenth and eighteenth centuries (which she identifies as the *érudit* and *philosophe* republics of letters) primarily in terms of political orientation. The focus of late seventeenth-century scholars was inward; the public which they cared about was each other. 'Although the increase of knowledge was an avowed goal ... the benefit of the larger society was not a major concern.'[11] Their Enlightenment heirs, however, celebrated knowledge as power, believing that they could use it to change the world by encouraging political reform in the public sphere, and moral reform in the private. It is in terms of this growing sense of a wider social obligation that we must locate Dena Goodman's description of the 'seriousness of purpose' of the Enlightenment republic of letters.[12]

This redefinition of the republic of letters in terms of its relations to its wider social context was reinforced by the increasingly commercial nature of British society. In their studies of different aspects of mid eighteenth-century literary culture, critics such as Jerome Christensen and Frank Donoghue identify the sophisticated nature of the book trade as a key reason for the erosion of the insularity of the older *respublica literaria*. Authors' perception of their work as property forced them to negotiate a complex array of pressures and opportunities which brought them into closer contact with a widening reading public that was no longer composed solely of other authors. The effects of these developments were double-edged. They reinforced authors' location within a much wider nexus of relations that included publishers and readers, but at the same, they could also alienate authors from their readers by immersing them within a bewildering network of impersonal exchanges that substituted financial reward for the earlier spirit of mutuality. But whether these commercial developments were viewed positively or negatively, observers agreed that like the growing campaign for political reform, they had transformed the republic of letters in a fundamental way.[13]

Jurgen Habermas traces this shift in authors' primary concerns in terms of the changing meaning of the word 'publicity' from the earlier feudal sense of the stylized 'aura' of the aristocrat to the rise of the more modern sense of publicity as a cultural domain 'whose decisive mark was the published word'. Building on the traffic in news that was established along early trade routes, territorial rulers mobilized the press as an important organ of public authority. Eventually, however, the absolutist government of the mercantile state 'provoked the critical judgement of a public making use of its reason'. Reversing its originally hegemonic role, the public sphere of the printed word 'was now casting itself loose as a forum in which the private people, come together to form a public, readied themselves to compel public authority to legitimate itself before public opinion'.[14]

Habermas's account of this historical shift in the meaning of the word 'publicity' from aristocratic aura to communicative process is analogous to Michel Foucault's sense of a shift from an earlier epoch in which power functioned by displaying itself in rituals such as public executions to a disciplinary form of power – symbolized by Jeremy Bentham's plans for a panopticon – which reversed this dynamic by emphasizing the visibility of the subjects rather than the rulers. Whereas Foucault's sense of this historical shift is pessimistic (modern life as a prison), Habermas emphasizes the liberating aspects of this version of publicity in which political subjects 'were to think their own thoughts, directed against the authorities'.[15]

Importantly, however, Habermas also stresses that the public sphere was in no way reducible to the literary sphere. The literary sphere was important as a means of fostering a process of 'self-clarification' which enabled a community of private individuals to recognize themselves as a public. This domain included both the actual practice of letter writing, through which 'the individual unfolded himself in his subjectivity', and the fictional counterpart of this practice, the epistolary novel. Although the political public sphere was constituted through this process of self-discovery, it was rooted in a wide array of formal and informal practices and modes of association that went far beyond the literary sphere.[16] These included various forms of local government and other civic institutions, such as hospitals and charity organizations, theatres, museums, and concert halls, learned and philanthropic societies, organized debating societies and meeting places, such as coffee houses, where the latest news could be discussed. Print culture was only one aspect of a complex array of social relations enabling critical discussion.

As the reform movement in Britain accelerated in the 1780s and 1790s, however, critics attributed an increasingly political role to literature that went far beyond the subjective and therefore private task of facilitating a process of self-interpretation: it was the single most effective means by which people could engage each other in a rational debate whose authority all governments would be compelled to recognize. In this more political guise, literature functioned as a kind of group project where the goal was to project the interests of the group so clearly onto the public consciousness that relations of power would give way to questions of morality.

Political Justice may have been notorious amongst critics who saw little reason for enthusiasm in the growing restlessness for reform, but amongst its advocates, Godwin's ideas about the role of litera-

ture were far from unique. Reformers were united by their sense
of the contradiction between the closed system of formal politics
and the liberating force of a free press as an enabling dialectic
fostering a growing critique of the hegemonic order. And they
were convinced that history was on their side. The *Analytical Review*
shared Godwin's interfusion of pessimism and optimism about
current social conditions, a blend which guaranteed the heroic role
of literature (and authors) as an 'engine' capable of alleviating
oppression:

To dispel those clouds of ignorance, and to disperse that mass of errour,
which have hitherto been so baneful to society, ought to be the first
business of enlightened minds. It is only by giving men rational ideas of
the nature of society, and of the duties and interests of human beings,
that the obstacles to the progress of human happiness are to be removed.
When such ideas are thoroughly disseminated, reason will soon triumph
over tyranny without external violence, and under the auspices of freedom general prosperity will arise.
 Towards the accomplishment of this great end the labours of many
eminent writers have, of late years, been directed. Their works have been
sought with avidity, and read with attention; and the influence of their
speculations has already been visible in the active spirit of inquiry, which
has been excited amongst all ranks of men. (22 (1795): 545)

Paying tribute to the same process, Mary Hays insisted that the
gradual pace of the dawning of truth was a sign of strength rather
than weakness. Human faculties, enfeebled by the continued
effects of prejudice, could not immediately adapt themselves to
'the sudden splendour' of the full force of these 'just and liberal
notions'.[17] The magnitude of these transformations did not make
them seem any less inevitable though. The *Monthly Review* allowed,
in their account of an English translation of Volney's *Ruins,* that
the arrival of a new era 'when the whole race will form one great
society' was not 'speedily to be expected'. But the undeniable fact
was that 'even now ... a new age opens; an age of astonishment
to vulgar souls, of surprize and fear to tyrants, of freedom to a
great people, and of hope to all the world' (6 (1791): 553). In *The
Proper Objects of Education* (1791), which was originally given as a
talk at the Dissenters' Meeting Hall at the Old Jewry, Joseph
Priestley agreed that '[i]n science, in arts, in government, in
morals, and in religion, much is to be done ... but few ... are able,
and at the same time willing, to do it' (2). But like his reformist

contemporaries, Priestley insisted that the 'times are fully ripe for ... reformation' (23), and mocked those who resisted the inevitable dawning of truth:

The late writings in favour of liberty, civil and religious, have been like a beam of light suddenly thrown among owls, bats, or moles, who, incapable of receiving any pleasure or benefit from it, can only cry out, and hide themselves, when the light approaches, and disturbs them. But may this light increase, and let all who are offended by it retire into whatever holes they think proper. (36–7)

By juxtaposing the enormity of entrenched prejudice with the 'sure operation of increasing light and knowledge', reformers implied that the conservatives' greatest error was their inability to see the futility of clinging to inherited traditions as the primary guide to future progress. 'Can ye not discern the signs of the times?' asked Anna Barbauld.[18] By transforming the dynamics of the current age into a semiotics writ large, Barbauld converted history itself into a text in the precise image of the reformist dream of publicity: universally available and potentially educational.

Many reformers also shared Godwin's more particular emphasis on the role of literature in promoting 'the collision of mind with mind', rather than simply communicating the epiphanies of inspired individuals – or what amounted to the same thing, unexamined ideas – to the reading public. The *Monthly Review*, which celebrated Priestley as someone who, 'by a sort of collision, strike[s] from reluctant minds some sparks of truth' (5 (1791): 303), offered its own pages as a place where these sorts of exchanges might find a home: 'As discussion is that collision of minds by which the sparks of truth are often excited, we are always desirous of promoting the operation of this mental flint and steel, provided it be used with politeness and good temper' (33 (1800): 371). Mary Hays argued that 'the truth must ... like the pure gold, come out uninjured from a trial by fire, which can consume only the dross that obscured its lustre'.[19] Intellectual investigations must themselves be open to an unrestricted process of investigation in order that their assumptions might be tested, and their positive contributions extracted. What was not truth was intellectual dross, which would be consumed by those exchanges out of which truth would ultimately emerge.

What remained constant for the advocates of this vision was the

connection between the ideal of liberty and the improvin
of what Mary Wollstonecraft called the 'rapidly multiplie
of the productions of genius and compilations of learning, k
them within the reach of all ranks of men'.[20] Exchanges i
might lead to new ideas, but literature's role as a means of p
ing new forms of knowledge needed to be balanced against its
other function as a medium for the diffusion of these ideas
throughout society. Using the example of Russia, the *Monthly
Review* warned that where the various fields of learning did not
become 'naturalized to the soil ... of national culture', they
existed in a state which resembled 'a greenhouse, in which exotics
are kept alive by artificial warmth ... In such circumstances, they
certainly do honour to the liberality and taste of those who are at
the expence of preserving them: but they are of little service in
adorning and fertilizing the country' (4 (1791): 481).

Godwin's insistence that unrestricted discussion was the surest
guarantee of liberty was reinforced by the conviction of many
reformist authors that vice was a result of ignorance. Properly
educated, even the most hardened criminal would recognize that
his true interests lay in obeying the laws of his society. Catherine
Macaulay argued that '[t]here is not a wretch who ends his miser-
able being on a wheel, as the forfeit of his offences against society,
who may not throw the whole blame of his misdemeanours on his
education'.[21] William Wordsworth's and Samuel Taylor Coleridge's emphasis on the capacity of reading to make us more fully
human through the exercise of the imagination finds its Enlightenment antecedent in the stress on education as a basis of individual and social reform. By fusing personal virtue and political liberty in a single redemptive process, reformers were able to counter
the conservative argument that genuine political reform was
impossible without a prior reform in the character of the people
themselves. In its review of Godwin's *Political Justice*, the *Monthly
Review* insisted that because 'individual and general *ignorance*' was
the source of 'all the oppression that exists among mankind ... A
general diffusion of knowledge [was] the only remedy for these
evils' (9 (1793): 311). This diffusion of knowledge was frequently
equated with the development of a set of rational standards of
opinion within and even between nations – a unanimity that was
not necessarily ever fully achieved but which was understood to
exist none the less as a kind of vanishing point to which all debates

were inescapably destined. Those who dissented from this optimistic position were owls, bats, or moles, who were free to scurry into whatever dark recesses they could find.

However amorphous this sense of inexorable historical progress may have been, these developments were recognized as being singularly dependent on technical advances in the print industry.[22] In *Letters on Education* (1790), Catherine Macaulay argued that the 'advantages of printing, by rendering easy the communication of ideas, giving an universality to their extent, and a permanence to their existence, will ever be found a sufficient remedy against those evils which all societies have experienced from the superstitions of the weak, and the imposing craft of the subtle' (323). Thomas Holcroft placed a similar emphasis on 'the art of printing' in the defence of this progressivist vision of history which his protagonist makes to the cynic Stradling in *Hugh Trevor* (1797):

> When knowledge was locked up in Egyptian temples, or secreted by Indian Brahmins for their own selfish traffic, it was indeed difficult to increase this imaginary circle of yours: but no sooner was it diffused among mankind, by the discovery of the alphabet, than, in a short period, it was succeeded by the wonders of Greece and Rome. And now, that its circulation is facilitated in so incalculable a degree, who shall be daring enough to assert his puny standard is the measure of all possible futurity? (352)

Holcroft's account of Western culture, from the wonders of Greece and Rome to the final glimpse of utopian futurity, is structured by its juxtaposition of Western traditions with Egyptian and Indian tyranny. But it is also informed by a teleology that bridges two historical epochs characterized by two different types of print in an irreversible march of social progress. From printing as a signifying system capable of reproduction to print as the mechanized basis of that reproduction, technical advances in the art of written communication foster democratic advances as a direct result of the dissemination of knowledge. D'Israeli was less confident of the effects of 'the invention of Printing', but he none the less acknowledged that it was fundamentally reshaping society by diffusing new ideas throughout a growing reading public which included 'those whose occupations had otherwise never permitted them to judge on literary compositions'.[23]

The printing press made it possible to produce large editions relatively cheaply and quickly, but the virtual space of the public

sphere which this created remained dependent on a growing network of lending libraries, reading rooms, reading societies, coffee
houses, debating societies, and on the beginnings of a national
postal system efficient enough to facilitate the circulation of
books, newspapers, and pamphlets.[24] This infrastructure spanned
the major cities and the provincial towns, and embraced, in varying degrees, both the polite and the poorer classes.[25] Richard
Altick notes that the more exclusive libraries, which charged fees
and were often attached to the 'literary and philosophical societies' which sprang up in the larger towns, were complemented by
numerous book clubs composed of members who banded together
to share the cost of books, and by the commercial libraries which
lent popular literature (generally novels) at accessible prices.
Altick's warning against overestimating the extent of the diffusion
of reading beneath the level of artisans and small shopkeepers is
probably true for those areas of literature whose price and length
limited their accessibility.[26] But it overlooks the enormous eighteenth-century demand for chapbooks, as well as for newspapers,
which by the 1790s carried extensive reports of parliamentary proceedings.[27] It also underestimates the effects of those formal and
informal associations and practices which helped to extend the
privileges of print culture amongst the lower orders.

The provision made in the Pitt government's 1789 bill to
increase the stamp tax against hiring out newspapers for a mini-
mal charge suggests a nervous awareness by the government of a
potentially large body of working-class readers.[28] The tradition of
tavern debating, especially in London, made it possible for anyone
who could afford the sixpence fee to be a part of the same
exchange of ideas about current topics that was identified by many
as the most important function of literature.[29] Whatever their
more political concerns, the Sunday night meetings of the London
Corresponding Society offered members of this class a chance to
participate in reading and discussion groups.[30] These expansionary
dynamics reinforced links between literate and non-literate social
groups, who were able to hear pamphlets and newspapers read
aloud in the taverns. All of these factors reinforce Stuart Curran's
observation that 'the sense that history was being made, or
remade, on a world scale was universal; so was the recognition
that it did not actually occur until it happened in print'.[31]

This ideal of literature as a public sphere was universalizing in the claims that were made for it, but this did not, of course, mean that it was universally embraced. It was generally associated with the reformist middle class, and particularly with Dissenters such as Richard Price, Gilbert Wakefield, George Dyer, Godwin, Priestley (praised by the *Analytical Review* – which was in turn published by another famous Dissenter, Joseph Johnson – for possessing 'a mind unincumbered with the shackles of authority, richly stored with knowledge, long exercised in liberal speculation, and . . . superior to artifice and disguise' (9 (1791): 52–3)), Helen Maria Williams, Anna Barbauld, and Hays.[32] Kramnick notes that because large numbers of English Dissenters had emigrated to the America, those 'who remained in England constituted about 7 percent of the population. But those 7 percent . . . were at the heart of the progressive and innovative nexus that linked scientific, political, cultural, and industrial radicalism'.[33] Rational Dissenters and their beliefs, values, and language permeated the non-establishment literary and social circles of the day, and had considerable influence over a wide area of printing and publishing. They 'resorted to literature and publishing as sources of income because many other professions were denied to them by the Tests'.[34]

Debarred from politics by their faith, and in the case of Williams, Barbauld, and Hays, by their sex as well, Dissenters discovered in literary achievements both a form of self-legitimation and a vehicle for promoting political change. They could establish their credentials as citizens fit to participate in the political sphere by demonstrating their abilities and their integrity within the literary republic. In doing so, they frequently contrasted the moral worth of 'the peaceful walks of speculation' with 'the crooked and dangerous labyrinths of modern statesmen and politicians'.[35] In *An Address to the Opposers of the Repeal of the Corporation and Test Acts* (1790), Barbauld turned political loss to strategic advantage by comparing the selfless integrity of literature with the corruption of formal politics:

You have set a mark of separation upon us, and it is not in our power to take it off, but it is in our power to determine whether it shall be a disgraceful stigma or an honourable distinction . . . If, by our attention to literature, and that ardent love of liberty which you are pretty ready to allow us, we deserve esteem, we shall enjoy it . . . If your restraints operate towards keeping us in that middle rank of life where industry and virtue most abound, we shall have the honour to count ourselves among that class of the community which has ever been the source of manners, of population and of wealth. (22–3)

For many observers, these differences between the industrious and virtuous middle classes and the indolent aristocracy were reflected in the different approaches of the educational institutions attended by their sons. Whereas a foreign visitor to Oxford was reportedly amazed by a degree examination in which 'the Examiner, candidate, and others concerned passed the statutory time in perfect quiet reading novels and other entertaining works', Dissenting academies such as Warrington, Exeter, Hackney, and Manchester were widely popular with the prosperous middle class for their efforts to offer a more practical and thorough education which included large components of the natural and applied sciences, philosophy, theology, and politics. In his *Letter to the Right Honourable William Pitt on the Subject of Toleration and Church Establishment* (1787), Priestley argued that '[w]hile your universities resemble pools of stagnant water secured by dams and mounds, and offensive to the neighbourhood, ours are like rivers, which, while taking their natural course, fertilize a whole country' (20). Priestley pioneered the study of history and geography at a university level while teaching at Warrington, and – after being driven from Birmingham by the riots of July 1791 – gave free lectures in chemistry and history at Manchester, where the student body included William Hazlitt from 1793 to 1795.

Importantly, Dissenting academies held their lectures in English rather than Latin, drawing on a range of English sources which were more easily and rapidly consulted, and more modern in their range of thought. Gauri Viswanathan has argued that English Studies were first formally implemented in India in the early nineteenth century. It is not disagreeing with this to add, as McLachlan and Robert Crawford do, that the informal roots of English studies lie in those programmes of polite literature or *belles lettres* which were frequently taught in Britain's social and geographical margins – the Scottish universities and the 'provincial, northern, non-metropolitan' settings of many of the academies.[36] It is in these political and institutional terms that we must read Peter Hohendahl's argument that '[l]iterature served the emancipation movement of the middle class as an instrument to gain self-esteem and to articulate its human demands against the absolutist state and the hierarchical society'.[37]

However coherent it may have seemed as a result of its adversarial status though, the reform movement remained a heterogeneous social body divided along lines of class as well as gender. In his analysis of the role of theory in the political developments of the period, David Simpson argues that

> for Tom Paine and his followers, as for their Enlightenment precursors, rational method was a liberating and demystifying energy, a way beyond the illusions of social, political, and religious conventions, which it exposed as just that: illusions ... [T]he naturally reasonable mind had only to be shown the truth for the truth to spread and prevail.[38]

The political aspirations of radical reformers such as Paine and the leaders of the London Corresponding Society overlapped with the professional ambitions of middle-class authors who were equally intent on mobilizing these ideas in order to legitimize their own reformist ambitions. Instead of either conflating these two groups or seeing them as wholly distinct, it is more important to view them as internally differentiated and multiply overlapping social constituencies, whose shared ideas about the role of literature led to a strategic entanglement and a mutual nervousness about the nature of their alliance in the polarized atmosphere of the mid-1790s.[39] Maintaining this focus on the heterogeneity of the reform movement, and remembering the points of commonality between many middle-class reformers and conservatives, usefully complicates the oppositional vision which structures approaches such as Olivia Smith's none the less valuable *The Politics of Language, 1791–1819*. As Isaac Kramnick puts it, '[i]n the last half of the eighteenth century ... we find antagonistic interests and conflicting ideologies that require more than the dichotomy of plebeian and patrician'.[10] Kramnick situates his argument in opposition to what he describes as E. P. Thompson's more polarized view, but in 'Eighteenth-Century English Society: Class Struggle Without Class?' Thompson argues in strikingly similar terms that 'when the ideological break with paternalism came, in the 1790s, it came in the first place less from the plebeian culture than from the intellectual culture of the Dissenting middle class, and from thence it was carried to the urban artisans' (163–4).

By tracing both the complex and often controversial relations between these elements of the reform movement, and their various points of opposition and collusion with their mutual opponents, for whom the word 'reform' became increasingly intolerable, I want to develop a more intricate understanding of the sorts of claims that were being made on 'literature' in the period. Emergent or developing ideas about the nature of literature were shaped by both the areas of overlap and the differences between these various elements of the political struggles in the period. Conservative authors and journals were in many ways sympathetic to ideas about literature as an engine of progress. At times, this was because the rhetoric of 'improvement' was too compelling to be seen to despise; elsewhere, it was because this spirit of improvement included priorities which conservative authors genuinely embraced. A correspondent to the *Gentleman's Magazine*, a periodical which was no friend to the sorts of political reforms advocated by the likes of Godwin, Priestley, Wollstonecraft, or Hays, none the less proudly cited this diffusion of learning as a source of national pride: 'Knowledge, which was long confined to few, is now universally diffused, and is not lost in empty speculation, but operates upon the heart, and stimulates more active and new modes of benevolence' (58 (1788): 214). The *Gentleman's* stressed, though without the political emphasis of these Enlightenment reformers, a similar sense of the need for this diffusion of learning throughout society:

To what end was the learning of a few whilst it was confined to a few? Moroseness and pedantry. To what end was the Gospel, whilst its moralities were veiled by pomp or mysticism? Superstition or hypocrisy. They are now universally disseminated for the happiness of all. And we have now in our power more genuine felicity than was ever known at any former period. (61 (1791): 820)

The *British Critic* could similarly announce that '[e]very publication which tends to the abridgement of labour, and the promotion of accuracy, must be acceptable to the literary world' (it gave the particular example of logarithms), but it was unlikely to endorse the sorts of connections between literature and the cause of political reform espoused by liberal and radical authors (3 (1794): 1). The progressive power of literature was, as we have seen, frequently associated with the cause of political liberty, but again, the interpretation of this relationship depended heavily on whether liberty was understood to refer to the present state of

society, and so to achievements that lay in the past, or to the goal
of transforming present conditions, guided by a vision of a better
future.

Conservative critics took pride in the fact 'that, in almost every
branch of science and literature, the industry and abilities of our
countrymen have rendered themselves conspicuous' (*BC* 4 (1794):
417). Nor were they unwilling to advocate the freedom of the
press. The *Gentleman's* allowed, in a hostile review of Thelwall's
Rights of Nature, that the republic of letters was a sphere within
which '[e]very member... however obscure, possesses the most
unbounded right to discuss with perfect freedom the opinions and
reasoning of every other' (67 (1797): 55). The *British Critic* offered
its own cautious endorsement of the political importance of 'an
ample publication of authentic documents to convey correct information' in the context of its support for the dissemination of conservative pamphlets (2 (1793): 152). Freedom of the press was
too important a touchstone of English liberty to be seen to oppose.
It was more effective to try to beat the radicals at their own game,
as Hannah More did with her *Cheap Repository Tracts*, by using literature as a means of reaching the hearts and minds of the lower
orders. And as the prosecution never tired of repeating in
seditious-libel trials, respect for the liberty of the press demanded
that it be defended as actively as possible from its greatest enemy,
which was not the threat of state intervention, but a licentiousness
which had betrayed the important social role which literature
ought to play.

UNENLIGHTENED MEN

The respect of conservative journals such as the *British Critic* and
the *Gentleman's Magazine* for the importance of the dissemination
of learning ought to caution against too-easy generalizations about
the ways that political contradictions of the period were mediated
by ideas about literature. The *Gentleman's* and the *British Critic*
were not opposed to reform, but they generally chose to concentrate on those non-threatening causes such as the reformation of
manners in what they saw as a profligate age, or the reformation
of those social structures which were intended to offer relief to
the poor. As the situation polarized, however, the word 'reform'
became increasingly linked with the so-called Jacobin thinkers,

in marked contradiction to the positions adopted by conservative authors and journals. The reformist vision of literature found its most influential critique in Edmund Burke's *Reflections on the Revolution in France* (1790), and it would be echoed, in one way or another, in the reactions of conservative intellectuals to the social and political turmoil which marked the 1790s.[41]

Insisting that he was 'influenced by the inborn feelings of my nature, and not being illuminated by a single ray of this new-sprung modern light',[42] Burke mocked the grandiose ambitions of the Enlightenment reformers whose debates he dismissed as the 'shallow speculations of the petulant, assuming, short-sighted coxcombs of philosophy' (109). English liberty was not to be identified with this spirit of innovation but, on the contrary, with 'the powerful prepossession towards antiquity, with which the minds of all our lawyers and legislators, and of all the people whom they wish to influence, have always been filled' (76). Customs were a greater guarantee of liberty than reason, which meant that literature ought not to be considered in terms of unrestrained debate, but as the repository of the wisdom of past generations. It was a 'history of the force and weakness of the human mind', an accumulation of inherited wisdom which served as both a monument to the grandeur of past generations and a potent reminder of the imperfection of the human character (292). The logical consequence of the reformers' ideas would not be the dawning of some wonderful era of enlightened liberty, but the demise of serious intellectual activity: 'No part of life would retain its acquisitions. Barbarism with regard to science and literature, unskilfulness with regard to arts and manufactures, would infallibly succeed to the want of a steady education and settled principle' (183). Unrestrained investigation led not to a newly harmonized sense of private interests but to the erosion of those unconscious affinities upon which social order was wholly predicated.

Nor was this simply because truth, the boasted prize of 'this new conquering empire of light and reason', was somehow hostile to the idea of social harmony (151). On a more fundamental level, Burke rejected the very capacity of these debates, carried on within the republic of letters, to have anything to do with truth. This autonomy, which was supposedly central to these intellectual exchanges, was, he argued, the source of the reformers' greatest problems. Fond of distinguishing themselves and lacking the sobering influence of any genuine political responsibility, these men of letters would pursue innovation for its own sake, rather than as a consequence of genuine debate about important social issues. 'For, considering their speculative designs as of infinite value, and the actual arrangement of the state as of no estimation, they are at best indifferent about it. They see no merit in the good, and no fault in the vicious management of public affairs; they rather rejoice in the latter, as more propitious to revolution' (129). Burke regretted that of the list of men elected into the *Tiers Etat*, 'of any practical experience in the state, not one man was to be found. The best were only men of theory' (90). Seduced by the apparently unlimited power of reason, these advocates of the Enlightenment were misled into an irrational and dangerous confidence in 'the personal self-sufficiency' of their own ideas (182). Instead of adequately respecting the accumulated knowledge of previous generations, they prided themselves on the unparalleled wisdom which characterized their own debates. Proper respect for established customs, on the other hand, bound individuals to the greater wisdom of the community.

These 'men of theory' were not dangerous simply because they were naively optimistic or relentlessly sceptical. Instead, Burke traced a hegemonic shift in which the 'monied interest' had begun to challenge the social dominance of the landed classes (205). Inseparable from this was the rise of a new breed of writers, 'the political Men of Letters' (205). Rejecting their claim to a disinterested commitment to the general good, Burke contended that '[t]hese writers, like the propagators of all novelties, pretended to a great zeal for the poor, and the lower orders', in order to stir up popular opinion against the *ancien régime*, whose status they opposed, not because it was tyrannical, but because they felt their own aspirations impeded by it (210). By striking at the twin pillars of stable government – religious faith and a respect for the state – they had deliberately fostered an atmosphere of unrest which had resulted in their greatest triumph, the revolution itself. Unlike many conspirators though, men of letters enjoyed the prominence that was inevitably attached to the equation which they had insisted on between their own literary efforts and the public good:

What was not to be done towards their great end by any direct or immediate act, might be wrought by a longer process through the medium of opinion. To command that opinion . . . they contrived to possess themselves, with great method and perseverance, of all the avenues of literary fame. Many of them indeed stood high in the ranks of litera- ture and science. The world had done them justice; and in favour of general talents forgave the evil of their peculiar principles. This was true liberality; which they returned by endeavouring to confine the reputation of sense, learning, and taste to themselves or their followers. (208)

These authors had concealed their plot by maximizing their visi- bility, keeping themselves, like a purloined letter, in the fore- ground of the affairs of the nation. No one had adequately recog- nized the true nature of their private agenda because they had so insistently identified themselves with the public good. This emphasis on publicity, however, was merely part of the conspiracy. Contrary to the openness which ought to characterize the republic of letters as a sphere of unrestrained debate, 'a spirit of cabal, intrigue, and proselytism, pervaded all their thoughts, words, and actions' (213). The 1790 edition of the *Annual Register*, which Burke had once edited, and which he had been involved with until only a few years earlier, reprinted his charge of conspiracy under the title 'Political Effects of the Junction between the great monied Interest and the philosophical Cabals of France' (32 (1790)). In the preface to the 1792 edition it repeated the claim that '[b]y means of the press, the grand forum in which all public affairs were agitated, ... the minds of men were alienated from kings, and became enamoured of political philosophy' (iv).

Nor were these points missed by any of those writers who agreed with Burke's assessment of the dangers of unrestrained enquiry, and of the worthlessness of abstract speculation. The *Anti-Jacobin* magazine managed to compress most of these arguments and rhe- torical strategies into the preface of its first edition in 1797. Appealing for the support 'of ALL who think that the PRESS has been long enough employed principally as an engine of destruc- tion', it similarly suggested that authors, fond of making an impression, were so attracted to the idea of innovation that they had corrupted print culture (1 (1797): 9). 'Novelty', it suggested, was so much more important to this modern breed of authors than 'TRUTH' that their own commitment to the truth was itself a novel proposition (2). This was not the only echo of Burke's *Reflections*:

We have not arrived (to our shame, perhaps, we avow it) at that wild and unshackled freedom of thought, which rejects all habit, all wisdom of former times, all restraints of ancient usage, and of local attachment;

and which judges upon each subject, whether of politics or morals, as it arises, by lights entirely its own, without reference to recognized principle, or established practice.

We confess, whatever disgrace may attend such a confession, that we have not so far gotten the better of long habits and early education, not so far imbibed that spirit of liberal indifference, of diffused and comprehensive philanthropy, which distinguishes the candid character of the present age, but that We have our feelings, our preferences, and our affections, attaching on particular places, manners, and institutions, and even on particular portions of the human race . . .

In MORALS We are equally old fashioned. We have yet to learn the modern refinement of referring in all considerations upon human conduct, not to any settled and preconceived principles of right and wrong, not to any general and fundamental rules which experience, and wisdom, and justice, and the common consent of mankind have established, but to the internal admonitions of every man's judgement or conscience in his own particular instance. (3–6)

Like Burke, the *Anti-Jacobin* rejected the rationalist juxtaposition of a 'true' knowledge of individual and collective interests with that false consciousness which went by the name of prejudice. Because all beliefs were culturally determined, they were necessarily rooted in the contingencies of history. Nor were they any worse for being so. The proposition that they could be replaced by ideas developed in the abstract sphere of intellectual debate was founded on a radical and dangerous misunderstanding of the human condition. Rejecting the reformist emphasis on reason as a threat to the social good, the *Anti-Jacobin* revelled in the same common-sense rhetoric as Burke.

In his exploration of the analogous position of 'theory' within cultural–political debates at the end of the eighteenth and twentieth centuries, David Simpson argues that this emphasis on the artificiality of theoretically developed ideas proved to be a rhetorically effective way of decrying the attempt to raise new questions reflecting the interests of people who were not supposed to take an interest in these matters.[43] Human experience, the argument runs, is too complex to be reduced to formulas derived from these sorts of political agendas. Ideas which did not grow imperceptibly out of generations of inherited experience were hardly likely to be the source of constructive social interventions. In *A Second Letter to the Right Hon. Charles James Fox, upon the Matter of Libel* (1792), John Bowles argued that in unsettled times, society could not afford to indulge idle speculators: '[t]heory, however fair, and however specious, is in such cases an *ignis fatuus* which leads toward destruction' (v–vi). T. J. Mathias agreed, in *The Pursuits of Literature* (1797), 'that *theoretical perfection* in government and *practical oppression* are closely allied' (III, 5).

Reformers did their best to rebut these denunciations. The *Monthly Review* protested against the paradox that those who were quickest to denounce theoretical speculation were also the greatest enemies of the sorts of experimentation which could give those theories some practical grounding:

as it has been long settled with respect to other branches of science, so one would suppose it must likewise be admitted with respect to this, that the way of experiment is the best and surest method of investigating truth. At least it might be expected that this would be unanimously maintained by those politicians who seem, from their conduct, to think it a sufficient refutation of the strongest arguments and most legitimate reasonings, to urge in opposition, that what has been advanced is mere *theory*. Yet so it is, that those who are the most forward to cry *theory*, on the first suggestion of an improvement, are often the foremost to prevent its being brought to the test of experiment, and reduced to practice, by setting up the shout of *innovation!* by displaying the great danger of departing from *precedent*, and by expatiating on the profaneness of violating the sacred institutions of *antiquity*. (7 (1792): 325)

In a review of a published sermon entitled *The Danger of too Great an Indulgence of Speculative Opinions*, it posed the question, 'to which of the *dark ages* are we returned, that we hear in every quarter, the cry of the danger of speculative opinions?' Such a doctrine, which was 'fit only for the gloomy cell of monastic ignorance', ran counter to Britain's own impressive history of philosophical enquiry:

After all that free inquiry has done for the world, from the time of the reformation to the present day, and after all the blessings that science, in the persons of her favoured sons, her Bacons, her Newtons, and her Lockes, has bestowed on mankind, are we still to be told that to indulge in speculative opinions, is *impious, absurd,* and *dangerous?* (*MR* 10 (1793): 115–16)

Ultimately though, the cries against innovation and against the disrespect of 'the new philosophy' for established authorities drowned out those who were prepared to give 'theory' a chance. Arthur Young, a leading agrarian reformer but, by 1793, no friend of democratic political reform, struck a popular chord when, like

Burke, he confessed to a natural antipathy to theory: 'I have been too long a farmer to be governed by any thing but events; I have a considerable abhorrence of theory, of all trust in abstract reasoning; and consequently I have a reliance merely on experience, in other words, on events, the only principle worthy of an experimenter,'[44] Theory was another word for that which remained untested, which as any English farmer could tell you, compared badly indeed with those tried and trusted ideas which testified to the importance of personal experience as a source of genuine knowledge.

In the face of the optimism inspired amongst reformist authors by the virtually unbounded prospect of futurity, conservative writers offered a reverence for history as an impressive accumulation of wisdom – or, in more melancholy moods that recalled Burke's lament for the death of chivalry – a dispirited sense of belatedness in the face of inevitable cultural decline. 'The true Augustan age of Britain is past', the *Gentleman's* wrote in its review of Mathias's *The Pursuits of Literature*, 'and the decline and fall of science, and every good system, is hastening on, beyond the power of man, however superior his intellects and powers, to stem the tide' (66 (1796): 940). The finest relics of past literary greatness, it intimated in a review of a new publication of Milton's *Comus*, could only offer the consolation of the memory of better times in the face of a strange and alienating sense of modernity. 'To us, who have almost outlived antient times, and stand on the brink of the precipice of modern ones, every illustration of antient history and manners must afford delight' (*GM* 68 (1798): 703).[45]

The excesses of the French Revolution were cited as proof that if the reform movement was inspired by a spirit of futurity, it was a future which was never to arrive. The appealing linearity of the reformers' progressive historical vision was reinterpreted as a rise and fall scenario in which the power of print culture was both blessing and curse, a cultural force leading civilized nations out of the wilderness of tyranny and superstition only to return them to an equally barbaric condition known as the 'modern' age. A pamphlet entitled *A Brief Reply to the Observations of Ben. Bousfield, Esq. On Mr Burke's pamphlet, Respecting the Revolution in France* (1791) argued that 'the fumes of a capricious unsettled zeal for liberty have enveloped [England] in utter darkness' (iii). A correspondent of the *Gentleman's Magazine* protested in similar terms against society's 'progress from barbarism to civilism, and its relapse from civilization into barbarism; which retrogation seems to be the glory of the present race of *philosophers*' (63 (1793): 224). In a pamphlet entitled *Slight Observations Upon Paine's Pamphlet* (1791), Thomas Green expressed his 'disgust', having changed 'the air and comfort of the country, for the business of London', to discover that, as a result of the feverish debates ignited by Paine's work, 'the people here are actually mad, and I am apprehensive, almost literally speaking, of being bitten' (1). No sooner had he seated himself in his usual coffee house, Green explained, than he was pelted with 'a multitude of questions' about Burke's and Paine's literary efforts 'with an eagerness which astonished me' (2).

The appropriation of the title of 'philosophy' by reformist authors typified all that their critics found most offensive about the pseudo-scientific association of literature with the supposed omnipotence of reason.[46] Nor did it help that this emphasis on philosophy highlighted the intellectual indebtedness of these reformers to the French *philosophes* such as Voltaire and Diderot. Mathias argued that '[t]here is one description and sect of men, to whom more than common reprehension is due, and who cannot be held up too frequently to the public scorn and abhorrence. I mean the modern philosophers of the French system.'[47] Citing Priestley's '*King-killing* wishes and opinions' as an example of the views of these modern philosophers, he suggested that the time had come when 'the swarm of free thinking and democratical pamphlets with which the public has been pestered' outweighed the evils of censorship.[48] In his satirical poem *The Unsex'd Females* (1798), Richard Polwhele referred to '[p]hilosophism, the false image of philosophy . . . a phantom which heretofore appeared not in open day, though it now attempts the loftiest flights in the face of the sun' (10). The *Gentleman's*, in a review of Abbé Barruel's *Memoirs, Illustrating the History of Jacobinism*, suggested a similar opposition between 'the words *Philosophism* and *Philosophists*', which characterized 'the sect of Voltaire', and 'the honourable terms of *Philosophy* and *Philosopher*', which were being overshadowed by these pretenders to knowledge (68 (1798): 151).

Conservative critics suggested that the inflated self-image of reformist authors had, ironically, led to the devaluation of serious research. In a published version of a sermon preached on 19 April 1793, a day appointed for a general fast, Walter King denounced what he described as 'a sort of independence of mind, a disdain of all superiority' that could be traced back to the age's exaggerated faith in individual ability.[49] These '*philosophers*', the *British Critic* agreed in a review of Godwin's *Enquiry concerning Political Justice*, lacked the humility that ought to be consistent with real intellectual endeavour: ✍

few pretend to deny the present to be an indolent and superficial age, though at the same time they will extol it as informed and enlightened; putting these detached assertions together, we have something very like the truth; which is, that it is an indolently informed and superficially enlightened age: despising all former wisdom, chiefly from not knowing it precisely; and free in assertion rather than enquiry, merely from that impudence which ignorance alone produces, and from a childish love of novelty, unchecked by fear of consequences, or veneration of any principles. (1 (1793): 308)

Faced with this era of mediocrity, the *British Critic* countered with their own ironic vision of futurity. So great was the arrogant superficiality of enlightened philosophers such as Godwin, that it would necessarily be left to a future age, when the proper task of intellectual enquiry would once again become the rightful goal of learned endeavours, to redeem the abuses of the present:

There is much reason to apprehend, that if this *enlightened* age should be succeeded by times of real wisdom and of sound research, the general laugh of posterity will attend those high pretensions which a few have uttered with such courage, and multitudes have admitted with such *levity*. (1 (1793): 308)

A correspondent of the *Gentleman's*, satirizing the hyperbolic expectations of these new philosophers, wryly congratulated England on the good fortune of this 'vast increase of *genius*'. For himself, though, he admitted,

I am almost tired of seeing so many geniuses, and heartily wish we had a peace on the Continent, that I might retire to some quarter where I could meet with a few plain, dull fellows like myself, and not run the risk of being knocked down by a Genius in every turning'. (69 (1799): 199)

As the French Revolution developed, reformist authors became identified, not merely with the atheistic tradition of Voltaire, but with the Jacobins themselves. The *Anti-Jacobin* magazine, whose name enshrined this negative identification, insisted that its satirical efforts were required precisely because literature had as strong an influence as it did. The *Gentleman's Magazine* warned that the threat of 'these new-fangled doctrines, this strange and hetero-geneous philosophy, which has deluged France with blood', was especially insidious because however greatly Britain's martial bravery could be depended upon to repel invaders in honest combat, ideas could never be similarly contested: 'Our native force and native courage would prompt us to avoid no encounter in the martial field: but what would even the magnanimity of Britons avail against the venom of poison mysteriously prepared, and com-municated with the malignant silence of assassins?' (63 (1793): iii). The intellectual route was a kind of stealth attack which ran against the grain of British ideas about fair play in military affairs. It was an unfair battle because these ideas insinuated themselves invisibly like a poison rather than challenging British defences in any forthright way. Regardless of the nature of the ideas them-selves, 'theory' could be denounced as a very un-British manoeuvre whose real purpose was to attack the existing structures of auth-ority without becoming involved in anything that could reasonably be described as a fair fight.[50] In practice, of course, attacks on 'foreign ideas' referred just as much to the enormous circulation of radical pamphlets which originated and found their target audi-ence in the British working-class reading public. But the identifi-cation of 'theory' – and all of the abuses that were associated with it – as foreign, provided effective ammunition against those social constituencies which lay outside of established ideas about the limits of the informed reading public; groups whose illegitimacy as members of that public was, for their critics, revealed in their abuse of the press.

All of this was reinforced by the contributions of authors who, like Burke, argued that this Jacobin philosophical tradition, far from being simply naive, had manipulated a tone of universal ben-evolence in order to further its own interests. Two books, Abbé Barruel's *Memoirs, illustrating the History of Jacobinism* (1797) and John Robison's *Proofs of a Conspiracy against all the Religions and Governments of Europe* (1798), reminded English reading audiences of Burke's more literal charge of conspiracy.[51] Barruel argued that the conspirators had dedicated themselves to spreading atheistic books across the continent. More dangerously still, in order to further their mischief they had seized on the *Encyclopédie*, which, because of its authoritative status, was all the better calculated for the dissemination of subversive ideas. And, led by none other than Monsieur d'Alembert, the infidels had taken control of the French Academy, converting it into a bastion of atheism.

The conspiracy which John Robison felt he had unearthed, an infidel society called the Order of Illuminati, intent on toppling all existing forms of government and religion, originated within the Masonic Lodges in Germany. But the organization had spread, Robison warned, throughout the civilized world 'under the specious pretext of enlightening the world by the torch of philosophy, and of dispelling the clouds of civil and religious superstition which keep the nations of Europe in darkness and slavery' (11) – a transformation which would rid the world of 'government, subordination, and all the disagreeable coercions of civil governments' (205). None of this was to be trusted though, Robison explained, since the Illuminati's Enlightenment rhetoric was only a means of imposing a greater tyranny than existing regimes had ever contemplated. Robison reproduced letters allegedly written by the different conspirators which suggested that, like their French counterparts, the Illuminati had seized on literature as the most suitable medium for luring new initiates:

We must bring our opinions into fashion by every art – spread them among the people by the help of young writers. We must preach the warmest concern for humanity, and *make people indifferent to all other relations*. We must take care that our writers be well puffed, and that the Reviewers do not depreciate them; therefore we must endeavour by every mean to gain over the Reviewers and Journalists; and we must also try to gain the booksellers, who in time will see that it is their interest to side with us . . . A learned or literary society is best suited to our purpose, and had Free Masonry not existed, this cover would have been employed; and it may be much more than a cover, *it may be a powerful engine in our hands. By establishing reading societies, and subscription libraries, and taking these under our direction, and supplying them through our labours, we may turn the public mind which way we will.* (191–5)

Robison's investigation of this conspiracy was intended to be taken literally, but his analysis of British culture slipped into a more figurative level of interpretation in which the Illuminati became a symbol of deluded Enlightenment thinkers, and an explanation for the ills of literature generally. Joseph Priestley, he explained, was a perfect example of the true extent of this influence: 'This writer has already given the most promising specimens of his own docility in the principles of Illuminatism, and has already passed through several degrees of initiation' (482). Whether these conspiracies were to be taken as genuine, or whether they were simply to be read as an effective way of conceptualizing the inadequacies of reformist thinkers, they foregrounded the danger of unchecked freedom of debate generally, by reminding readers of Burke's connection of the abuse of literature with the origins of the French Revolution. As Burke had himself warned in his references to Price, those who disagreed with this reformist view could ill afford to ignore it. It was, for both its supporters and detractors, the focus of the most important debates of the period about the nature of literature.

PRINCIPLES AND PRACTICE

Arguably, these denunciations of the reformist ideal of literature could be recontained within the limited relativism of the belief that 'no man can write down TRUTH', which emerged instead as the gradual product of unrestrained debate (*MR* 14 (1794): 393). Far from signalling the subversion of the public sphere, such criticisms could be celebrated as ironic examples of its true potential – collisions of mind with mind that helped to clarify the central role which literature played as an engine of social progress. Burke's *Reflections* was frequently praised for having stimulated so extensive a debate about the rights of man. The *Analytical* used its review of Paine's *Rights of Man* as an opportunity to make precisely this point:

The public, or rather mankind in general, have very considerable obligations to Mr Burke, for bringing under review and discussion in his celebrated publication, so many topics of the highest importance to human happiness. Fortunately for the present age, politics and government are no longer mysteries enveloped in the dark shades of divine right and feudal prejudice; in the present dispute men will be taught by their interests to determine on which side the force of argument preponderates. (9 (1791): 312)

The charge that this Enlightenment vision encouraged each individual to value his own little stock of knowledge over the inherited wisdom of previous generations could similarly be put down to the misunderstanding of critics who failed to see that reformist thinkers thought of truth as the product of an ongoing exchange of ideas *between* individuals – a process which did not, in any case, negate the importance of knowledge inherited from the past.

There were, however, several developments in the 1790s which changed the terms of the debate in ways that reformers could not accommodate. Most obvious was the increasing state presence, which included specific pieces of legislation, the sharply increased number of politically motivated arrests, the interruption of mail between suspected dissidents, the widespread use of spies, threats to revoke the licences of publicans who continued to host politicized debating societies and to carry reformist literature, and cooperation with loyalist groups intent on intimidating reformist activities.[52] There were attempts to curb these state interventions. Fox's libel bill, which gave juries the right to decide on whether a piece of writing was seditious, passed into law in May 1792, and was widely hailed as a victory for the freedom of the press. But it was more than offset by the King's Proclamation condemning 'wicked and seditious writings . . . tending to invite tumult and disorder', issued on the same day that Fox's bill received its third reading in the House of Lords.[53] Thomas Erskine's successful defence of Thomas Hardy, John Horne Tooke, and John Thelwall in the 1794 treason trials was similarly overshadowed by the suspension of *habeas corpus* early in 1795, and by Grenville's and Pitt's bills to curb seditious and treasonable practices – the so-called 'gagging acts' – later that year. I will turn to these aspects of the struggle to determine the social role of literature below, but it is equally important to emphasize a more subtle discursive shift that undermined the central propositions of reformist ideas about literature.

In practice, freedom of the press referred to the absence of a state licensing body. All citizens were free to publish their views, but if these views were intemperately expressed, they were subject to the charge of seditious libel. As Sir William Blackstone put it, 'the liberty of the Press . . . consists in laying no *previous* restraints upon publications, and not in freedom from censure for criminal matter when published'.[54] The potential criminality of particular pieces of writing was premised on an indefinite but strongly perceived distinction between those publications that were speculative, or designed to participate in an exchange of ideas, and which therefore deserved protection from the law, and those works that were merely designed to inflame the minds of disgruntled sectors of society, and which therefore deserved to be punished with the full weight of the law. Learned works whose composition required a considerable amount of time, and which targeted a selective audience through both their price and their writing style, and which were not therefore 'liable to excite popular commotions', were to be distinguished from those more dangerous pamphlets, essays, and periodical publications that were 'written in a short time ... circulated at a moderate expense, and [had] an immediate action upon the public mind'.[55] This distinction, Thomas Erskine pointed out in a speech delivered to the Friends of the Liberty of the Press in January 1793, was as important as it was indefinite: 'The extent of the genuine Liberty of the Press on *general* subjects, and the boundaries which separate them from licentiousness, the English law has wisely not attempted to define; they are, indeed, in their nature undefinable.'[56] The interpretative boundaries must be determined in each particular case, but the distinctions upon which the decision must be based remained broadly understood. Erskine, for instance, expressed his surprise at having to defend the Dean of St Asaph in 1784 for publishing what he insisted was 'the *first abstract speculative writing, which has been attacked as a libel since the Revolution*'.[57]

The problem with this arrangement was not merely that, until the passing of Fox's libel law in May 1792, the decision as to whether a piece of writing constituted libel was left to the determination of the judge rather than the jury. Nor was it simply that the indefinite nature of the distinction between these two types of writing could be easily manipulated by judges and specially picked juries responding to the growing spirit of alarm. What was more difficult for reformers to counter was the increasing association of precisely those types of work, which, as 'abstract speculative writing', ought to be entitled to exemption from prosecution, with the 'Jacobin' or 'new philosophy' that was thought by many to be most dangerous to the security of the state. The very qualities which could, in the past, be argued to entitle a piece of writing to exemption from legal reprimand came to be the defining qualities of those works which for many critics posed the greatest danger to the security of the state. Within the courtroom of public opinion, if not always in the legal courts themselves, speculative writing, instead of being defined in opposition to seditious writings, became seen as a style of enquiry which was deeply implicated in the practice of fomenting unrest.[58]

Other elements of the distinction remained unchanged. The size, cost, and difficulty of any piece of writing still protected many radical authors from prosecution. The point was frequently repeated that the use of accessible language at a cheap enough price, designed to capture the attention of the disenfranchised, was more of a crime than were the seditious ideas that were being offered. The *Gentleman's Magazine* allowed that Richard Brothers would have had nothing to fear if he 'had written in a more respectable manner', but, it warned, 'it should seem [Brothers's writings] are calculated to worse ends, and written for the understanding, and adapted to the purchase of the lower class' (65 (1795): 208).[59] The *British Critic* made the same point in the opposite way when it suggested that Godwin's *Political Justice* might escape prosecution because it was written in a style that was not likely to attract the attention of the most dangerous sectors of the reading public.[60] 'Secure in these great pledges of obscurity', the *British Critic* suggested,

full many a copy have we seen with its title page exposed in a window, with its leaves uncut, till flies and dust had defaced its open front, and many an one, perhaps, shall we see descending from the flies above to those of subterranean London, guiltless of having seduced one wavering mind, or excited even a wish to prosecute, much less to persecute, the author. (1 (1793): 307)

Having criticized the Jacobin tendencies of Holcroft's *Hugh Trevor*, the *British Critic* similarly suggested that 'the length of the tale (for these three volumes are only the beginning of Trevor's sorrows) is the only chance it has of not rendering its writer answerable for a great deal of mischief' (4 (1794): 71).

Related to the distinction between speculative and seditious works was the equally important and homologous distinction between ideas and actions, which also rested upon the issue of social class. Central to the claim for the autonomy of literature as a public sphere free from government control was the conviction that rational individuals were capable of exchanging ideas, however radically misconceived, without being tempted into acting on them. Social improvement, it was frequently stressed, was the almost passive and apparently inevitable result of the pursuit of learning. Knowledge, properly diffused, was sufficient in itself to storm the barricades of tyranny.

Critics warned, however, that this distinction between thought and action was being undermined by the distribution of literature designed to appeal to the labouring masses. '[I]n vulgar minds', the *British Critic* suggested, 'the transition from contempt and dislike to acts of violence is but too easy' (7 (1796): 262). Thomas Erskine, prosecuting Thomas Williams for publishing a cheap edition of *Age of Reason*, offered a longer meditation on the importance of confining potentially inflammatory literature to readers who understood the significance of this distinction between thought and action:

An intellectual book, however erroneous, addressed to the intellectual world upon so profound and complicated a subject, can never work the mischief which this Indictment was calculated to repress. – Such works will only incite the minds of men enlightened by study, to a closer investigation of a subject well worthy of their deepest and continued contemplation. – The powers of the mind are given for human improvement in the progress of human existence. – The changes produced by such reciprocations of lights and intelligences are certain in their progression, and make their way imperceptibly, by the final and irresistible power of truth ... But this book has no such object, and no such capacity: – it presents no arguments to the wise and enlightened; on the contrary, it treats the faith and opinions of the wisest with the most shocking contempt, and stirs up men, without the advantages of learning, or sober thinking, to a total disbelief of every thing hitherto held sacred; and consequently to a rejection of all the laws and ordinances of the state, which stand only upon the assumption of their truth.[61]

The audience targeted by *Age of Reason* would be misled into drastic courses of action because they lacked the advantages of education necessary, not only to distinguish helpful from destructive ideas, but also to understand that ideas, properly digested by enlightened minds, would achieve the desired effects without recourse to action. Unable to govern themselves, they would be inclined to challenge the political authority of their own government.

The difference was not that the enlightened understood, unlike their less educated counterparts, that ideas could be reflected upon without necessarily being put into action; the real difference was that the enlightened understood that this _was_ a form of action. As the *Analytical Review* put it, reason would 'triumph over tyranny without external violence' (22 (1795): 545). Or as Erskine had expressed it somewhat more poetically, 'such reciprocations of lights and intelligences ... make their way imperceptibly, by the final and irresistible power of truth'.[62] Reason acted by asserting itself in the form of broadly held opinions; its lessons did not, therefore, need to be acted upon in any direct way. The mistake of the unenlightened was to misconceive of the nature of this inseparability of thought and action. Because they lacked an adequate education, they could be stirred into irrational behaviour. Their response was unnecessary, however, not because action ought to follow debate at a suitable distance, but because they ought to recognize that the two apparently very different processes were really only a single phenomenon.

However radical his vision of social change might have been, Godwin's views about the role of literature as an engine of reform were based on a strong sense of this distinction. 'It is the characteristic of truth', he argued, 'to trust much to its own energy, and to resist invasion rather by the force of conviction than by the force of arms', which would be to 'give birth to deformity and abortion'. Nor was Godwin free from a connected sense of the identity of those who failed to understand this distinction. 'Society, as it presently exists in the world', he explained:

> will long be divided into two classes, those who have leisure for study, and those whose importunate necessities perpetually urge them to temporary industry. It is no doubt to be desired, that the latter class should be made as much as possible to partake of the privileges of the former. But we should be careful, while we listen to the undistinguishing demands of benevolence, that we do not occasion a greater mischief than that we undertake to cure.

The reparation of social injustice required that the privileges of learning be extended to the people who had previously been denied them, but one of the effects of social inequality was that those who lacked these privileges were unfit to be trusted with them. In trying to extend the power of knowledge to those who were incapable of properly understanding the reflective nature of this power, benevolent people faced the possibility of 'propagating blind zeal, where we meant to propagate reason'.[63] To seek redress because one was *too* thoroughly unrewarded within existing social relations, according to this cautionary stance, was to be disqualified from doing so.[64]

As the radical reform movement gathered pace in the years

following the publication of *Political Justice*, Godwin became hardened in his certainty about the importance of respecting these sorts of distinctions, and about the social identity of those groups who threatened the sovereignty of reason. In his *Considerations on Lord Grenville's and Mr Pitt's Bills concerning Treasonable and Seditious Practices* (1795), he used familiar terms in defending the freedom of the press in the face of legislation that was widely seen to encroach upon it:

A doctrine opposite to the maxims of the existing government may be dangerous in the hands of agitators, but it cannot produce very fatal consequences in the hands of philosophers. If it undermine the received system, it will undermine it gradually and insensibly; it will merely fall in with that gradual principle of decay and renovation, which is perpetually at work in every part of the universe.[65]

Nothing could be more natural than this process of change, which would be virtually unnoticeable, manifesting itself only through those larger and unstoppable processes of universal evolution. None of this was automatic, however. The freedom which was central to the unconstrained play of reason must be as strictly limited in its access as it was absolute in degree:

reform is a delicate and an awful task. No sacrilegious hand must be put forth to this sacred work. It must be carried on by slow, almost insensible steps, and by just degrees. The public mind must first be enlightened; the public sentiment must next become unequivocal; there must be a grand and magnificent harmony, expanding itself through the whole community. There must be a consent of wills, that no minister and no monopolist would be frantic enough to withstand. This is the genuine image of reform; this is the lovely and angelic figure that needs only to be shewn, in order to be universally adored.[66]

The democratic tone of this call for the development of unequivocal public opinion was balanced against the selective nature of those who were to be entrusted with instigating and stimulating these processes. The angelic figure of reform was too pure to be sullied by the wrong hands. It was precisely this sense of distinction which William Burdon singled out for praise in his defence of Godwin in his pamphlet, *Various Thoughts on Politics, Morality, and Literature* (1800):

Mr Godwin's is not a noisy, tumultuous address to the passions of men, calculated to set the world in an uproar, but a calm, rational system, intended to develope and improve the judgement, and therefore slow in its operation, and silent in its effects: it is addressed to the individual in his closet, and not to the multitude in camps, and courts, and crowds. (35)

For his many advocates, Godwin's *Considerations* was a perfect statement of precisely this disposition towards peaceful change. Signed by 'A Lover of Order', it objected equally to those pieces of government legislation that would encroach upon the sacred liberty of the press, and to those illegitimate groups whose activities had given occasion to the two bills.

More particularly, Godwin identified those sacrilegious hands that would lay hold of the angelic figure of reform with a group whom many acknowledged to be the unspecified target of the 'two bills', the London Corresponding Society. For Godwin, the LCS (based, he pointed out, on the Jacobin Club in Paris), and other political societies like it, were the apostasy rather than the consummation of his vision of radical change. These groups recruited 'from the poorer classes of society', welding them into an 'extraordinary machine':

it has forced itself upon public notice, by the immense multitudes it has collected together in the neighbourhood of the metropolis, at what have been stiled its general meetings. The speeches delivered at these meetings, and the resolutions adopted, have not always been of the most temperate kind. The collecting of immense multitudes of men into one assembly, particularly when there have been no persons of eminence, distinction, and importance in the country, that have mixed with them, and been ready to temper their efforts, is always sufficiently alarming . . . It is not, for the most part, in crowded audiences, that truth is successfully investigated, and the principles of science luminously conceived. But it is not difficult to pronounce whether the political lectures that are likely to be delivered by an impatient and headlong reformer, are entitled to approbation.[67]

Literature's role as an 'engine' had nothing to do with those groups which operated as a 'machine'; quite the opposite, Godwin's 'public opinion', however unanimous it must ultimately be, was wholly distinct from mass meetings or movements in which the private identity of each participant was obscured. Those who failed to recognize the difference between private readings and public meetings, which was broadly homologous to the difference between ideas and actions, and between speculative and seditious writings, were the enemies rather than the advocates of reform

[handwritten note: Distinction not made clear – Abuse by conserv]

because they failed to appreciate that reason was intimately connected with the reflective process of *literary* debate. This position,
ensuring the purity of reform by articulating the traditional distinction between those types of exchanges which ought to be
exempt from legal attentions and those which required these
attentions, ought to have maintained for Godwin that freedom
which his own literary efforts required. And indeed, unlike many
of his contemporaries, Godwin was never arrested for his writings.
The problem, however, was that this distinction, like the distinction between speculative and seditious writings, was one of the
casualties of the 1790s. In his *A Second Letter to the Right Hon.
Charles James Fox, upon the Matter of Libel* (1792), Bowles argued
that the characteristics which many felt ought to protect an author
from the law could be used to conceal far more sinister intentions.
Because a seditious text 'does not display its real tendency but by
means of a connect [*sic*] with something else … and though in
appearance it be merely speculative', he warned, 'it may be prac-
ticably intended, under the mask of theory, to disturb the peace
of society, and to produce public heats, tumults, and insurrections'
(44). Nor was the problem simply that publications which seemed
to be inspired by legitimate intentions could actually be designed
with the opposite purpose in mind. More fundamentally, the
reformist emphasis on free debate as a process capable of producing cultural truths precluded the possibility of deciding in any final
way what the nature of legitimate intentions should be. In its
review of George Dyer's *An Address to the People of Great Britain, on
the Doctrine of Libels, and the Office of Jurors*, the *Gentleman's Magazine*
argued that uncontrolled enquiry was characterized, not by the
inflexible opposition between discourse and practice, but by the
easy transition from free ideas to unrestrained actions:

The rock on which such assertors of the *truth* split is the want of distinguishing between *speculative* and *practical* truth. In order that their opinions may be established, all others are to be admitted, – is the great
preliminary article of their creed. They forget that, whether society be
in a civilized or uncivilized state, it cannot subsist while men are allowed
to say what they please of each other, which must finally lead to *doing*
what they please to each other. (69 (1799): 320)

The problem with reformers such as Dyer, the *Gentleman's* suggested, was that they wanted to limit the effects of their emphasis
on the free play of reason by situating it within a framework that

dictated what counted as rational enquiry. Once people had been granted the power to determine their interests for themselves, however, this foundationalist recourse to distinctions which could help to limit this freedom became negotiable as well. Far from promoting social stability by reconciling the authority of the government with the opinions of the people, the freedom of expression championed by advocates of reform would only intro-duce a note of permissiveness that would in turn open the flood gates to the wholesale neglect of any restrictions whatsoever on individual behaviour. Like Mathias in *The Pursuits of Literature*, cor-respondents of the *Gentleman's* were quick to cite the destruction of Priestley's house and library in the Birmingham riots of July 1791 as proof that whatever Priestley's own beliefs, freedom of ideas and ungoverned actions were points on a dangerous con-tinuum of licentiousness rather than alternative forms of inter-vention.

In its review of Godwin's *Considerations*, the *Gentleman's* suggested that Godwin's support for freedom of expression, however much he himself might oppose these dynamics, played directly into the hands of those who could least be trusted with the control of public opinion: 'This is begging the question ... who will stop the pro-gress of one man's reasoning to another and perhaps a worse man's acting, upon such occasions?' (66 (1796): 142). Far from precluding seditious actions, the *Gentleman's* argued, the unchecked exchange of ideas tended to provoke them. Worse, Godwin's argument, pushed to its logical extremes, failed to offer any obvious way of stabilizing political authority in order to rule on the legitimacy of these actions. Once people had subscribed to the idea of unconstrained debate, who was to deny the legitimacy of other people's more dangerous ideas about the limits within which all interaction was acceptable?

Nor was Godwin always identified as a member of that mis-guided community of thinkers who erroneously but honourably believed in the possibility of preserving the difference between ideas and actions. Despite his best efforts to distinguish himself from potentially violent insurrectionists, Godwin was often denounced by conservative critics as one of the radicals' greatest spokesmen. Mathias warned that in the hands of 'Mr Godwin and other speculative writers', ideas and actions were inseparably intertwined:

I can laugh at their metaphysics, and even be amused with their panto-
mime fancies, *as such*. But when I know that their theories are designed
to be brought into action, and when they tell us, that they hate violence,
bloodshed, revolution, and misery, and that truth and happiness are their
objects . . . I declare from private conviction and from public experience,
that I oppose the admission of their doctrines, whether recommended by
Thomas Paine or William Godwin.[68]

Mathias stressed that he was not against freedom of the press.
But unlike 'the speculators of former times', modern theorists
tended to publish in ways which transgressed the boundaries that
protected literature from inflammatory propaganda:

The lucubrations of Montesquieu and Locke were given as the result of
long experience and continued meditation, and were designed to produce
not subversion, but *slow* and gradual reformation, as the various states
of Europe would admit. The writers of these days on the contrary, throw
out their ideas *at a heat*, and intend they should be brought into *immediate*
action.[69]

Mathias did not so much reject the distinctions offered by Godwin
between speculative and seditious writings, and between ideas and
actions, as turn them back against Godwin in the way that Godwin
had done with the LCS. The end result was the same: the opposition between ideas and actions could no longer ensure the integrity of radical political authors, however committed they may have
seemed to be to limiting themselves to rational exchanges.

More than Godwin or any other writer in the period, it was 'that
rude and left-handed fencer, Thomas Paine', who did the most to
confuse these distinctions, both by the themes and style of his
writings, and by the sorts of audiences that they attracted (*GM* 66
(1796): 397). Part 2 of *Rights of Man* (1792), for which Paine was
tried, announced on its title page its aim of 'combining Principle
and Practice'. This intention, for many of Paine's critics, was
embodied in the vulgarity of his writing style, which catered to
those who were unable to reason adequately upon these matters,
and by his decision to issue part 2 in a cheap sixpenny edition, at
the same time reissuing part 1 at the same price.[70] As E. P.
Thompson argues, it was Paine 'who put his faith in the free operation of opinion in the "open society".[71] Olivia Smith similarly
suggests that Paine's achievement was the creation of a style
which, for disenfranchised but politically motivated readers, 'suddenly brought one's own language into the realm of the literary'.[72]

But it was equally true that for Paine, the exchange of ideas could never be abstracted from the issue of social intervention. Nor, Paine might have added, was this position unique to radicals. The class-determined interpretation of the ideal of free speech confirmed that ideas were *always* reinforced by particular forms of social pressure.

The threat that critics identified in Paine's efforts to target a plebeian audience was reinforced by the industriousness with which many reform societies disseminated abridged versions of *Rights of Man* and *Age of Reason*. In *Radical Satire and Print Culture*, Marcus Wood warns that it 'has not been sufficiently recognized that for working people in the 1790s *The Rights of Man* [*sic*] would frequently have been read not in the form of the lengthy pamphlet, which in its combined form ran to some 120 tightly printed pages, but in highly simplified forms which included broadsides, chapbooks, handbills and selections' (94). The deliberate circulation of Paine's work was, as Smith notes, an example of the inseparability of ideas and actions: the political clubs were strengthened by the popularity of Paine's work and also helped to reinforce his popularity by publishing cheap editions of his writing (60). For Paine, the test of the importance of any work was the extent of its diffusion amongst an eager reading public. In the introduction to part 2, he bragged that unlike Burke's *Reflections*, part 1 of *Rights of Man* had sold 'not less than between forty and fifty thousand' copies (177). Because of its echoes of traditional Enlightenment ideas about literature as a medium for the communication of knowledge, his point was vital. Implicit in it was the suggestion that, for his critics, this very process of diffusion had become a test of criminality.

The anonymous author of *A Defence of the Constitution of England against the Libels that have been lately Published on it; Particularly in Paine's Pamphlet on the Rights of Man* (1791), offered his own pamphlet as 'a way of guarding the people against *those who offer them poison*' (5), an antidote designed 'to prevent the effect of immediate surprize on weak minds; and to bespeak their attention to the discussions and measures of reasonable men, even those who advance the principles which are adopted by Paine, but who advance them like Scholars and Gentlemen' (33–4). Another anonymous pamphlet entitled *Remarks on Mr Paine's Pamphlet, Called the Rights of Man* (1791), reiterated the distinction between ideas

and the forms of communication which made those ideas dangerous. 'Men of sanguine temper' could safely exchange 'violent opinions' because, regardless of how little else they agreed upon,
'speculative' thinkers understood the importance of confining
their message to other speculative thinkers (5). But the security
of this arrangement had been compromised by the vulgar writing
style of authors such as Paine, and by the efforts of reformist
groups to subsidize the dissemination of 'six-penny pacquets of
sedition, for the study of a common people, but lately and scarcely
emerging from the darkness of ignorance' (6–7). Paine's book, the
author suggested, was very similar to a weapon popular in France
which, ironically, was also called the Rights of Man:

[It] was sold at a reduced price, and contained within itself every principle of human annoyance. – It was something like a loaded whip, of
about five feet in length, and concealed a cut-and-thrust sword.

By this contrivance every man was enabled to purchase for *a few hours*,
a thing which armed him with power to knock down, cut, and stab his
fellow creatures, as he pleased. – *It was long, heavy, pointed, sharp, and cheap.*
(80)

For the author of this anonymous pamphlet, as for other loyalist
critics, price reduction (when it was radical rather than conservative literature that was being subsidized) not only emphasized the
author's and bookseller's desire to spread poison throughout
society, it highlighted the unnatural status of the book's
readership.

This would not have been as great a problem as it was except
for what Alan Richardson has provocatively explored as the 'democratization' of reading – the development of new reading audiences eager for political information but lacking, according to
their critics, the necessary education.[73] In *A British Freeholder's
Address to His Countrymen, on Thomas Paine's Rights of Man* (1791),
George Mason argued that 'the greatest difficulty to me is to find
any passages in Paine's Book deserving animadversion. Some
degree of literary taste is almost universal in Britain: – I mean
with those who can read; and who would write to those who cannot?' (13). For Mason, this universality of literary taste ought to
neutralize the vulgarity of Paine's book. But there is an instructive
confusion in his terms of reference, since Paine was, after all, writing precisely to those individuals who were traditionally excluded

from accounts of the reading community, but who were eager for
political literature all the same.

For some critics, this confusion was precisely the point. In the
advertisement to part 4 of *The Pursuits of Literature* (1797), T. J.
Mathias repeated the conviction he had already expressed in part
3, that 'LITERATURE, *well or ill conducted*, IS THE GREAT ENGINE *by which*,
I am fully persuaded, ALL CIVILIZED STATES *must ultimately be supported
or overthrown*'. This was increasingly the case, he argued, because
the changing patterns of readership had blurred existing calcu-
lations about the positive and negative potential of literature as a
sphere for the exchange of ideas:

> I am now more and more deeply impressed with this truth, if we consider
> the nature, variety and extent of the word, Literature. We are no longer
> in an age of ignorance, and information is not partially distributed
> according to the ranks, and orders, and functions, and dignities of social
> life. All learning has an index, and every science its abridgement. I am
> scarcely able to name any man whom I consider as wholly ignorant. We
> no longer look exclusively for learned authors in the usual place, in the
> retreats of academic erudition and in the seats of religion. Our peasantry
> now read the *Rights of Man* on mountains and moors and by the way side;
> and shepherds make the analogy between their occupation and that of
> their governors. Happy indeed, had they been taught no other compari-
> son. Our *unsexed* female writers now instruct or confuse us and them-
> selves in the labyrinth of politics, or turn us wild with Gallic frenzy.
> (IV, i–ii)

Mathias was as clear as Mason was hesitant about the entanglement of the issues of political authority, literary taste, and potential readerships, but his conclusions about literature as 'the great
engine' capable of deciding the fate of nations were just as pessimistic. The image of '*unsexed* female writers', a popular one
amongst critics of the reform movement, as we shall see in chapter
4, suggested for many the worrying extent to which these changes
in the role of literature constituted a crime against nature itself.
Nor, Mathias argued, did traditional arguments about the distinctions between safe and dangerous forms of literature – such as
price, length, accessibility – continue to hold:

> It is not enough to say, a book is bulky or voluminous, and therefore can
> have no effect upon the mass of the people, because that opinion is not
> true. Such a book can not only be abridged and dispersed abroad, but a
> man like Thomas Paine, with a rude, wicked and daring manner of think-

ing, and with vulgar but impressive language, may blend the substance of the opinions with his own, and in a short popular tract make them familiar and intelligible to every apprehension. (III, 1–2)

What radical reformers celebrated as the democratization of reading, conservative critics denounced as a seditiously intended disruption of the legitimate boundaries of traditional readerships, which effectively negated literature's constructive potential as a spur to critical debate.

THESE PROSECUTING TIMES

By addressing readers who were not traditionally assumed to constitute the target audience of important political writings, and by announcing on the title page of *Rights of Man*, part 2, his own sense of the interpenetration of principles and practice, Paine offered a new and radically different interpretation of the role of literature as a force for social change. Nor was Paine an isolated figure in these developments. The London Corresponding Society, which took an active role in promoting Paine's writing, also dedicated themselves to circulating their own works as widely as possible in order 'to diffuse political knowledge' amongst those elements of the populace which did not traditionally figure in constructions of the public.[74] The LCS's resolutions, which had already been 'published in the newspapers' by the Society for Constitutional Information, 'were afterwards published by the London Corresponding Society itself, in the form of hand-bills, and thousands of them were distributed in London, and throughout the country'.[75] Defamed by John Reeves's Association for the Protection of Property Against Republicans and Levellers, the LCS published an *Address to the Nation* 'vindicating their character from the base lies propagated against them . . . The copies were printed in the form of large broadsides, and posted up in various parts of London'.[76]

As the arrest and conviction of the bill sticker who posted the *Address* might suggest, this widened definition of literature as an engine of change was contested, not only amongst a growing number of pamphlet writers, but with equal attention, in a series of highly publicized trials. Publication, because it ensured the circulation of ideas amongst an informed reading public, was a cornerstone of the ideal of literature as a public sphere, but it also exposed the author to the full rigour of the law. As the prosecution argued in Joseph Gerrald's sedition trial:

in themselves the speeches are not criminal. The resolutions, if locked up in the breast, the speeches, if uttered to the winds of the desart, the writings, if concealed in our repositories from human observation, are neither criminal nor obnoxious to punishment . . . [T]he man who writes, without attempting to disseminate, or to publish, a seditious composition, may remain in the country as an innocent citizen; and, however disaffected in secret to government, will still enjoy the protection of its laws.[77]

Ideas, in order to shape public opinion, needed to be diffused throughout society, but the growing numbers of people who could read – and who, more dangerously, appeared eager to read – but who could not be *trusted* as readers, meant that it was precisely the dissemination of ideas which ensured the author's potential criminality.

Some authors and booksellers offered their own legal battles as protests against the intrusion of the state. Daniel Isaac Eaton made a virtual career out of it throughout the 1790s, frequently publishing the judicial proceedings as independent texts. He was indicted on 3 June 1793 for selling *Rights of Man*, part 2, and again on 10 July 1793 for selling Paine's *Letter Addressed to the Addressers*. He was acquitted both times, and subsequently published an ironical pamphlet, *The Pernicious Effects of the Art of Printing upon Society, Exposed*. In 1794 he was tried for including a story about a gamecock 'naming our lord the king' in his journal *Politics for the People, or a Salmagundy for Swine*,[78] and then again in the same year for publishing Pigott's 'Female Jockey Club', and was acquitted both times. In 1796 he was in court again for publishing Pigott's *Political Dictionary* and then for *Duties of Citizenship*. He revived his efforts when public unrest began to grow again in the 1810s, republishing an edition of parts one and two of *Age of Reason* in 1811. When in 1812 he was tried and found guilty for publishing part 3, he was sentenced to eighteen months in jail and to stand in the pillory where he was cheered by the crowd.[79]

Trials such as these became the subject of enormous public interest. During Thomas Hardy's treason trial in 1794, which Lord Chief Justice Eyre described as an 'extraordinary case, which can hardly be judged of by the common rules on which we proceed in cases of this nature',[80] the audience spilled out onto the street:

The streets were seemingly filled with the whole of the inhabitants of London, and the passages were so thronged that it was impossible for the Judges to get to their carriages. Mr Erskine went out and addressed the multitude, desiring them to confide in the justice of the country; reminding them that the only security of Englishmen was under the inestimable laws of England, and that any attempt to overawe or bias them, would not only be an affront to public justice, but would endanger the lives of the accused. He then besought them to retire, and in a few minutes there was scarcely a person to be seen near the Court. No spectacle could be more interesting and affecting.[81]

In his *Memoir* (1832), Hardy recalled the public reaction to the news in even more dramatic terms which united virtually all British citizens in a single joyous recognition of his – and by extension, their own – escape from the progress of tyranny:

Immediately on the words 'NOT GUILTY' being pronounced by the foreman of the worthy jury, the Sessions House, where the Court sat, was almost rent with loud and reiterated shouts of applause. The vast multitude that were anxiously waiting without, caught the joyful sound, and like an electric shock, or the rapidity of lightning, the glad tidings spread throughout the whole town, and were conveyed much quicker than the regular post could travel, to the most distant parts of the isle, where all ranks of people were anxiously awaiting the result of the trial. (53)

Hardy's description of people waiting 'anxiously' for the news in 'the most distant parts of the isle' reimagines the bourgeois dream of universality in the more extensive terms embraced by the radical reformers: a nation waiting to participate in a unified expression of joy over the failure of an attack on the promoters of liberty. The respect of the general populace for the sovereignty of the judiciary amplified Erskine's argument in the courtroom that the actions of Hardy in particular, and the political societies in general, reflected a widened rather than a damaged respect for the difference between ideas and actions. Their behaviour was consistent with the plan 'adopted by the Prisoners, of surrounding Parliament (unwilling to reform its own corruptions), NOT by armed men, or by importunate multitudes, but by the still and universal voice of a whole people CLAIMING THEIR KNOWN AND UNALIENABLE RIGHTS'.[82] The fluidity with which the trial's audience spilled out beyond the space of the courtroom into the street reflected the way that the trials, as authoritative judgements on the nature of literature, were themselves recuperated as literary texts which invited readers to play the role of juries, deciding, within the sphere of the literary republic, on the merits of what had transpired within the public space of the courtroom. The bottom line of public debate, these trials seemed to indicate, was the law. But publications of the trials, and the debates which inevitably surrounded them, suggested that the law itself, as fully as it ought to be respected, was none the less subject to the long-term influence of what Mary Favret has described as 'a higher law, an ideology of the public will'.[83]

Ironically, trials of seditious literature made it possible to publish excerpts or whole copies of those works legally as part of the proceedings of these trials. In his *Autobiography* (1824), another member of the LCS, Francis Place, recalled the complexities generated by these interdiscursive shifts in the case of Thomas Williams's trial for publishing an edition of *Age of Reason*:

> On the verdict being given Lord Kenyon said. 'I have observed several persons from curiosity taking notes of what passed here. This publication is so shocking that I hope nobody will publish this: I mean that a general detail of it will not make any part of that publication. Nobody who has any regard to decency, nobody who has any regard to their own interest will endeavour to disseminate this publication by publishing what has passed to day'. Lord Erskine however corrected his speech for the Morning Chronicle and it was of course published the next day. (171)

Erskine's prosecution of Williams was greeted with dismay by those who saw him as an advocate for freedom of the press. Whatever Erskine's sense of the limits of this freedom, however, his respect for the necessary importance of the press, correctly used, was reflected in his decision to publish a corrected version of his speech in the *Morning Chronicle*. Thomas Spence employed a more radical version of the same approach when he read out the whole of his pamphlet, *The Restorer of Society to its Natural State*, during his trial in 1801. It may have helped to lose Spence the trial (he was sentenced to a year in jail and fined twenty pounds), but it enabled him to reproduce the pamphlet legally as part of his subsequent publication, *The Important Trial of Thomas Spence*, which became a standard text in radical collections.[84]

The circulation of radical political tracts helped force the question of the relationship between the laws against seditious writings, the supposed autonomy of literature, and the growing readership that lay outside of the traditional boundaries of the

reading public. Acting in his more usual and better remei
capacity of advocate for the defence in the trial of Paine for
of Man, part 2, Thomas Erskine had argued that 'the cause re
itself into a question of the deepest importance to us all
NATURE AND EXTENT OF THE LIBERTY OF THE ENGLISH PRESS'. It was, in
other words, a case which went to the heart of the struggle to
define literature in terms of the related questions of political authority and the reading community. Paine, living in France by the
time of his trial, made the same point in a letter to the Attorney-
General: because of his personal absence from the country, the
real object of prosecution must have been *'the rights of the people of
England to investigate systems and principles of government'*.[85]

Erskine argued that the case was straightforward. It was wholly
unaffected by the question of the extent to which other people
may have gone to disseminate copies of *Rights of Man*. All of this,
whatever its consequences, had nothing to do with the task of
determining whether Paine was guilty of seditious libel. What
mattered, Erskine argued, in terms which perfectly reflected the
reformist ideal of the republic of letters, was whether Paine really
believed that what he was urging was in the best interests of the
country:

The proposition which I mean to maintain as the basis of the liberty of
the press, and without which it is an empty sound, is this; – that every
man, not intending to mislead, but seeking to enlighten others with what
his own reason and conscience, however erroneously, have dictated to
him as truth, may address himself to the universal reason of a whole
nation, either upon the subject of governments in general, or upon that
of our own particular country … All this every subject of this country
has a right to do, if he contemplates only what he thinks would be for
its advantage, and but seeks to change the public mind by the conviction
which flows from reasonings dictated by conscience.[86]

Whereas Erskine rejected the idea that the nature of the book's
readership, whether it was determined by the author's style of
writing or by the efforts of others to spread the work, could in any
way affect the question of the work's legal status, the counsel for
the prosecution argued that the question of audience provided
clear evidence of Paine's seditious intentions. The fact that Paine
had not been arrested for part 1 of *Rights of Man*, he explained,
was proof that he actually agreed with Erskine about the freedom
which ought to be accorded to disinterested authors. What made

part 2 different was not so much any variation in the book's message as the separate issue of the ways in which the book had been circulated.

> This particular publication was preceded by one upon the same subjects, and handling, in some measure, the same topics ... Reprehensible as that book was, extremely so, in my opinion, yet it was ushered into the world under circumstances that led me to conceive that it would be confined to the judicious reader, and when confined to the judicious reader, it appeared to me that such a man would refute as he went along.
>
> But, Gentlemen, when I found that another publication was ushered into the world still more reprehensible than the former; that in all shapes, in all sizes, with an industry incredible, it was either totally or partially thrust into the hands of all persons in this country, of subjects of every description; when I found that even children's sweetmeats were wrapped up with parts of this, and delivered into their hands, in the hope that they would read it; when all industry was used, such as I describe to you, in order to obtrude and force this upon that part of the public whose minds cannot be supposed to be conversant with subjects of this sort, and who cannot therefore correct as they go along, I thought it behoved me upon the earliest occasion, which was the first day of the term succeeding this publication, to put a charge upon record against its author.[87]

Ultimately, what was on trial was the question of whether ideas ought to be judged on their own merit, or whether they could be tried in terms of the probable or possible future actions of those who were influenced by them. Nor was a book to be judged by any negative effects which it unwittingly triggered, but by its circulation amongst a readership, who were themselves implicitly being judged according to their potential to embark on such a calamitous course of action. For the jury, the image of a page from *Rights of Man* used as a wrapper for child's sweetmeats – the ultimate symbol of radicals' attempts to corrupt the minds of the innocent – was vivid proof of Paine's seditious intentions. The foreman rose to interrupt the prosecution before its reply to Erskine's defence, explaining that the jury was already unanimous in its decision that the prisoner was guilty.

In July 1798, Charles Fox wrote that he considered the sentencing of Joseph Johnson to nine months in jail for selling an anti-war pamphlet written by the elderly Dissenting minister, Gilbert Wakefield, who himself received a two-year sentence, to be 'a death blow to the liberty of the press'.[88] This vision of literature received an even more eloquent eulogy in a silence that is embedded in the third edition of Godwin's *Political Justice*, which appeared in late 1797 without the section entitled 'Literature'. Even for a radical middle-class reformer like Godwin, it had become too risky to advocate such a position publicly. The ideal of literature as a public sphere had been edited out of Godwin's text just as, on a wider discursive level, it was being edited out of history. The arrests of a seemingly endless series of authors, publishers, and booksellers, all of them evidence of what Thomas Spence referred to as 'these prosecuting times',[89] and the flood of legislation designed to curtail the easy circulation of cheap literature, brought home for many intellectuals the reality that literary publications were the one place where 'this right to discuss with perfect freedom the opinions and reasoning of every other' manifestly did not exist (*GM* 67 (1797): 54–5). Public opinion would continue to grow as a force within the political public sphere after 1800, but this was paralleled by the diminution of the scope and authority of the republic of letters. Conservatives' success in mobilizing public opinion in the 1790s reinforced the strength of the political public sphere at the expense of literature as it had been defined in the previous two or three decades.

These obituaries for the press were slightly premature. The unrest that marked the years following the end of the Napoleonic war, the Peterloo Massacre, and the Queen Caroline affair recuperated many of the same issues about literature which had been fought out during the 1790s. William Cobbett responded to the growing agitation by reducing the cost of his journal, the *Political Register,* and renaming it the *Weekly Political Pamphlet* (familiarly known as 'Twopenny Trash') in November 1816.[90] And trials such as William Hone's once again became important platforms for the articulation of a radical democratic position.[91] In some ways, the stakes involved in the struggle to rethink the limits of the reading public were considerably higher by the 1810s because, as E. P. Thompson argues, it had by then become financially possible to maintain a self-sustaining literary community of 'full-time agitators'.[92] William Hazlitt offered an exemplary account of the reformist vision of the social importance of a free press in his 1828 essay, 'The Influence of Books on the Progress of Manners':

The reading public – laugh at it as we will, abuse it as we will – is, after all (depend upon it), a very rational animal, compared with a feudal lord and his horde of vassals ... The owner of a baronial castle could do as he pleased, as long as he had only to account to his tenants, or the inhabitants of the adjacent hamlet, for his unjustifiable proceedings, to crush their feeble opposition, or silence their peevish discontent; but when public opinion was brought to bear upon his conduct, he could no more stand against it than against a train of artillery placed on the opposite heights to batter down his stronghold, and let daylight into its dark and noisome dungeons. Just so the Modern Philosophy 'bores through his castle-walls, and farewell LORD!'[93]

The description is gloriously untarnished by the blows that this ideal of literature had suffered in the last decade of the eighteenth century. The power of literature transforms not only disparate individuals into a unified body of readers sharing the same opinions about what they read; it converts the selfish and narrow-minded individual into the perfect citizen: 'an *ideal* and abstracted, and therefore a disinterested and reclaimed character'.[94]

Like Burke in the early 1790s, various critics took to the field to defend the social order against these disruptive influences. Robert Southey argued that liberty had been reduced to licentiousness by agitators who contradicted their own emphasis on the importance of freedom of expression by '[a]ddressing themselves to the passions of the vulgar'.[95] Coleridge's second *Lay Sermon*, which appeared in 1817, focused its attack on radical leaders such as Cobbett, Leigh and John Hunt, and Hazlitt. In a pamphlet entitled *Reflections on the Liberty of the Press in Great Britain* (1820), Friedrich von Gentz – the German translator of Burke's *Reflections* – warned that the

vilest libellers have, with unexampled effrontery, erected their standards in opposition to the Government, not merely in the streets of London, but in every city great and small, in every town and village ... The disorganising principles which the periodical pamphleteers, particularly those of the common order, instil into the lower classes of the people, are truly alarming in their nature; but still more alarming, when it is considered that the men who promulgate them, exercise an unbounded control over the opinion of millions of readers, who cannot procure the antidote of better writings.[96]

There would be no final word on these debates, but the growing threat of state intervention on one side, and an alarmist recognition of the potentially revolutionary consequences of this new reading public on the other, helped to perpetuate a climate of

suspicion which made it difficult to believe in Hazlitt's utopian \
vision of literature as a force capable of refashioning nations ⌇
according to the interests of the people. The ideal of literature as
a public sphere had run aground on political anxieties about the
sector of the populace which could reliably be included within the
reading public, and on a deep suspicion that theoretical abstrac-
tions were politically dangerous rather than liberating.

These were not the only tensions haunting the republic of letters. In the next chapter I want to turn away from this account of
the ways that debates about literature were shaped by the often
turbulent effects of the French Revolution, and look more closely
at the beliefs which inhered in the idea of print culture as an
information revolution with excesses and anxieties of its own. The
Enlightenment ideal of literature as a means of generating and
diffusing new ideas collapsed partly under the weight of the
overtly political stresses that we have already examined, but also
as a result of these superficially non-political tensions. As Mathias's comment that '[a]ll learning has an index, and every science
its abridgement' within a warning about the political dangers of
a mass readership suggests, these effects cannot ultimately be separated.[97] The tensions which each of these revolutions produced
were mutually reinforcing.⬚

In part 2 I will look more directly at the plebeian and female
reading publics rather than simply encountering them as the
demonized Others of polite culture. But first it is necessary to
detour through an account of this information revolution which
reflected the interests and ambitions of the (largely male) professional middle classes because I want to stress that the backlash
against these new entrants, even where it was staged in overtly
political terms, was shaped by literary developments which threatened the social distinction of authors as well as the security of
the state. Indeed, it was often precisely because these subaltern
communities – workers and women – mimicked rather than
opposed the Enlightenment rhetoric of the middle classes at a
time when those ideas were already unravelling that they had to
be so loudly denounced for irrationality.

CHAPTER TWO

Men of letters

It is always with peculiar pleasure that we take up the work of a professional man; since, from men of experience, we can generally look, with confidence and safety, for useful instruction. Theory may dazzle us for a moment with splendid visions, which vanish 'ere they fully meet the eye: but from practice we reasonably expect more substantial information.

Monthly Review, January 1796

NOBLE MINDS

The October 1796 edition of the *Gentleman's Magazine* included an alleged letter entitled 'Affecting Address of a Poor Student'. It was a kind of job application. Relying on the *Gentleman's* concern for 'the *distressed* of various descriptions', the correspondent announced that he was anxious 'to procure a situation in life which is not of the common kind, and, therefore, not likely to be obtained by common means'. His problems, he explained, had to do with a love of reading:

From a *boy* ... I have been particularly fond of *study*, and the love of books increases with increasing years. Unfortunately for me, my finances are too narrow to enable me to enjoy that learned leisure, which is peculiarly adapted to my inclinations ... With a mind not uncultivated, and inclination thus ardent in pursuit of knowledge, I find myself ill-calculated to undertake any servile employment in order to live. (66 (1796): 808)

His fondness for study had rendered him unfit for and unwilling to pursue any more menial occupation, but he was none the less having difficulties capitalizing on his literary pursuits in any remunerative way. In a word, he had become overqualified; his intellectual credentials and the lifestyle expectations they encouraged were out of step with his occupational prospects. Having '[a]rrived to a time of life when most men consider their destination in the world as fixed', he found himself without a home, friends, or money, and 'little acquainted with any of the various ways of procuring a subsistence' (808). More grating than any of these hardships, he continued, was the knowledge that, had he 'been *fairly* used, there would have been no necessity for me to seek a maintenance by the medium I now do' (ibid.).

Unjustly treated by a world which refused to reward his sense of cultural elevation in any practical way, he was forced to appeal to the readers of the *Gentleman's Magazine* because, 'being in the *literary* department, it seems to me, that one of the most probable means to obtain the completion of my wish is to make it known through the medium of that Magazine which is most read by *literary men*' (808). Driven by hardship, he was reduced to offering himself for employment, preferably as 'librarian and secretary to some nobleman, private tutor to the children of some gentleman of fortune, or amanuensis to some literary man, who, from whatever cause, may wish for such an assistant' (ibid.). Such a life would both allow him to earn a living through the application of his intellectual skills and afford him leisure time to continue to indulge in his love of study.

He was, in other words, a gentleman in need of an income writing to other more prosperous gentlemen in the pages of a periodical whose very name testified to the inherent connection between literary taste and social status. However much he might have staged this appeal as a kind of debt that was owed to him because of his predilection for study, his plea was fundamentally conservative: higher learning and the upper classes had a naturally harmonious relationship within which he had so far failed to be included, but this was better viewed an oversight than as an indictment of existing social relations. His letter was a request for personal employment rather than a demand for social transformation.

This student's crisis coincided, however, with a more radical struggle by authors to re-imagine their social status by insisting on a set of values which identified the middle class rather than the aristocracy as society's moral centre, and the energetic transactions of print culture rather than the privileged leisure of a landed elite as the cornerstone of the general good. The image of the Romantic writer as outcast implies a certain haughtiness towards any mundane place within the working world, but I want to suggest that the dominant image of the author in the 1790s was more closely tied to what was perhaps the most powerful ideological achievement of the long middle-class revolution: the prestige of the professional. Such a claim shifts the focus of our attention away from the myth of the Romantic poet to a very different discursive network, but it also situates that network within a different political context.

The struggle to define literature according to various social and political perspectives (a struggle whose implications we are still living with today) was inseparably related to the professional ambitions of authors to establish the prestige of their position. Journals such as the *Monthly Review*, *Monthly Magazine,* and the *Analytical Review* – all broadly sympathetic to reform and naturally inclined to believe that professional authors were the best means of achieving this – made the point on repeated occasions and in a number of ways. 'In a period like the present of high intellectual culture', the *Monthly Review* suggested, 'when the speculations of literature are diffused with a celerity and brought into action with a boldness hitherto unknown, the profession of an author is becoming one of the most important and most responsible of human employments' (12 (1793): 77). But it was not just the reformist journals that championed the importance of professional authors. Conservative journals may have opposed their counterparts' political interpretation of this position, but they tended to share their predisposition towards a particular form of what Pierre Bourdieu has described as 'cultural competence'.[1] Marilyn Butler's suggestion that '[w]ithout having a radical editorial stance, the *Gent's Mag* managed by its very representativeness to reflect middle-class attitudes that could become egalitarian and oppositional (in relation to an aristocratic government) in the last three decades of the century', must be qualified by an emphasis on the magazine's extreme hostility to the reform movement in the 1790s.[2] But her point that, without intentionally embracing radical positions, the *Gentleman's* could adopt 'oppositional' stances as a consequence of its middle-class perspective, highlights the extent to which the far more gradual middle-class revolution, which developed throughout the century, established a certain degree of common ground between authors who sometimes differed greatly in their views on more pressing political issues. Indeed, the possibility that the 'letter' from the poor student was intended to be read satirically reinforced rather than departed from this professional orientation. For radical and conservative authors such as William Godwin and T. J. Mathias, who none the less agreed in their description of literature as a powerful 'engine', political differences were framed within a shared assumption about the importance of authors as the professional group who – for better or worse – were in charge of this machine.

What was at stake was less the transformation of the author into someone fit for inclusion within the polite classes (though many critics worried that this was also happening) than a redefinition of this social elite in terms of intellectual industriousness. 'Nothing is more certain', Burke insisted in the *Reflections*, 'than that our manners, our civilization, and all the good things which are connected with manners, and with civilization, have, in this European world of ours, depended for ages upon two principles . . . the spirit of a gentleman, and the spirit of religion'.[3] Arguably, the question of the social identity of a gentleman constituted one of the central focuses of these revisionary struggles. The late eighteenth century was, of course, an age when those who could afford to were overwhelmingly dedicated to reproducing this identity by purchasing and adopting whatever possessions and behaviour were identified with the aristocracy.

Authors were involved in this process in a slightly different way. Critiques by radicals such as Paine, Spence, and Cobbett – which treated the aristocracy as 'a separate class parasitic on the nation' – were complemented by the more measured criticisms of middle-class reformers. They were generally more interested in appropriating than abolishing the privileges traditionally accorded to the aristocracy, though they justified these privileges on the basis of merit rather than inherited titles or – like middle-class *arrivistes* – newly purchased manor houses and carriages.[4] It was, however, a mode of appropriation which depended upon a levelling rhetoric. The *Monthly Review* suggested that the cultural dynamics of the 'general diffusion of wealth and the dissemination of knowledge' made it unlikely that the reverence for '*noble birth*' which flourished 'in ages of ignorance and despotism' would survive unweakened (11 (1793): 394–5). Such a message was unimpeachably democratic: whereas aristocratic privilege excluded even those who had acquired wealth through their own efforts, the diffusion of knowledge empowered increasing numbers of people who were willing to exert themselves.[5] But far from levelling all distinctions, the emphasis on the social benefits of literature re-established these distinctions in terms of professional merit rather than birth. The diffusion of knowledge might well undermine the respect that was traditionally paid to noble birth, but as the agents who made this process possible, authors enthusiastically advertised themselves as the new social superiors.

Mary Favret notes that many authors inferred that precisely because they *were* both industrious and disinterested, they constituted a 'spiritual aristocracy' which simultaneously rejected the elitist guarantees of inherited titles and referred to their own endeavours in terms of 'nobility' and 'elevation'.[6] Arthur O'Connor compared the 'unnatural mass of inflated vanity' of 'an aristocracy ... in whom a ready born pre-eminence has stiffled [*sic*] every exertion of the mind' with *'the aristocracy of reason'*.[7] The *Monthly Review* insisted about William Gifford, the future editor of the *Quarterly Review*, that 'he possesses what ancestry cannot bequeath, great talents and *a noble mind*' (40 (1803): 1; emphasis added). Not only was Gifford's low birth no blemish on his achievements, the *Monthly* continued, it was evidence that this nobility of mind afforded him a greater degree of self-reliance than aristocratic birth could ever offer. The political emphasis on the moral independence of the individual remained intact; it was simply being redefined in terms of the individual's integration within, rather than distance from, the relations of production.

Gareth Stedman Jones's claim that in Britain, 'unlike France and America, republican vocabulary and notions of citizenship never became more than a minor current', is contradicted by a growing body of writing which focuses on the importance of republican ideas within British political thought in the eighteenth century.[8] But it also overlooks the centrality of classical republican ideas to conceptions of culture which functioned as a means of legitimating new forms of social distinction.[9] The discourse of the republic of letters was, properly speaking, a bourgeois variation of the more internally coherent discourse of classical republicanism. Knowledge, for those who advocated this position, became a kind of property – a necessary precondition for engaging in debates about questions of general or civic importance in a way that corresponded to landed wealth's status as a prerequisite for political participation within civic humanism. Like landed wealth, the knowledge of the man of letters was a form of (symbolic) capital which existed outside the unstable fluctuations of commerce. And, again like landed wealth, it was presumed to suggest a concern for the general rather than the individual good.[10] Unlike landed wealth though, the knowledge of literary men was assumed to circulate throughout society. Men like Joseph Priestley may well have possessed minds that were 'richly stored with knowledge', but this was felt to be the guarantee of a liberal nature precisely because knowledge could not be hidden away but, by its very nature, tended to be diffused amongst the reading public (*AR* 9 (1791): 53).

Not all critics accept this argument for the historical importance of classical republicanism in the eighteenth century. In *Republicanism and Bourgeois Radicalism*, Isaac Kramnick allows that it has served as a useful correction to over-generalizations about the influence of Lockean individualism, but he also argues that this revision goes too far when classical republicanism 'becomes the organizing paradigm for the language of political thought in England ... throughout the [late eighteenth] century' (166). Kramnick argues that liberalism, as a 'modern self-interested, competitive, individualistic ideology emphasizing private rights', had far greater relevance in a period of commercial growth driven by a confident middle class than did a 'classical-Renaissance ideology emphasizing selfless duty-based participation in the communal pursuit of the virtuous public good' (35). Other critics agree that Kramnick's general history of political thought was particularly true of the literary marketplace as an urbane nexus of private interests saturated with a modern, cosmopolitan, and forward-looking commercialism that had little to do with the elite, public-minded ethos of classical republicanism. Roy Porter argues that 'the real intelligentsia was not chairbound but worked in the market place. Ideas were a trade, produced for a wide popular readership.'[11] Authors may have espoused the importance of disinterested virtue in their writing, and even sought to practise it in their personal lives, but it was a luxury that they could not afford in their professional careers in a commercial sector that was dominated by market forces. *Political Justice* may be remembered as the one text of the 1790s which most forcefully championed the possibility of virtuous behaviour inspired by a sense of the general good, but Godwin also recognized that his choice of subject matter 'was more or less determined by mercantile considerations'.[12]

There are, however, two qualifications that need to be made. The first is that the strength of Kramnick's evidence mitigates against the clarity of his historical conclusions because it is so rigorously selective. The result is a highly monological version of middle-class consciousness. Surveying the same middle-class Dissenting tradition in *Godwin's Political Justice*, Mark Philp stresses the Dissenters' emphasis on virtuous conduct in terms that are much closer to republicanism's emphasis on a duty-based concern for the general good. Reflecting on Godwin's personal experience of a community of mutually reinforcing relations within the intelligentsia, Philp argues that 'Godwin wrote as if a republic of virtue was possible because he lived in a community which attempted to realise the basic principles of such a republic' (216). They may have been embedded within a network of commercial pressures and opportunities appealing to individual self-interest, but middle-class authors were also capable of envisioning themselves as an autonomous social formation, characterized by their shared commitment to virtuous conduct on behalf of society as a whole.

Reading Kramnick's and Philp's accounts of the same middle-class Dissenting tradition against each other highlights the extent to which the debate about the relative importance of republicanism or liberalism has encouraged a critical bifurcation that disguises a significant amount of common ground which existed between these discourses. The discrepancy between Philp's and Kramnick's depictions of the Dissenting middle class foregrounds the importance of understanding the connections and tensions between these alternative discourses within the views of a social class that embraced an overlapping network of shared and diverging beliefs. Both versions are present in Habermas's account of the bourgeois public sphere as the product of a traffic in commodities and news between private individuals, but which was ultimately 'of Greek origin transmitted to us bearing a Roman stamp'.[13] Rather than experiencing the discourses of republicanism and liberalism in mutually exclusive terms, many expressions of what we might now describe as an eighteenth-century middle-class ideology were hybrids of these two views, fusing a commitment to the self-motivated individual with a nostalgic belief in public virtue. However incompatible they may have been theoretically, they were fused together within the heteroglossia of cultural change.

This relation was complicated by the fact that classical republicanism was not the only, or even the leading, inspiration for a commitment to public virtue. As Leonore Davidoff and Catherine Hall have suggested, Christianity offered individuals both an institutional structure and a moral rationale for public work based on a selfless devotion to the greater good. If middle-class men and women lived in a world that denied them 'substantive public power' regardless of their success in their own careers, their most common response was to create 'their own associations and networks which gave meaning to their lives and in the process challenged the existing apparatus of power'. Equally importantly, Christianity offered a logic of public service which compelled its members to involve themselves in the various public roles. 'Men's claim to act as stewards and trustees for God, to demonstrate their faith through their church and chapel duties, their public works and their business practices, provided a basis for later claims for other kinds of influence and power'.[14]

The republic of letters and religious faith mirrored each other but they also overlapped. Many notable writers were profoundly Christian and many noted Christians – particularly women, whose opportunities within the Church were limited – turned to writing and as a way of serving their faith. Christianity also encouraged a redefinition of the role of the gentleman that reinforced the revisionary efforts of professional writers. Davidoff and Hall argue that whereas masculinity, 'in gentry terms, was based on sport and codes of honour derived from military prowess, finding expression in hunting, riding, drinking and "wenching"', middle-class thinkers driven by a religious influence were intent on establishing 'a new kind of male identity' based on 'the kind of public action which confirmed a manly presence based on moral authority rather than physical prowess or the power of wealth and office'.[15]

For many, however, the literary community, with its overriding commitment to the progress of learning, was powerfully informed by, but never wholly reducible to, the motivating power of Christian faith. Republicanism sometimes functioned as an overt faith in itself, but in terms of literature, it manifested itself more powerfully as a network of assumptions and practices which collectively defined a professional community – the republic of letters – whose essential feature was this commitment to serving the public good through the promotion and diffusion of knowledge – a disposition which underpinned authors' broader strategic commitment to transposing the civic humanist ideals of disinterested behaviour and panoptic social knowledge from the loftier rhetoric of aristocratic detachment into the idiom of professional life.

My second qualification to Kramnick's argument, which emerges out of this dialogic version of a middle-class culture, is that it was precisely authors' immersion within the individualist ethos of commercial society that made classical republicanism attractive as a mediating language capable of establishing an important cultural role for authors: an identity-in-difference which situated authors both within and above the division of labour. To put this another way, the discourse of classical republicanism gained its value as a descriptive paradigm precisely because it did *not* accurately reflect the ethos of modern commercialism which necessarily characterized eighteenth-century literary production. It enabled authors to say something unique about themselves, to argue for a privileged discursive position by recuperating the possibility of disinterested commitment to the general good – a quality that was traditionally viewed as the sole prerogative of an elite minority distinguished by landed wealth.

The key to this revision of the symbolic importance of their occupational status was an alignment of professional activity with an Enlightenment reverence for 'knowledge' as an abstract force whose effects were bound up with the public good. In *Power and the Professions in Britain, 1700–1850*, Penelope Corfield provides a context for understanding the ambitions of professional authors in her exploration of the more general rise of the professional classes, whose interests were reflected in 'the development of knowledge based service industries' in the period (179). Butler similarly argues that this dynamic was reinforced by 'the period's massive investment in knowledge' generally.[16] The exertions of professionals and men of commerce both contributed to the good of the whole society, but unlike their commercial counterparts, whose primary concern was ultimately the self-interested pursuit of profit, professionals could claim to be motivated by an interest in the good of society as a whole – a motivation that could be easily and powerfully identified in terms of their commitment to the development of knowledge.

Authors' insistence on their location within the professional ranks was complicated, however, by a further distinction within the professions. As Corfield also suggests, the rise of professions such as law, medicine, and engineering was reinforced by their development of self-governing organizations capable of regulating the conduct of their members. But if these disciplinary organizations were central to professional claims to social distinction on the basis of their high moral integrity, then authors were clearly faced with the troubling fact that their profession was not only impossibly anarchic, it seemed to be getting worse. Access was wholly dependent on the increasingly easy process of being published, and the issue of standards was caught up in wider debates about the uneven tastes of modern readers.

In light of this problem, the regulatory tendency implied by the appeal of classical republicanism's emphasis on a disinterested elite provided authors with the symbolic means of identifying their own profession as a distinct cultural field which none the less represented everyone's best interests. Just as importantly, it set 'the good author' apart from those other authors who paid no regard to these ideals. If professional accreditation could not be established through specific regulations, then ideology could achieve what bureaucracy could not. Goldgar argues that late seventeenth-century authors appealed to the communal standards of the republic of letters as proof that it was 'in some ways separate from the rest of society'.[17] The symbolic value of this claim was reinforced in the next century by the Enlightenment's emphasis on the broader social importance of learned knowledge. What was good for literature was good for the nation and, when it functioned properly, literature behaved like a nation, but one that fitted this classical (rather than a modern liberal) description.

Such a reading complicates John Barrell's claim for the prevalence of 'the belief that in a complex, modern, commercial society, a society divided by the division of labour and united only by the pursuit of wealth, the opportunities for the exercise of public virtue were much diminished'.[18] This was certainly true, but those who celebrated literature as an engine of improvement were actively reimagining the possibility of exercising public virtue in a way which stressed the importance of being both rooted within the division of labour *and* disinterested.[19] Inevitably, adapting an aristocratic ideology to highlight their own professional achievements involved authors in certain contradictions, but as Kramnick suggests, the alternative ideology of middle-class liberalism was fundamentally contradictory anyway. Surveying middle-class reformers' considerable interest in fostering the 'improvement' of their plebeian inferiors, Kramnick notes:

For all its commitment to emancipation and liberation, its zeal to free human beings from political, spiritual, and economic restraint . . . bourgeois radicalism . . . casts an ominous shadow of discipline, regimen, and authority. Though these radicals preached independence, freedom, and autonomy in polity and market, they preached order, routine, and subordination in factory, school, poorhouse, and prison. In its liberating aspect, bourgeois radicalism was bent on toppling the aristocracy; in its repressive aspect, it was determined to improve the poor.[20]

Focusing on Thomas Day's connections with the Birmingham Lunar Society, Kramnick similarly comments that '[o]ne might expect that a Rousseauean primitivist would have little to do with these apostates of industrialism and science, but the two tendencies could exist side by side, and indeed in the same person.' It is within this complex web of discursive tensions and associations that we have to locate the republican aspect of the republic of letters. It may not have been 'the organizing paradigm for the language of political thought in England', but it provided a powerful metaphorical tool for authors interested in asserting their own professional autonomy and social importance.[21] If the discourses of classical republicanism and commerce were ultimately incompatible, the second half of this chapter argues that these tensions were experienced by many authors, not as a conflict between two ways of seeing the world, but as a crisis in literature itself. Such a move simultaneously confirmed a republican nervousness about the morally corrosive effects of luxury, and reinforced the myth of the heroic role of public-minded authors struggling to rid society of both the inherited fetters of aristocratic prejudice and the excesses of commercial abundance.

The greatest challenge in professional authors' attempts to represent themselves according to the terms of classical republicanism lay in the difficulties created by employing an ideology of leisure as description of their occupational commitments. To suc-

ceed in this discursive translation, authors would need to lay claim
to the two central characteristics that were formerly attributed to
the aristocracy: a disinterested concern for the general good, and
a panoptic social view capable of offering general rather than particular knowledge. Freed from a dependence on any occupational
commitments, which would have located them within the division
of labour, aristocrats possessed a wider view of their society than
was available to those individuals who, immersed within the division of labour, were capable of only local forms of knowledge.
And far from being tempted by selfish designs, landed wealth was
assumed to be so extensive and enduring that it was naturally
consistent with the long-term good of the nation itself. According
to this view, aristocrats were above the possibility of political contradiction. In order to appropriate this rhetoric as a means of
legitimating their own industrious self-image, professional authors
would need to invert both of these distinctions. These two shifts,
and the tensions which they created, are the subject of the next
two sections.

THE MIDDLE RANKS

Faced with the apparent contradiction between their financial
dependence on their work and the claim that they were motivated
by disinterested concerns, authors inverted the equation between
selflessness and leisure by insisting that they worked *because* they
were disinterested.[22] This was achieved partly by the growing
equation of 'knowledge' with the general good, and partly, as Mary
Favret has suggested, by converting the reality of many authors'
poverty into a virtue. Conservative critics may have rejected the
politicized terms used by reformers to explain the social role of
authors, but they shared a sense of both the public importance of
those individuals who were promoting 'the mental progress of
[the] country' in a responsible manner, and of the fact that these
authors were motivated by a disinterested love of learning (*BC* 5
(1795): i). Isaac D'Israeli cited the number of authors who 'perished in poverty, while their works were enriching the booksellers'
as proof that their motivation was the public good, rather than
private gain.[23] T. J. Mathias agreed: 'Whoever would do a public
service, must forget himself. His remuneration is from within.'[24]
'Book-making', or writing motivated by a desire 'for the immediate

profit', the *British Critic* warned, could only ensure the inferior
quality of a work, and therefore had no legitimate place within
the republic of letters. 'It is not till the subject in a manner forces
itself upon him, from the fullness of his knowledge, that a writer
who values his reputation will undertake to handle an abstruse
branch of science' (6 (1795): 238). As Maria Edgeworth emphasized in her eulogy for the publisher Joseph Johnson, professionals
were distinguished not by their unique types of labour, but by the
fact that their labour was uniquely motivated:

> His lib'ral spirit a *Profession* made,
> Of what with vulgar souls is vulgar Trade.[25]

Literary figures might occasionally find that their work generated
sizeable incomes but, because work of real merit could never be
motivated by selfish ends, this would necessarily be a happy consequence of their efforts rather than a driving incentive. Whereas
classical republicanism distinguished between the possibility of
disinterestedness and the limitations of any sort of professional
work, these sorts of comments implied that authors worked *because*
they were disinterested. Embedded within and dependent upon
their individual fields of enquiry, they were none the less contributing to the good of all.[26]

  This claim to disinterestedness was doubled on the global level
in writers' emphasis on the republic of letters as a community
which transcended national boundaries. This spirit of generosity
was not universal. The *Gentleman's Magazine* congratulated its
'countrymen' on the fact that '[i]n the confusions of *politicks* and
the *rights of men* ... Literature is retreating to our island, as her
safest refuge; and that to the libraries formed by our own Literati
we are daily adding those of our neighbours' (61 (1791): 156). But
especially amongst those sympathetic to reform, authors routinely
underlined their pretensions to disinterestedness by emphasizing
their selflessness on a national level. Journals such as the *Analytical*
congratulated themselves for promoting the diffusion of foreign
literature at a time when the 'evils of war' were obstructing 'the
free circulation of the productions of mind through the general
republic of letters' (23 (1796): 248).

  In their account of a translation of Vivant Denon's *Travels in
Upper and Lower Egypt*, the *Monthly* allowed that '[s]ince the chief
object of the French, in their invasion of Egypt, was the annoyance

of our eastern possessions, we cannot but approve the vigorous measures employed by our government to drive them from their conquest'. Their political allegiance 'as Englishmen' established, however, they also insisted that

> as members of the republic of letters, and as general philanthropists, we may find some reason for regretting that sound policy would not permit us to allow the French to remain in possession of Egypt; because it is a part of the world which has been imperfectly examined.

If this placed them in what seemed like an untenable position, they explained that this was only because Napoleon had failed to recognize the wisdom of subordinating his desire to 'conquer Egypt' to his 'liberal and scientific' ambitions (39 (1802): 149). To be disinterested was to be beyond selfishness, but because this presupposed having the wisdom to recognize the importance of *being* disinterested, it was clearly not something that applied to everyone.

Like the purer forms of civic humanism, within which the opportunity for exercising public virtue was uniquely the prerogative of the possessors of landed wealth, this hybridized version of the discourse was empowering precisely because its universalizing tone disguised what continued to be a set of highly selective cultural assumptions. As Barrell puts it, the discourse of classical republicanism 'could be used to distinguish a liberal middle-class from its inferiors, in just such a way as, unadapted, it had distinguished a liberal ruling-class from a middle-class now claiming to be its equal in virtue'.[27] This middle-class version still included amongst the vulgar those members of the lower orders who were traditionally excluded from polite society. But it also included in this category many of those people whose very privileges, so central to older perceptions of the polite classes, tended to discourage studious application. Rejecting the traditional distinction between the polite and vulgar elements of society, Mary Wollstonecraft explained, in her *Vindication of the Rights of Men*, that by 'the vulgar, I mean not only to describe a class of people, who, working to support the body, have not had time to cultivate their minds; but likewise those who, born in the lap of affluence, having never had their invention sharpened by a necessity are, nine out of ten, the creatures of habit and impulse'.[28] Never to have worked was just as detrimental to the development of one's intellectual faculties

as having done nothing but the most menial sort of work. Both
extremes tended to diminish the individual's capacity for rational
self-government. 'Surveying civilized life', she repeated later in
the text,

and seeing, with undazzled eye, the polished vices of the rich, their insin-
cerity, want of natural affections, with all the specious train that luxury
introduces, I have turned impatiently to the poor, to look for man unde-
bauched by riches or power – but, alas! what did I see? a being scarcely
above the brutes, over which he tyrannized; a broken spirit, a worn-out
body, and all those gross vices which the example of the rich, rudely
copied, could produce.[29]

This emphasis on intellectual capability as the defining characteristic of that moral integrity which was required of any individual
who wished to exert her- or himself in matters of public importance applied to readers as well. In *Proper Objects of Education* (1791),
Priestley emphasized that the educational efforts of the Dissenting academies were aimed primarily at 'the middle classes . . .
The lowest of the vulgar will not easily be brought to think on
subjects wholly new to them. As to the persons in the highest
classes of life, they are chiefly swayed by their connections and
very seldom have the courage to think and act for themselves'
(39). The *Monthly Magazine* celebrated its popularity in similar
terms as

a pleasing proof, that the case of liberty is not in so deserted a state as
some of its desponding friends have imagined; and that, whatever may
be the change in the sentiments of the higher classes, and the ignorant
apathy of the lowest, the middle ranks, in whom the great mass of information, and of public and private virtue resides, are by no means, disposed to resign the advantages of liberal discussion, and extensive
enquiry. (5 (1798): 1)

Whereas traditional formulations of civic humanism distinguished
sharply between those social groups who were capable of exercising public and private virtue, the widened focus of this bourgeois
adaptation located 'the great mass' of both public *and* private
virtue, which it implicitly equated with the possession of 'information' rather than landed wealth, in the hands of the middle
class.[30]

   If society was too minutely stratified to allow for accurate divisions along lines of class, these boundaries could none the less be

constructed differentially through representations of the morally profligate upper and lower orders.[31] The perceived connection between a familiarity with literature and the Enlightenment dream of 'improvement' offered the professional classes a way of establishing their position as the new moral centre by addressing themselves to the urgent task of curing what the *Analytical Review* referred to as 'the discontent of the poor and the pride of the rich' (14 (1792): 528). Harold Perkin has argued that '[t]he middle ranks were distinguished at the top from the gentry and nobility not so much by lower incomes as by the necessity of earning their living, and at the bottom from the labouring poor not so much by higher incomes as by the property, however small, represented by stock in trade, livestock, tools, or the educational investment of skill or expertise'.[32] Professional authors were able to turn both of these distinctions to their advantage by insisting on the need to earn a living as a positive social characteristic rather than a necessary evil, and by highlighting the fact that they did so by means of an intellectual rather than a manual vocation.

By characterizing the lower orders, who toiled in the sorts of jobs and for the sorts of reasons that did not qualify them for inclusion within the civic elite, as morally degenerate rather than as a group whose social grievances might legitimately inspire their own more radical reformist ambitions, middle-class writers were able to subsume their social inferiors as part of their reformist project – evidence of their liberality which simultaneously denied the possibility of widening the nets of political agency any further to include their social inferiors. The *Analytical Review* warned that '[t]here is no subject that will more frequently affect or surprize the thinking mind than the little attention which is paid in this country to the morals of the profligate and the poor' (7 (1790): 438). Noting that 'to excite the spirit of industry, and to rear the infant poor to early habits of labour and attention, were objects that well deserved the patronage and the encouragement of every liberal and enlightened member of society', it praised the Philanthropic Society, 'which, founded on the wise and benevolent principle of preventative policy, is established for the purpose of rescuing children from the abodes of infamy and wretchedness, and of rendering them, by proper instruction and discipline, useful members of society' (10 (1791): 196).[33] Whatever right intellectuals may have possessed 'to discuss with perfect freedom the opinions and reasoning of every other', instilling a sense of subordination and an awareness of the folly of discontent remained the goal behind most advocates' ideas about the education of the poor (*GM* 67 (1797): 55).[34] 'Principles, not opinions, are what I labour to give them', reassured Hannah More.[35]

At the other end of the scale, the moral preeminence of the aristocracy was increasingly dismissed as having been perverted by the 'infection of . . . ostentatious luxury and effeminacy'.[36] 'To attempt to reform the poor while the opulent are corrupt', More cautioned, was 'to throw odours into the stream while the springs are poisoned.'[37] However conservative More may have been in her defence of the existing class structure against radicals such as Tom Paine, her announced need to improve it by ridding the upper and lower orders of their corrupting influences was deeply rooted in the ethos of middle-class evangelism. Within the emphasis on 'industriousness' that characterized English nationalism in the eighteenth century, the absolute leisure ensured by landed wealth could be dismissed as idleness leading to effeminacy – the antithesis of civic character – rather than privileged as the basis for independence of mind and comprehensive social knowledge. As the *Monthly Review* put it, '[i]dleness is the cause of most of the calamities that afflict mankind, but industry is the source of many blessings and solid advantages: the former either producing or feeding our vices; the latter counteracting or destroying them; and in their stead, sowing the seed of every virtue' (15 (1794): 291).[38]

Criticism of the aristocracy was reinforced by the claim that they had abandoned one of their most important functions – the patronage of learning. John Pinkerton, who campaigned for an Academy of National History and for the founding of public libraries, blamed the deplorably low state of the study of English literature on the lack of support from the upper classes.[39] A correspondent to the *Gentleman's Magazine* expressed the hope 'that our Great will return to their former taste for true glory; that the characters of jockey and gambler will one day not be thought absolutely necessary to complete a nobleman and a gentleman; but that the solid patronage of literature may be admitted to claim some attention' (58 (1788): 126). Like the pressures for parliamentary reform, this reinterpretation of the relative importance of the aristocracy had been building throughout the second half of the century. Citing their lack of patronage for important literary projects in his *A Grammar of the Persian Language* (1771), Sir William Jones identified the nobility's negative opinion of 'learning as a subordinate acquisition, which would not be consistent with the dignity of their fortunes, and should be left to those who toil in a lower sphere of life', as evidence of this malaise (II, 125). Samuel Johnson's defiant letter to the earl of Chesterfield notwithstanding, authors often argued that systems of patronage needed to be reinvigorated rather than dismantled. To do so, however, required that the aristocracy be reformed. And since it was the virtuous exertions of middle-class authors which were most likely to achieve this, the argument also implied that it was the author, rather than the aristocrat, who ought to be the privileged moral centre of the relationship. In his 1753 *Essai sur la société des gens de lettres et des grands*, d'Alembert articulated this shift when he argued that men of talent should show 'exterior respect' for men with titles, but nobles should show a 'more real' respect for the talented.[40]

The aristocracy's literary role was not to be limited to patronage. Through the 'study of polite letters', Jones suggested, 'persons of eminent rank . . . instead of relieving their fatigues by a series of unmanly pleasures, or useless diversions, might spend their leisure in improving their knowledge, and in conversing with the great statesmen, orators, and philosophers of antiquity'.[41] Because this was not a project which they were naturally inclined to embark on, however, they needed to be encouraged by those who had already learned the value of studious enquiry. Citing the 'manly dedication prefixed to these volumes, and the rational preface which explains the tendency of them', the *Analytical Review* praised Priestley's recommendation, in his *Experiments and Observations on Different Kinds of Air*, of 'the study of nature and experimental philosophy to the prince of Wales, and to men of fortune and leisure, as the surest means of enlarging their views, and withdrawing them from sensual pleasures' (8 (1790): 370).

By offering these sorts of judgements, professional authors rewrote classical republicanism's bias towards the transcendent position of the aristocracy, which was traditionally assumed to guarantee them an 'equal wide survey' of all society, as an enfeebling remoteness from the domain of intellectual production which fostered a narrow rather than a comprehensive perspective.[42] Reviewing Lord Montmerre's collection of essays on Irish political issues entitled *The Crisis*, the *Monthly Review* praised him for being 'free from the prejudices that might naturally be expected in a member of the aristocracy; his manly mind has enabled him to surmount them' (17 (1795): 11). A 'peculiar characteristic as to their turn of thinking, as well as their composition and arrangement, frequently distinguishes such from those ... who, having dedicated their time and talents assiduously to study, are considered as authors by profession', the *Analytical* agreed in its review of Thomas Pennant's *Description of London*. Reading it, the reviewer was 'not without sometimes feeling an involuntary smile arise at occasional singularities of expression, or oddness of thought' (10 (1791): 22). Professional authors were not to be judged in these matters by their social superiors, but were themselves to act as appreciative, though perhaps slightly bemused, judges of gentlemen of fortune and leisure, secure in their role as intellectual superiors.[13]

The social identity of professional authors was not defined solely in terms of their relationships with the higher and lower orders though. Their conflicted relationship with the aristocracy, which emphasized social distinction but in a manner that was based on individual merit, was mirrored in their equally ambivalent relationship with the commercial sector. Once again, Burke, sharpened by his antagonistic edge, was an astute observer of the situation. The 'new description of men' called 'the political Men of Letters', whose frustrated ambitions he identified as the real source of the French Revolution, had 'formed a close and marked union' with another emergent social category, 'the monied interest'.[44] For Burke, it was the interpenetration of their interests, rather than the tensions between them, which characterized relations between the two groups. This was certainly true to an extent. Commerce and literature, both of which were felt to value individual productivity, were frequently cited as related manifestations of the prosperity of late eighteenth-century England.[45] As J. G. A. Pocock suggests in *Virtue, Commerce, and History,* such a view was necessarily premised on a progressive view of history which focused on the accumulated benefits of advanced civilization rather than on the decline of public virtue, which republican thinkers tended to emphasize:

When the polite man of commercial and cultivated society looked back into his past, what he necessarily saw there was the passions not yet socialised, to which he gave such names as 'barbarism' and 'savagery'; and his debate against the patriot ideal could be far more satisfactorily carried on if he could demonstrate that what had preceded the rise of commerce and culture was not a world of virtuous citizens, but one of barbarism'. (115)

For those who shared this view, the market was both the means by which an industrious individual could rise in the world and the cultural force which made the diffusion of knowledge possible. Frederick Augustus Fischer argued in *Travels in Spain* that 'litera-ture and the book-trade are as it were two sisters, that mutually aid and encourage each other' (quoted in *MR* 41 (1803): 270). Samuel Johnson referred to the bookseller Robert Dodsley as his 'patron'.[46] Such a point may seem straightforward, but it suggests that we ought to avoid any simple acceptance of Terry Eagleton's argument that one of the reasons for the gradual disintegration of the public sphere was its invasion 'by visibly "private" commer-cial and economic interests'.[47] The literary sphere did not need to be 'invaded' by economic interests because, as many commen-tators understood it, it was already premised on market relations. The ongoing debate about copyright foregrounded authors' claims to ownership of their literary productions as intellectual prop-erty[48]. In his study of the effects of the debate on ideas about authorship, Alvin Kernan speculates that the Romantic myth of the autonomous creator has its roots in the stress that many authors placed on the property rights of the individual writer.[49]

Nor should we assume that commerce and literature rep-resented two highly distinct fields of socio-economic endeavour that were capable of judging one another across some clearly delineated cultural divide. Instead, they intersected in the mixed and multiple functions which often characterized the role of indi-viduals in the book trade. Reviews tended to be run by publishers who were eager to promote book sales – by 'puffing' their own publications if they were unscrupulous but, more legitimately, by fostering a sense of the importance of keeping up to date with the state of literature generally.[50] In doing so they helped to constitute the figure of the learned middle-class reader, who, in turn, helped to consolidate the importance of print culture. As Bourdieu puts it, 'the consumer helps to produce the product he consumes, by a labour of identification and decoding'.[51]

In many towns, the printer of the local newspaper was also a bookseller, who not only sold books but lent them.[52] Nor, outside of the major cities, were many shops devoted exclusively to books. Instead, provincial bookstores were forced by their more limited market to offer books as one of the many products they stocked.[53] James Raven similarly notes that:

[m]any traders offered other services to help insure against financial hardship or to draw attention to their stationery, books, publications, or printing and binding operations. Many bookshops exchanged old books for new, sold ink, vellum, paper hangings, household wares, musical instruments, and lottery tickets, or served as a clearing-house for local information and services. For well over a decade [Thomas] Hookham acted as ticket-broker for the Hanover Square and St. James's Park assemblies and concerts.[54]

A. S. Collins notes that a sense of community between authors and their commercial counterparts was grounded in authors' presence around the tables of publishers and in the shops of booksellers. Joseph Johnson's coterie of reformist authors is well known. Crabbe's *Memoirs* recalls a dinner with 'Messrs. Longman & Co. at one of their literary parties', and Thomas Holcroft could frequently be found in Debrett's bookshop.[55] Historians of the bourgeois public sphere have similarly linked the growing importance of print culture with the development of a social infrastructure of commercial establishments such as private libraries, reading groups, and coffee houses.[56]

Middle-class Protestantism embraced both a capitalist work ethic and a respect for learned knowledge.[57] The *Analytical Review* suggested that successful British merchants, many of them among 'the most liberal and enlightened men that have appeared in Europe', were distinguished not only by success in their chosen field, but often by their 'love of science', their 'patronage of learned men', and the example they provided of their 'integrity and virtue' (5 (1789): 129). The two groups, guardians of the growing storehouses of knowledge and industrial wealth, converged in institutions such as the Society for the Encouragement of Arts, Commerce, and Manufactures in Great Britain, and the Birmingham Lunar Society, in which intellectuals such as Joseph Priestley, Thomas Beddoes, and Erasmus Darwin mixed with pioneer industrialists such as Josiah Wedgwood, Matthew Boulton, and James Watt, the inventor of the modern steam engine.[58]

Relations between the two sectors, however, were haunted by

the doubts which many authors expressed about the corrosive effects of commerce on public virtue. Authors may have re-imagined public virtue in terms of occupational commitments, but this widened definition remained antithetical to the selfishness of those individuals for whom profit was an end in itself.[59] The *Analytical Review* warned, in the same review which praised the potential benefits of commerce, that 'the love of money [becomes] a mean passion, when money is pursued for its own sake' (5 (1789): 129). In *Memoirs of Emma Courtney* (1796), Mary Hays depicted this difference between the two groups – those who apply themselves in ways that develop a sense of personal worth and those interested only in amassing personal wealth – in her account of the meeting between Mr Melmoth, 'the haughty, opulent, purse-proud, Planter, surrounded by ostentatious luxuries', and his guest, the intellectually accomplished Mr Harley:

Mr Harley received the formal compliments of this favourite of fortune with the easy politeness which distinguishes the gentleman and the man of letters, and the dignified composure which the consciousness of worth and talents seldom fails to inspire. Mr Melmoth, by his awkward and embarrassed manner, tacitly acknowledged the impotence of wealth and the real superiority of his guest. (108–9)

The meanness of spirit of anyone driven by financial greed, and the ostentatious display of this wealth once it had been accumulated, were as emasculating as the efforts of authors were morally strengthening. Mr Melmoth may have acquired the trappings, but Mr Harley possessed the personal character, of a gentleman. Nor was it simply a matter of the way the two men conducted themselves. Their opposite stances on the issue of slavery – Mr Melmoth made his fortune in the West Indies; Mr Harley is an eloquent opponent of the slave trade – provide an indication of the very different effects that their pursuits have had on their moral character. The man who was enslaved to profit would naturally tend to be sympathetic to the idea of slavery; the man of letters, because his efforts were fostered by a spirit of moral independence, would be quick to respect other individuals' rights to the same personal liberty.[60]

Republican thinkers shared a distrust of commerce as a source of luxury that was likely to encourage moral and political corruption. Some republican reformers, such as Paine and Thelwall, adopted qualified pro-commercial stances which aimed at securing a more equitable vision of economic justice. But others, such as Godwin, insisted that commercial growth, and the heightened demand for luxury goods which this created, merely added to the burden of the labouring poor without generating any corresponding increase in pay.[61] Influenced by the scepticism of his republican mentor, Jean-Jacques Rousseau, Thomas Day expressed a similar ambivalence about the Janus-faced nature of commerce in his *A Letter to Arthur Young Esq. on the Bill now depending in Parliament to prevent the Exportation of Wool* (1788):

In its origin, [commerce] is a gentle river gliding silently along its banks, and dispensing fertility to every soil it visits: a little farther advanced, it is a salutary inundation, that may sometimes impede the labours of agriculture, but repays with usury the damage it occasions: in its last stage, I fear, it is too apt to become an impetuous torrent, that threatens destruction in its course, and bears away liberty, public spirit, and every manly virtue. (17)

The equivocal nature of this relationship between the professional and commercial sectors of the middle class is perhaps nowhere better illustrated than in Wollstonecraft's *Letters Written during a Short Residence in Sweden, Norway and Denmark* (1796), where it was personified in her conflicted relationship with Gilbert Imlay. 'England and America', she admitted in a letter written while she toured the Scandinavian countries as the representative of one of Imlay's business ventures, 'owe their liberty to commerce, which created a new species of power to undermine the feudal system. But let them beware of the consequence; the tyranny of wealth is still more galling and debasing than that of rank'. 'You may think me too severe on commerce', she warned in another letter written during the same trip, 'but from the manner it is at present carried on, little can be advanced in favour of a pursuit that wears out the most sacred principles of humanity and rectitude.'[62] Wollstonecraft's more negative opinions must be read in terms of her already strained relationship with Imlay. However, taken together with her own admission of the liberating effects of commerce, and with her speculation that the sales of *Letters Written during a Short Residence* might give her much needed personal independence, they represent the two faces of the contentious relationship between authors and their commercial counterparts.

More important than stressing the distinct natures of literature and commerce is the interpretive task implied by the claim that the attempt to determine the 'exchange rate of the different types of capital is one of the fundamental stakes in the struggles between class fractions [*sic*]'.[63] Whatever the differences between these two elements of the middle class, many critics stressed both the productive friction of their interaction and the impossibility of their disentanglement. Indeed, it was in many ways the dynamic interpenetration of these three groups – the aristocracy and the professional and commercial communities – as interdependent and partially antagonistic forces, that helped to reshape the related definitions of the polite classes and the political community, and, because of the increasing identification of these latter groups with the reading public, the idea of literature.

THE FANTASY OF THE LIBRARY

The claim to disinterested virtue was not in itself enough to ensure the successful translation of classical republican ideals and distinctions into middle-class terms. However far the ideal of aristocratic leisure had given way to an alternative emphasis on industriousness, the intellectual division of labour into increasing forms of specialization complicated the ability of professional authors to offer a model of comprehensive knowledge in opposition to the loftier style associated with the panoptic vision of the aristocracy. In what was often felt to be an increasingly atomized society characterized by growing anxieties about complex social relations dominated by private rather than public interests, the inability to respond to what seemed to be the demise of this panoptic cultural perspective constituted a crisis of social knowledge that would help to define the claims of authors to cultural authority. Only by responding adequately to this crisis could authors appropriate the language of classical republicanism. In order to do so, however, it was necessary to demonstrate that the republic of letters was not simply an entanglement of endless different fields of study which perfectly reflected these anxieties about social fragmentation, but an internally unified body of knowledge capable of transcending its own division of intellectual labour.

For Burke, the issue of specialization was no anxiety; it was a straightforward problem. Being situated within the division of labour, he argued in his denunciation of the *Tiers Etat*, ought to disqualify people from participation in the civic sphere:

Their very excellence in their peculiar functions may be far from a qualification for others. It cannot escape observation, that when men are too
much confined to professional and faculty habits, and, as it were, inveter-
ate in the recurrent employment of that narrow circle, they are rather
disabled than qualified for whatever depends on the knowledge of mankind, on experience of mixed affairs, on a comprehensive connected view
of the various complicated external and internal interests which go to
the formation of that multifarious thing called a state.[64]

Within the discourse of civic humanism, the particular excellence
of a professional was wholly inconsistent with those matters of
wider importance which characterized the public sphere of civic
service. As Pocock explains it, 'the landed man, successor to the
master of the classical *oikos*, was permitted the leisure and autonomy to consider what was to others' good as well as his own; but
the individual engaged in exchange could discern only particular
values'.[65]

Even for those literary professionals who insisted that the development of any sort of useful knowledge required intellectual exertion in a necessarily limited area, the equation of the limits of a
single occupation with public virtue remained a continuing source
of anxiety. However liberating knowledge may have been seen to
be generally, systematic research within any particular field could
be enslaving rather than ennobling. The popular assumption that
the crippling long-term effects of any form of manual labour suggested a corresponding set of mental constrictions that undermined the individual's capacity for comprehensive thought was all
too easily suggested by images such as William Cowper's description of Charlotte Smith, '[c]hained to her desk like a slave to his
oar'.[66] Alexander Crichton worried in *An Inquiry into the Nature and
Origins of Mental Derangement* (1798) that, like 'shoemakers, who
not only live a sedentary life, but sit constantly bent', and 'glass-
blowers, who are exhausted by intense heat, severe work, and hard
drinking', professional authors 'who neglect all exercise, and live
too much retired', were vulnerable to the 'dreadful malady' of melancholy (II, 235).

Anxieties generated by the intellectual division of labour could
be resolved, however, by an emphasis on the 'scientificity' with
which these disparate forms of knowledge were organized: a kind
of fantasy of the library or, in an even more concentrated form,
the encyclopedia, in which the usefulness of the various forms of

writing depended on their collection and organization into a single internally coherent body of knowledge.[67] As Alvin Kernan puts it, the 'library focuses the intellectual world and provides a paradigm of consciousness, what a society knows and how it knows it'.[68] It is perhaps in terms of this emphasis on the need for a rigorous organization of literature that we might consider Ludmilla Jordanova's point that 'science and literature are united in their shared location within cultural history'. If, as Jordanova argues, historical analysis of these fields of knowledge is too often undermined by an inadequate sense of the 'crucial connections' between them, then this can be remedied not only by emphasizing the large areas of overlap between these now distinct fields, but also by a sense of the belief in the scientific rigour with which these various fields of literature could be organized into a unified whole.[69]

David Simpson has argued that it

is one of the ironies of English social and intellectual history that the very bourgeois orders that appear to have had a use for the methodical manner were more anxious to identify themselves with the immethodical habits of their social superiors; the history of aesthetics in the eighteenth and nineteenth centuries (and beyond) is marked by the politically disenfranchised middle class projecting itself into an imaginary posture of gentlemanly disinterest.[70]

By situating these observations within the discursive struggle which inhered in contemporary debates about the nature of literature, this irony becomes a bit easier to understand. Whereas the comprehensive knowledge of the aristocracy was premised on their distance *from* the division of labour, professionals were necessarily situated within it. The only way that the panoptic vision of the aristocrat could be emulated, therefore, was through an alternative emphasis on the overarching unity of the various specialized areas of intellectual endeavour: two different versions, one individualist and the other communitarian, of the same comprehensive ideal. If the professional classes were to appropriate the language of classical republicanism, then, as Barrell puts it, 'a new kind of knowledge was required, and a new kind of knower'.[71]

What was essential was the availability of a further body of scientific expertise which, because its sole concern was the organization of knowledge, would be capable of coordinating the various specialized focuses. It was in this regard that the *Monthly Magazine*'s obituary of Samuel Paterson celebrated his role in the recent emergence of 'the science of literary history, and the art of bibliography':

The knowledge of bibliography and literary history bears, perhaps, the most recent date, in the annals of the human mind: it is the happy result of those persevering inquiries into the intellectual and active powers of man, through which we have been able to refer to their common stock, and to trace back to their root the manifold, diverging, and apparently unconnected branches of the tree of knowledge; and it is also the immediate consequence of that overgrowing and amazing scientific wealth, from which we have endeavoured to take the most valuable materials, and the most conducive method, for our exertions and improvement. It was duly experienced ... how an exact partition of labour, and a convenient method of classification, could assist the powers of judgement and of memory; and how this very method of classification might be subservient to the arrangement of a library, or, in other words, to the regular and local disposition of objects that are the occasion of our ideas, and give a fuller scope to our faculties. (15 (1803): 43)

This science of the proper organization of the various branches of the tree of knowledge was both an important form of knowledge in its own right, and the key to appreciating the underlying unity of the endless different fields of intellectual enquiry. And because it was scientific, it was universal, capable of discovering the interconnection of every branch of knowledge, regardless of how disconnected they may have seemed. Mary Hays argued that '[e]very science ... beheld in the gross, resembles a loaded fruit tree in autumn; but as all the fruits and foliage are ramifications of the one, so all the departments of the other, may be reduced to a few first principles, and these comprehended, the whole is understood.'[72] In times of plenty, it could be difficult to see the trees for the fruit. It was important, therefore, that this intellectual plentitude be complemented by a corresponding study of the interrelationships of these various branches of learning in order that their unity might remain clear, even when it was no longer visible to the casual observer.[73]

Paterson's encyclopedic dream of an all-encompassing, scientifically arranged history of the different intellectual enquiries of endless people living in endless different times and places, all of them represented from a single panoptic perspective, was nothing less than impossibly totalizing:

He regretted that no system of universal bibliography and literary history had ever been exhibited ... He was aware that a work of this kind, capable of representing in one point of view the intellectual pursuits of several nations, and of an infinite number of individuals in every age; able to connect the scientific annals of each generation with their proper links; to notice in their due times, place and gradation, all the names who have gradually contributed to the improvement of the human mind, and to describe every publication, with the circumstances by which it was attended, would be utterly impossible for any man to execute ... The impossibility however of performing a complete work of this kind was not with him a reason why nothing should be undertaken towards effecting the purpose, if not by one man, at least by a society of men. (*MR* 15 (1803): 43–4)

Just as important as the infinite scale of the history envisioned was the fact that the information collected be organized in such a way that it was capable of being represented 'in one point of view' that was wholly available to the individual reader. No one could possibly cover enough ground, speak enough languages, take notice of the works of enough different generations in enough different places, to deliver the results which such a prospect demanded. But neither Paterson nor endless others who shared his encyclopedic spirit were deterred from trying to realize it in some limited form.[74]

It was, as Lawrence Lipking has noted, a profoundly colonizing impulse.[75] A series of articles in the *Gentleman's Magazine*, collectively titled 'THE ACADEMIC', argued that knowledge was not, as people too easily assumed, the opposite of cultural wilderness; unsystematized, the various forms of knowledge *were* a 'wilderness of conjecture'. But if authors could 'methodize and arrange for inspection [these] scattered ideas ... what a flood of light would burst on the regions of knowledge!' (62 (1792): 101). All that was necessary in this regard was that the rigour which characterized the individual sciences be applied to the metascience of bibliography. 'Without the aid of characteristic divisions', the *Monthly Review* warned, 'we can make no regular advances in the study of nature, or transmit any information relative to that study with precision to posterity' (42 (1803): 178). The potential anarchy of literature as a sphere of unrestricted investigation and debate had to be contained by the unifying power of truth on the one hand, and by the reassuring promise of scientific arrangement on the other.

This classificatory emphasis was reflected in the ambitious scope of books such as Andrew Kippis's *Biographia Britannica*, the *Encyclopedia Britannica* (1768–71), Samuel Johnson's *Dictionary* (1755) and *Lives of the Poets* (1778–80), Robert Henry's *The History of Great Britain, from the first Invasion of it by the Romans under Julius Caesar* (1771–93), and Charles Burney's *General History of Music, from the earliest Ages to the present Period* (1776). Nor was it only the most impressive works of the age, by eminent authors, and taking years of dedication, that exhibited this totalizing spirit. The July 1803 edition of the *Monthly Magazine* carried an advertisement on its inside cover for four books, all by the same author, William Mavor, LLD: '*A UNIVERSAL HISTORY, ANCIENT AND MODERN, comprehending a General View of the Transactions of every Nation, Kingdom, and Empire, on the Globe, from the earliest Account of Time, to the General Peace of 1802; The HISTORY OF ENGLAND, from the earliest Records to the Peace of 1802; The HISTORY OF ROME, from the Foundation of the City of Rome, till the Termination of the Eastern Empire; and, The HISTORY OF GREECE, from the earliest periods, till its Reduction into a Roman Province*'. In reality, texts such as Mavor's were simply compilations of various different sources of information, but they exuded a confidence about the seemingly limitless boundaries of any one project that coincides with Paterson's own totalizing ambitions.

However fiercely William Wordsworth may have asked, 'who shall parcel out / His intellect, by geometric rules?', it remained the case that this encyclopedic confidence manifested itself in a corresponding certainty about the importance of scientific rigour in studies of the individual mind.[76] The *Analytical Review* praised W. A. Accurst's *Essay towards a general Knowledge of Characters* for its systematic attempt to reduce the 'various phenomena of the human character' into 'a complete and regular classification' (2 (1788): 259). Samuel Stanhope Smith was praised in similar terms for his effort, in *An Essay on the Causes of the Variety and Complexion and Figure in the Human Species*, to 'class the faculties of the mind and the passions which swell in the heart' (*AR* 2 (1788): 431). Both reviews agreed that these classifying efforts were, like Paterson's dream of an all-inclusive system of knowledge, doomed to 'innumerable modifications' by the early state of this particular science (ibid). But, they also agreed, this only added to the importance of these projects, whose ultimate goal was no less than an attempt to answer the question of whether the 'world without' corresponded to 'that within' by discovering the structures which made these worlds intelligible (ibid). Erasmus Darwin fused the rigour of the scientist with the judgement of the critic in his similar claim, in *Zoonomia* (1794–6), that a 'theory' which could 'bind together the scattered facts of medical knowledge and converge into one point of view the laws of organic life', would simultaneously produce real improvements in medical practice and 'enable everyone of literary acquirements to distinguish the genuine disciples of medicine from those of boastful effrontery, or of wily address'. Such a development would also, he added, 'teach mankind . . . the *knowledge of themselves*'(2).

Properly understood, the republic of letters resembled an enormous library, divided into sections which were themselves subject to an endless process of methodical subdivision, each portion of the whole made up of books that were, ideally, organized on the same scientific basis. This emphasis was in turn reflected in the related stress on the cultural importance of real libraries. In his study of readership patterns in provincial England, Roy McKeen Wiles argues that 'there were book clubs, private societies which had their own libraries for use by members, cathedral libraries, practical libraries, parochial libraries, school libraries, and coffee house libraries, in addition to purely commercial libraries open to anyone who paid the usual fee'.[77] William Lane advertised in various newspapers that 'for any Person, either in Town or Country, desirous of commencing a Circulating Library; he always had, ready bound, several Thousand Volumes in History, Voyages, Novels, Plays, &c. suitable for that purpose', and he added that he would be 'happy instructing them in the manner of keeping a Reading Library'.[78] In his *Letter to the Right Hon. William Pitt, shewing how crimes may be prevented, and the people made happy* (1796), John Donaldson suggested that '[b]y converting the powdering room into a family library, printers, booksellers, and all the different branches of trade and manufactures connected with them, will be greatly extended, the people made wiser and better and the revenue much increased by the duties on paper' (11).[79] Libraries, for Donaldson, were positioned at the intersection of commerce and learning, and ought to be welcomed as a potential source of private and public virtue.

Libraries were both an important means of encouraging the circulation of literature throughout society, and a metonym for Enlightenment ideas about literature generally: what mattered was that they were universal in their scope, properly ordered, and available to all interested members of the reading public.[80] Many critics suggested that it therefore behoved those nations which prided themselves on a spirit of liberality and cultural achievement to administer their greatest libraries in a suitable manner. Left in a state of neglect or, what was frequently assumed to be the same thing, closed to learned individuals eager to avail themselves of these resources, they existed as testaments to the vacancy of aristocratic pageantry which enjoyed most respect in those ages characterized by mass ignorance and illiteracy. Only when the extensive holdings of national libraries were adequately organized and accessible did they become a symbol of the prosperity which print culture was helping to ensure throughout the civilized world. In its celebration of the decision of the government of France to publish 'Accounts and Extracts of all the Manuscripts in the Royal Library', *Monthly Magazine* noted that 'an anxious wish had long prevailed, that the immense stores of information which are locked up in various libraries of Europe, frequently inaccessible and unknown, should be communicated to the public' (15 (1803): 201). The *Analytical* celebrated the enlightened role of the Danish king, who had not only 'thrown open his great library for the use and inspection of every gentleman, who indulges a wish to be admitted', but had even permitted '[c]haracters of note ... to carry home with them such MSS or printed books as they chuse' (3 (1789): 1–2). Inspired by political antipathies, but similarly aware of the full importance of the proper use of libraries, a correspondent to the *Gentleman's* complained that 'PARIS, so much inferior to LONDON, in all other respects, daily offers, not only the King's library, but many others, where literary men may keep the *best company in the world, without dress or expence.* But, in London, *such company* cannot be approached without both, and scarcely then' (62 (1792): 791). It was insulting that England, which prided itself on a respect for individual merit, was overshadowed by revolutionary France, where all literary men were free to work in the king's library, unencumbered by more worldly concerns. 'Is this not', he asked, 'a national disgrace?'

In his collection of essays entitled *The Observer* (1791), Richard Cumberland offered a series of meditations on the same theme in ancient history. Under the rule of Pisistratus, he noted, the genius of Greece had manifested itself in the construction of the first public library, 'laying it open to the inspection and resort of the learned and curious throughout the kingdoms and provinces of the world' (I, 178). Like Pisistratus, 'Osymanduas', more famously immortalized by Percy Shelley for building a slightly less respected monument, converted one of the chief temples into a public library, inscribing an invitation upon the front to 'all his subjects to enter in and partake of his benefaction' (III, 61). This concern 'to provide against the mental as well as bodily ailments of his people' was so admirable, Cumberland added, that he would not 'hesitate to give *Osymanduas* more credit for this benefaction of a library, than if he had been founder of the pyramids' (ibid). However enlightened these efforts may have been, though, the Romans' liberality was greater still. Not only did they build public libraries, they wisely appropriated adjoining buildings 'for the use and accommodation of students, where every thing was furnished at the emperor's cost; they were lodged, dieted and attended by servants specially appointed, and supplied with every thing, under the eye of the chief librarian, that could be wanting, whilst they were engaged in their studies and had occasion to consult the books' (69).

The problem with all of this was that such liberal arrangements tended to have self-reinforcing, but ultimately destabilizing, effects. Libraries made literature easily available, but they also foregrounded what Kernan describes as 'the darker meanings of vast accumulations of printed books'.[81] The Enlightenment faith in the progress of knowledge was shadowed by the disruptive possibility of an endlessly accelerating, self-regenerating inflation of print which threatened to exceed any strategy for its assimilation. Regardless of other worries about the actual quality of books, the possibility that there were simply too many of them meant that civilized nations might be swamped rather than liberated by advances in print culture.[82] This concern was not particularly novel. In the March 1751 *Rambler* (no. 106), Samuel Johnson had reflected on the gloomier implications of impressive libraries:

No place affords a more striking conviction of the vanity of human hopes than a public library; for who can see the wall crouded on every side by mighty volumes, the works of laborious meditation, and accurate enquiry now scarcely known but by the catalogue, and preserved only to encrease the pomp of learning, without considering how many hours have been wasted in vain endeavours. (200)

Denis Diderot worried in 1755 about 'a future age' when 'the state of literature after the printing press, which never rests, has filled huge buildings with books' (quoted in Lipking, 154). Interestingly, Diderot's response was the production of his *Encyclopédie*, a text which would be able to assimilate the whole range of existing forms of knowledge in a methodical and therefore accessible manner.

The fact that these worries had existed for decades did nothing to eliminate suspicions that the production of knowledge was now accelerating more quickly than ever. It had become increasingly easy to imagine a scenario in which this dream of the library, the science of the various branches of literature itself, tilted over into the nightmare vision of an entire library catalogue stocked with nothing but the contents of other libraries. 'The materials of history are become so numerous', the *Analytical Review* warned, 'that it has been found necessary to make histories of themselves; and almost every nation has now its own Historical Library' (3 (1789): 523). In their review of John George Meusel's *Guide to the History of Literature*, the *Monthly Review* worried in strikingly similar terms:

The sources of knowledge are become so copious, and learning has assumed such a variety of shapes, that it requires a great portion of our time to *learn* even what it is that *may be learned;* and whence we are to obtain the details of each particular branch of universal science. This circumstance produced a new species of historical writing, called *Bibliography*; and the works on that subject only would fill a considerable library. (32 (1800): 466)

The dream of organizing all forms of knowledge into a single system could only be maintained if the records of these systems were arranged into a system in themselves, but spiralling levels of production were quickly reducing this vision to an early obsolescence. When the stores of knowledge became so great that bibliography alone could 'fill a considerable library', its totalizing ambitions were no longer a science but a kind of madness shared by those individuals who were deluded enough to believe that these seemingly limitless resources could still be properly assimilated.

Just as worrying as the growing quantities of books being

printed was their increasingly uneven quality, and the fact that public demand favoured the worse rather than the better sort. Reformist and conservative critics found common ground in their insistence that fashion represented all that was most frivolous and in need of moral improvement. Thomas Holcroft argued that '[o]f all the insolence that disturbs society, and puts it in a state of internal warfare, the insolence of fashion wounds and embitters the most.'[83] Literature was traditionally felt to offer a steadying antidote to this threat by teaching a respect for the importance of rational knowledge and personal virtue. The *Tatler, Spectator,* and *Guardian,* hailed by the *Gentleman's* as 'those exquisite papers, which were the delight of the most brilliant æra in our literary annals', were frequently associated with precisely this effect (58 (1788): 331). In his *Essays, Biographical, Critical, and Historical, illustrative of the* Tatler, Spectator, *and* Guardian (1805), Nathan Drake argued that the three journals had in themselves produced a new era of taste and virtue which confirmed the equation between the production of literature and the 'diffusion of private virtue and wisdom [which] must necessarily tend to purify and enlighten the general mass' (III, 398).

The problem by the end of the century, however, was that books were *too* popular; literature had become the darling of fashion. In an alleged letter to the *Gentleman's Magazine* entitled 'A modern Requisite towards the Character of a Gentleman', the 'correspondent' argued that literature had been cheapened, not by its obscurity, but quite the opposite, by the emphasis that was placed on it:

The pursuits of men are constantly varying with the varying fashions of the times in which they live ... In the days when the feudal spirit had possession of the public mind, it was deemed essential to the character of a *gentleman*, either to fight a duel, or to rescue a princess: – *now* ... if a man of fashion wish to distinguish himself, – *he writes a book.* – Should this fail, as it is odds but it do, he writes another; and then a third: still bearing in mind the maxim of the committee, – 'issue more paper'. (69 (1799): 740)

Within the fashionable world it had become publish or perish. The result was 'the many confused, incompetent, and ignorant works which we every day meet with' (ibid.). Employing another analogy to noble life, the correspondent explained that like 'a celebrated hunt in the interior of the kingdom' where the first question asked about newcomers was 'How many horses does he keep?', the merit of authorship was based wholly on the question, 'How many books has he written?' (ibid.). 'This superficial way of reading', he continued, 'produces an equally superficial way of thinking. – And thus men, becoming learned without labour, impose upon the multitude, and not unfrequently upon themselves' (ibid.). To make matters worse, the book trade, which had helped to foster the revival of literature, was a willing accomplice in its degradation:

> The *authors*, in alliance with the booksellers, avail themselves of the exterior recommendations of advertisements, – puffs, – vignettes, – title-pages, – superfine royal, – superb engravings, &c. &c. – while the *readers*, no less dexterous, – call in the assistance of indices, – extracts, – heads of chapters, – *converzationis*; and thus get the character of a book, and are enabled to quote from it, without the drudgery of perusal. (ibid.)

None of this meant that worthwhile authors and books no longer existed, but the problem remained that the seriousness of any work tended to diminish the size of its potential readership. In its review of Charles Mitchell's *Principles of Legislation* (which the *Annual Register* found important enough to reprint in its entirety), the *Monthly Review* warned that because 'the most useful publications are not always the most entertaining, those which are calculated chiefly for the instruction of mankind are rarely perused, except by the small circle of readers who are endowed with a clear understanding and sound judgement' (21 (1796): 121). Hays worried in a similar way that the literary standard 'which raises [books] in the eyes of the few, either sets them beyond the reach of the multitude; or, what is infinitely worse, renders them obnoxious to its hatred and persecution'.[84]

Novels attracted an extended audience, making them a popular form with both reformist authors such as Hays, Godwin, Holcroft, Bage, and Wollstonecraft, and conservative novelists such as Elizabeth Hamilton, Jane West, and Charles Lloyd.[85] Godwin announced in the preface to *Caleb Williams* (1794) that his use of the novel form represented an attempt to communicate political truths 'to persons whom books of philosophy and science are never likely to reach' (1). For women writers, the novel was both more accessible than the 'masculine' genres such as politics and history, and the medium through which they could reach the greatest number of their peers.[86] As Janet Todd puts it, 'for women in the later 1790s, reacting against their debasement by the sentimental myth and increasingly confident of their literary position, fiction seemed a way of inserting their works into culture as allegorical tales, ethical stories and active political agents'.[87]

More often, though, novels were denounced as an indication of the extent of the dangers flowing from literature's unrestricted popularity. The Enlightenment ideal of literature was premised on the rational impulse of readers who 'had only to be shown the truth for the truth to spread and prevail'.[88] But this presumed that readers *wanted* to see the truth when it was just as possible to spend their time on 'the vast, and rapidly increasing heap of insipid novels' whose sole intention was to distract rather than inform (*AR* 11 (1791): 215). In her 1788 review of Charlotte Smith's *Emmeline* for the *Analytical Review*, Mary Wollstonecraft warned against the dangers which 'young females' faced by reading 'those pernicious writings' which 'tend to debauch the mind, and throw an insipid kind of uniformity over the moderate and rational prospects of life.'[89] The *Monthly Review* complained that '[n]ovels spring into existence like insects on the banks of the Nile; and, if we may be indulged in another comparison, cover the shelves of our circulating libraries, as locusts crowd the fields of Asia. Their great and growing number is a serious evil: for, in general, they exhibit delusive views of human life; and while they amuse, frequently poison the mind' (2 (1790): 334). The dangers posed by circulating libraries, which were frequently cited as a symbol of the contagious effects of bad romantic novels, were, as Paul Langford argues, 'one of the standard clichés of the late eighteenth-century'.[90]

The problem was not confined to novels. Commenting on Robert Nares's *A Thanksgiving for Plenty, and Warning against Avarice,* the *Edinburgh Review* explained that '[f]or the swarm of ephemeral sermons which issue from the press, we are principally indebted to the vanity of popular preachers, who are puffed up, by female praises, into a belief, that what may be delivered, with great propriety, in a chapel full of visitors and friends, is fit for the deliberate attention of the public' (1 (1802): 128). Unlike sermons, travel writing has become an important focus of critical attention in our own age,[91] but as perceptive as these studies frequently are, they often fail to foreground the implication of travel writing in the wider crises of print culture. Reviewers in the period, however, were more forthcoming about these problems. Conflating the craze for 'books of Travels' with the more general excesses of literary production, a semi-annual Preface in the *British Critic* likened their task as reviewers to the same 'species of composition' – they were awash on a wide, wide sea of bad manuscripts. Like all travellers, the review explained, they were faced with hardships that were an inevitable portion of their journey. But mustering up the spirit of the true explorer, they intended to be 'kinder to our readers than the generality of travel-writers', who, desperate for any novel attraction in an already swollen market, detailed their 'hardships . . . at full length . . . [E]ven sea-sickness has been minutely and copiously described, as a new phenomenon, by a very late voyager' (12 (1798): iii). This kindness was not due to any lack of misadventure stories, the Preface added, but to their commitment as reviewers to the integrity of literature:

> We could indeed, were we disposed to indulge a satirical humour, amuse the public occasionally, by the recital of many lamentable adventures; the difficulties we encounter in one place, the ingratitude that assails us in another . . . But not perceiving that the cause of Literature would be benefited by such confessions, we are content with a harmless laugh among ourselves, and persist in our plan of laying the fair side only before the public, in our half yearly recapitulation. (iii)

So familiar were these problems that they could be evoked, not merely as nightmare, but as the stuff of urbane humour – an ironic awareness of the dangers of literary excess which never lost sight of the gravity of the situation.

Nor was it just that books capable of promoting rational understanding were being overshadowed by productions whose only role was to divert. Learning (as opposed to literary entertainment) had itself become something of a fashion, but, many critics feared, with the same enfeebling consequences. Nowhere was this more obviously the case than with the growing demand for abridgements and anthologies. 'In the present state of European Literature', the *British Critic* noted, 'every year produces, almost in every country, a vast accession of books . . . But new books are usually made up of the old materials; to which, if a little felicity of combination or illustration accede, it is as much as we can reasonably expect' (10 (1797): i). In its review of the modestly titled *A View of Universal History, from Creation to the Present Time*, the *Monthly Review* reflected at length on the double-edged nature of the problems created by these anthologizers:

Perhaps there never was a period in which abridgments of books on comprehensive subjects so much abounded as at present. Abridgments of
divinity, philosophy, history, and the *belles lettres*, are published almost
every month; and the writings of some of the most approved authors of
the last and present age have been garbled and retailed under the appel-
lation of BEAUTIES, &c: – the beauties of Johnson, Sterne, Goldsmith,
&c. This practice is justified by some plausible arguments; the strongest
of which seems to be that it peculiarly contributes to the diffusion of
knowledge; but whether a superficial knowledge thus acquired has not a
tendency rather to inspire vanity and self-conceit, than to enlighten the
understanding or to rectify the heart, may be questioned; and it must be
allowed, even by those who are most partial to such compendiums, that
they may tend to draw off the attention of young students from those
original writers, whose reputation has been consecrated by the approbation of successive ages, and who have ever been considered as our best
guides in the pursuit of wisdom, and her constant associate, virtue. It
has likewise been alleged that they may prove unfavourable to those
habits of application and attention, without which it is impossible to
make a real progress in any branch of learning: but, whatever may be
the force of such objections, abridgments are too flattering to the indol-
ence of mankind not to meet with readers and advocates: and after all,
they may really be of much use, by smoothing the way to knowledge, and
making it pleasant to those who might be discouraged from pursuing it
by more rugged and tedious paths. (20 (1796): 141–2)

Knowledge was only as useful as it was widely diffused, but when
extracts became a substitute for, rather than an incentive to, the
task of reading 'original authors', they fostered passive approaches
to studious enquiry which dulled rather than sharpened the individual's rational powers. Mathias warned that extracts had
'created more half-scholars than the world ever saw before ... It
is rather singular that the very mode which was adapted for the
revival of learning in the early ages, should now be followed with
the opposite effect'.[92]

Worse still was the fact that the growing popularity of these
sorts of collections tempted unqualified but opportunistic editors
into producing ill-assembled anthologies. A correspondent of the
Gentleman's was voicing a well-established opinion when he
denounced 'dealers in this piratical commerce [who] take every
opportunity they can seize, for converting the works of others to
their own emolument'. Inspired by greed, 'they mangle and pillage
them in an arbitrary manner' until the sources had become almost
unrecognizable (62 (1792): 131). Thomas MacDonald similarly

denounced the 'increasing multitude of literary mercenaries, through all their different ranks and degrees of prostitution, who, for the basest purposes, let out to hire some faculties of the soul with which Nature has ennobled man'.[93] So destructive was the lure of profit, the *Gentleman's* argued, that the once noble pursuit of literature had been reduced to 'the present science of book-making, from which the reader can learn nothing new' (66 (1796): 46). For his own part, the fabled Sylvanus Urban, editor of the *Gentleman's*, warned that a 'concern for the interests of Literature' compelled his reviewers 'to the severity of free and unreserved censure' of 'the propagators of frivolity and insipidity, whether under the titles of *Beauties, Flowers, Abridgements,* or of *Essays, Observations, Dissertations, Disquisitions, Sermons,* or under more specious and less hacknied titles' (58 (1788): 441).[94]

Behind these broader cultural anxieties lurked growing concerns about declining standards of authorial distinction. A 'letter' to the *Monthly Magazine* (probably by a staff writer) warned that the 'universality . . . with which [literature] is diffused throughout society . . . renders it less valuable . . . [A]rticles grow cheap, not in proportion to their insignificancy, but their abundance' (7 (1799): 110). Excessive literary production, the letter warned, had serious effects on the process of *learning,* because it encouraged people to read much rather than to read well. But it had even more serious effects on the social status of the *learned,* whose efforts were being eclipsed by the growing number of pretenders to their elite position. 'Great talents, indeed, in any condition of civilized society must inevitably confer a certain degree of power', it continued, 'inasmuch as they render their possessors either useful, or formidable: but scarcely any literary attainments would, I apprehend, raise a writer in these days, to the same degree of eminence and request, as Petrarch, Erasmus, and Politiano enjoyed, in their respective times' (ibid). If knowledge did not become rooted in the soil of the national culture, then according to the reformist priorities of the Enlightenment, it was difficult to see how the work of learned authors could be of any importance. But if everyone was able to turn author, it became equally difficult to see how 'real' authors were to preserve their sense of distinction.

At the heart of these issues, for many critics, were the growing effects of technical and commercial advances generally. For the relatively conservative readers and writers of the *Gentleman's Maga-*

zine, the situation was typical of the more general evils of 'this scribbling age, when every man who can write composes a pamphlet, and every journeyman bookseller erects himself into a publisher ... when the press and the sword are alike familiarly appealed to' (62 (1792): 934). Catherine Macaulay was more sympathetic to the reform movement, but she too acknowledged that 'advances in knowledge' were being wasted in 'a senseless course of dissipation, and an unwearied exertion to procure the means of luxury [which] diverts our attention from the objects of our true felicity, and renders us callous to the woes of others'.[95]

If, for literary heroes such as Steele and Addison, literature was an important means of affecting the nation's moral improvement, by the end of the century it had become embroiled in all of the negative effects of fashion which they had set themselves so industriously against. The republic of letters was threatened on one side by political upheavals which cast into question the claim of authors to freedom of expression and, on another side, by the growing popularity of fashionable literature, which effectively trivialized this freedom. Both problems made it increasingly difficult to argue for the paramount importance of literature as a public sphere whose greatest strength was its ability to facilitate the diffusion of knowledge; both tended to locate the source of these conflicts in emergent readerships whose judgement – whether it was because they were too preoccupied with serious issues, or because they were not serious enough – could not be trusted.

SOVEREIGNS OF REASON

If anxieties about the growth and uneven quality of literature highlighted the absence of any transcendent perspective from which this body of knowledge could reliably be viewed, periodicals were quick to offer themselves as a means of making this detachment possible. By providing a condensation of available texts arranged with careful attention to literary quality and proper classification, the periodicals characterized themselves as more portable versions of the ideal of the library. Journals such as the *Gentleman's Magazine* went even further by offering themselves as the embodiment of the public sphere, a meeting place of the 'numerous and very learned Correspondents' who were both readers and writers, and whose exchanges became all the more import-

ant at a time when war was disrupting communication with their
literary counterparts across the channel: 'We wish to hold out an
Olive-branch both in Literature and Politicks; and that an Armis-
tice may take place in the Territories of MR URBAN, even if it should
fail on the Continent of Europe' (64 (1794): iii–iv). The *Critical
Review* similarly suggested that at a time when politics and war
divided both whole nations and authors living within one nation,
a 'review of this kind, without the violence, the illiberality of party,
neither dictated by a bigoted attachment to old forms nor an
impetuous fondness for every innovation, cannot fail to be agreeable to the dispassionate reader, and will serve to connect, what
the practice of mankind has already united, the political and literary department' (1 (1791): iv).[96] By avoiding politics in the negative sense of party agendas, periodicals would be able to safeguard
what ought to be the sovereign influence of rational and informed
debate. In doing so, they projected themselves as 'a paradigm of
audience-making' – a guarantee of the continued importance of a
particular role for reading and the possibility of a particular type
of reader.[97] What remained essential was the transformation of
the disparate forms of learning into a unified body of knowledge,
untainted by warfare, party spirit, or personal prejudice.[98]

As Nathan Drake's comments about the *Tatler*, the *Spectator*, and
the *Guardian* suggest, periodicals had played an important role
in literary culture throughout the eighteenth century. A journal
entitled *The Present State of the Republick of Letters*, which appeared
in 1728, announced in the Preface to its opening volume a set of
goals that closely anticipates the self-descriptions of journals
dating from the end of the century. Declaring its primary 'design
of informing the Curious, by a kind of Journal, of what passes from
time to time in the Republic of Letters', it preceded to define the
broader utility of this function in terms of the Enlightenment
sense of the mutually reinforcing relationship between freedom of
the press and social liberty (i). Referring to the absence of a state
licensing board, it situated itself within this multiply advantageous
relationship between politics and print, which, in turn, found its
clearest expression in the sign of the nation:

'Tis to this happy liberty, both of conscience and the press, so much
envied by our neighbours, that we owe those many excellent books which
are daily printed in England. This has enabled us to make those discoveries and improvements in almost every part of knowledge, which have

gained so great a reputation to the English writers abroad, that our language is now studied by foreigners as a learned one. No Englishman can wish this liberty abridged, but he who envies the glory of his country, and the advancement of learning and truth. (ii)

By the 1790s, the combined pressures of political conflict, literary overproduction, and the tyranny of fashion demanded that the reviews play a more important role than ever if the claim for the connection between print culture, the dissemination of knowledge, and social progress was to survive. Beyond the continuing goal of encouraging the diffusion of learning by offering manageable introductions to the most important recent publications, reviews were now required to perform the more conservative task of preserving the coherence of the republic of letters as a unique cultural domain (and therefore of upholding the claims for the social distinction of authors) by taming those political and cultural pressures which threatened to erode literature's unique social function.

Periodicals claimed to encourage these ambitions by fulfilling three related tasks: organizing the massive literary output into systematic shape, selecting what was worthwhile and castigating what was not, and ensuring the permanent place of these productions in the memory of the reading public by presenting them on a monthly or quarterly basis in volumes which were intended to be bound and preserved in public and private libraries. Roper argues that the reviews

were not meant to be read for entertainment and thrown away. They were conceived as instalments of a continuous encyclopedia, recording the advance of knowledge in every field of human enterprise ... All the researches, speculations, discoveries, and achievements, of that age of progress were recorded in these journals by means of a systematic review of as many new publications as possible – ideally, of all.[99]

Like the science of bibliography, periodicals constituted both a single branch of the tree of knowledge and a potentially unifying study of that tree; they were a form of literature whose chief concern was the history of literature itself.[100] 'The true idea of a Literary Journal', the *Analytical* (whose full title was the *Analytical Review, or History of Literature, Domestic and Foreign, on an enlarged Plan*) asserted in the preface to its first volume,

is to give the history of the republic of letters ... ANECDOTES which may in any shape illustrate the History or Fate of a work, would be in no wise inconsistent with the plan of such a Journal. Facts, which admit of no doubt, can raise no controversy. In relating them, the Writers give no opinion of their own; they appear only as they ought to appear, the HIS-TORIANS of the Republic of Letters. (1 (1788): iv)

The dream of viewing universal literary history, the history of the republic of letters itself, from any single, all-encompassing per-spective, had begun to seem impossible, but, the *Analytical* implied, this idea could be recuperated in a periodical that was able to provide a suitably arranged series of accounts of this ongoing his-tory of literary production on a regular basis. The *British Critic* similarly likened itself to 'a library endowed sufficiently to collect all valuable productions . . . either for the general collector, or the more confined selector of literature' (5 (1795): i). The scientificity which characterized any properly organized and all-inclusive library offered periodicals a kind of quasi-legal authority capable of bringing order to the chaos of literary productions. The *Monthly Magazine* described its half-yearly retrospective as 'a general invi-tation [to readers] to repeat their visit of inspection to the *National Library*: we are now at leisure to conduct them in to the several apartments; and shall be happy to point out the acquisition which each has, of late, received' (7 (1799): 509). Nor were the benefits of these designs, or the potency of the metaphor of the library, missed by the reading audience. A letter to the *Monthly Magazine* from a correspondent who, 'engaged with the cares of [his] count-ing-house', valued his periodical collection as a 'little library' keep-ing him informed about the progress of learning attests to this (15 (1803): 211). Literary journals belonged on the shelf of any good library precisely because they contained the spirit of that library in their very form.

If their monthly presentation, however condensed and well organized, was still too voluminous, the *British Critic* went even further by offering, like the *Monthly Magazine*'s half-yearly visit to their '*National Library*', 'a still more compendious direction, less dry and barren than an index: but with little more than general hints concerning the merits of publications, the fuller accounts of which, may be found in the correspondent pages of the Review at large' (9 (1800): ii). The primarily selective function of the *British Critic*'s prefaces would supplement the relatively comprehensive goals of the monthly editions – a plan which was not unlike the vision of a history of the various literary histories or a library filled with records of the contents of other libraries. Instead of the image of the library, the *British Critic* employed the equally powerful metaphor of cultivation:

In forming a Garden, for utility or pleasure, men select their plants with care; the nutritive, the salutary, the elegant, are sought and studiously arranged, while the useless, the offensive, and the noxious are banished without scruple, and permitted to depend on chance for a despised and precarious existence. Into a Garden formed with this attention, we endeavour to conduct our readers, when we present them with our periodical preface. (4 (1794): iii)

Monthly reviews were intended to select the most worthwhile productions, but even this was a relative wilderness which required the more careful attentions of the prefaces. Though their 'monthly Criticisms' ranged 'through all the wilds of literature', their prefaces presented readers with still more condensed notices of only those literary plants that would 'contribute to their health, or at least to their elegant and innocent gratification' (iii).[101]

By offering a selective introduction to recent publications, reviewers could save readers the impossible task of acquainting themselves with everything new in order to discover what was worthwhile. And, by brandishing what the *Gentleman's* called 'the correcting lash of criticism', reviewers would be able to offer an informal type of censorship based on their power to persuade (66 (1796): 319). The *Analytical Review* stressed the importance of chastening writers who were guilty of 'that false taste for glittering tinsel, which was creeping in among our minor poets' (22 (1795): 158). For D'Israeli, the increasing ease with which anyone could be published meant that this disciplinary function was the singularly most important role of the reviewer:

In the last century, it was a consolation, at least, for the unsuccessful writer, that he fell insensibly into oblivion. If he committed the *private* folly of printing what no one would purchase, he had only to settle the matter with his publisher: he was not arraigned at the *public* tribunal, as if he had committed a crime of magnitude. But, in those times, the nation was little addicted to the cultivation of letters: the writers were then few, and the readers were not many. When, at length, a taste for literature spread itself through the body of the people, vanity induced the inexperienced and the ignorant to aspire to literary honours. To oppose these inroads into the haunts of the Muses, Periodical Criticism brandished its formidable weapon; and it was by the fall of others that our greatest geniuses have been taught to rise.[102]

Early periodicals were widely celebrated for fostering the revival
of learning by facilitating the sharing of knowledge, but with the
growing popularity of literature and the increasing ease with
which an individual could be published, the situation had reversed
itself. Now, reviewers had the opposite job of guarding the republic
of letters from inexperienced or ignorant interlopers who had
wandered into it because they either misunderstood the rigorous
intellectual dedication required of authors, or because they were
catering to an audience that either could not or would not privilege good writing.

The ability to offer a coherent introduction to current literature
by selecting and organizing the flood of publications into a kind of
ongoing library or studiously arranged garden, was not the only
way that periodicals were able to serve the republic of letters. In
order to provide a form of comprehensive knowledge, the lessons
offered by the escalating production of literature had to be not
only all-encompassing but enduring as well: marked not only by
the breadth, but by the constancy of their enquiries. The tree of
knowledge offered the unifying promise of a comprehensive vision,
not only because the tangle of its different branches could be
traced back to the same trunk, but because the metaphor implied
an equally assuring sense of historical continuity. These pretensions to a more enduring fame were invoked by a correspondent
to the *Gentleman's* who explained that he would have sent his letter
(which took issue with the idea 'that the author who writes in
support of the Government and receives an annual salary for his
literary labour, is a despicable character') to a newspaper except
that 'those publications are seldom looked upon more than as
mere *ephemeral* records' (65 (1795): 190). Sending his letter to the
Gentleman's, on the other hand, meant that 'the idea here suggested may have a more permanent duration, and may fall under
the eye of observation at some future day, when Gentleman's
Magazine is taken from the shelf for the amusement of an *idle*
hour' (ibid). So perfectly did periodicals organize and preserve
their accounts of print culture that they were capable of ensuring
the equation between literature and the progress of knowledge in
the present, and entertaining readers in some future '*idle* hour'
when currently urgent debates had been safely confined to the
past. The *Monthly Review* similarly announced that it had decided

to print an out of date notice of James Beattie's *Elements of Moral Science* because

our review answers a double purpose; its pages being not only read in order to learn what is passing in the literary world at the moment of their appearance, but often consulted in times long subsequent, as a regular history of literature, and a register of the publications that have issued from the press since its commencement, nearly half a century ago. (19 (1796): 398)

Contemporary readers could rely on a good periodical to keep them up to date with the latest publications. But future readers, who were also an important audience, required a comprehensive coverage which included even those texts that had already become objects of public familiarity by the time they were reviewed. Like the *Analytical Review*'s 'solitary student', journals addressed themselves to all civilized and refined nations, including those which were 'yet to rise, perhaps in an endless succession' (5 (1789): 163). So important was this regulatory role that the reviews were able to describe themselves as a kind of literary government, or what Samuel Pratt called *'the sovereigns of Reason'*.[103]

There were growing concerns, however, that periodicals were themselves behaving in ways that exacerbated the problems facing literature. One problem was that periodicals, which frequently advertised themselves as a useful way of dealing with the inflated number of publications, were themselves sharply on the increase. In 1788 the *Analytical Review* found it necessary to justify setting itself up 'at a time when Literary Journals are more numerous than useful' (1 (1788): i). The politics of the *Anti-Jacobin* were diametrically opposed to those of the *Analytical*, but it similarly acknowledged that 'some apology may perhaps be necessary for the obtrusion of a new Paper upon the World' (1 (1797): 1). They were intended to render the growing output of literature more manageable, but periodicals were themselves springing up in a manner which reflected, rather than counterbalanced, this problem. Marilyn Butler suggests that the number of journals and newspapers nearly trebled in the second half of the eighteenth century, from 90 in 1750 to 264 in 1800.[104] Leaving newspapers out of the equation, Patrick Parrinder argues that the number of journals offering literary reviews then doubled between 1800 and 1810, and reached a peak of at least thirty-one in the early

1820s.[105] Jon Klancher suggests that '[p]eriodicals alone represent[ed] an awesome task of critical reading; between 1790 and
1832 over four thousand journals were published in Britain, some
in many dozens of volumes'.[106]

More serious than the issue of their escalating numbers was the
changing style of the periodicals themselves. By the late eighteenth and early nineteenth centuries, people were already widely
convinced of the rise-and-fall scenario that Habermas has forced
into the centre of our own critical debates about the demise of the
public sphere. Not only were commentators aware of this scenario,
they had already developed a version-within-a-version of it in their
accounts of the fate of the periodicals. Because the staggering
quantity and increasingly uneven quality of publications threatened the Enlightenment equation between the production of literature, the diffusion of knowledge, and social progress, journals
had become useful as a kind of governing presence capable of
sustaining rational debate by selecting, organizing, and preserving
an ongoing introduction to the various departments of the republic
of letters. But corrupted by the temptations of a debased reading
public, and infected with the divisive and embittering effects of
party spirit, they too had embarked on a perhaps irreversible process of moral decline. Instead of saving literature from its own
destruction, they had compounded the inevitability of this
demise.[107] This account was reinforced by the submerged narrative
of the rise and fall of political republics such as Athens, Rome, or
more recently, revolutionary France: the republic triumphs over
tyranny in order to establish a democracy, but this democratic
impulse is abused by demagogues who exploit their position by
catering to the worst instincts of the public in order to pursue
their own limited interests.

Whatever the more positive role that it sometimes assigned to
critics, the opening edition of the *Analytical* offered a history of
the periodical press which coincided with this account. 'The true
design of a Literary Journal', the *Analytical* argued, was 'to give an
account of new publications, as may enable the reader to judge of
them for himself'. This role had been dutifully fulfilled by the
'most respectable of the earlier *Critics*', but it was now going
increasingly unheeded:

in later times, the writers of literary journals, flattered by the attention
paid to their decisions, and gratified by the influence they have obtained

over authors, have filled their publications with little else than their own opinions and judgements. The old Journalists appear, only to introduce their *Principals,* while the modern ones seem to mention these, only to bring forward *themselves.* (1 (1788): i)

Instead of guarding the republic of letters from the intrusions of those who were unqualified to belong, reviewers were abusing their position, using their literary authority to promote their own interests by addressing those who read chiefly for diversion. An article, purporting to be a letter written by a correspondent to the *Monthly Magazine,* agreed that 'there are too many readers who feel the greatest pleasure in this kind of reviewing; and the critics, sensible of this, endeavour to accommodate their criticisms to this vitiated taste, by throwing into their remarks as much of the *sal atticus* as possible' (6 (1798): 102).[108] There were, it allowed, still 'a few critics who have not quite lost sight of what may properly be called the *morality of criticism*', but they tended to 'find that their critiques are not so favourably received by the public as they deserve to be, from the want of that which they cannot bring themselves to make use of with the freedom of their less tender-hearted brethren' (ibid). The force of reason had given way to the tyranny of prescription, the progress of knowledge overshadowed by the rhetorical demonstrations of pugilistic critics who were all too eager to appease a reading public that attended to their opinions for all the wrong reasons.

The rise and fall of the periodicals, whose perceived role was itself rooted in the rise and fall of literature generally, was a familiar, almost predictable scenario. D'Israeli argued that '[j]ustice is administered by the Critics, frequently, with more adversity than justice. The people groan under the tyranny of these governors, particularly when they are capricious and visionary ... [N]o author can answer for his fate, when he once is fairly in their hands'. Like 'the Grand Monarque' himself, reviewers had emerged as a force capable of preserving the literary republic, but they had used their privileged position to give opinions that were appealing for their combative style at the expense of any attention to the literature itself.[109] Nor, for Protestant England, was France the only available example of this sort of tyranny. Samuel Pratt argued that it was impossible 'to conceive of a more useful institution than that of a Literary Journal, when conducted with various ability and inflexible justice'. But this role was threatened,

Pratt warned, by those 'critical usurpers, who with pontifical pride, fulminate their defamatory bulls against Genius and Learning, in ignorant pomposity or in rude impertinence'. These usurpers had reduced the *'Judgement-seat'* of criticism into 'a *secret Tribunal*' where judgements were issued without the slightest attempt at accuracy: 'the work which ought to be condemned is acquitted, and the production that deserves to receive distinguished honours, is, by this ungenerous artifice, supposed to be guilty of all the imperfections imputed to it'.[110] Such a development, Pratt implied, was more appropriate to the despotic tastes of Papists than to the spirit of liberty which animated British Protestantism.

Something was rotten in the republic of letters. And the source of this rot, most commentators agreed, was the small-mindedness of critics who had begun to act as demagogues in a republic whose spirit was wholly opposed to such behaviour. Worse still, critics warned, periodicals, the guardians of the disinterested world of letters, had been polluted by the divisive effects of party spirit. Literature's role as a public sphere was informed by a deep sense that it was non-partisan: whatever opinions authors may put forward were motivated by a concern for the general good. But a spirit of acrimony between individuals with different personal agendas had invaded literature, threatening the progress of learning. 'There is no passion which is so directly calculated to pervert the understanding, and to undermine the virtue, not only of individuals but of whole communities', the *Analytical Review* warned, 'as the rage of party. The most absurd fictions are credited, the . . . voice of truth is not heard' (16 (1793): 222). The 'letter' to the *Monthly Magazine* on the rise and fall of literary journals raised similar fears about the effects of party spirit. 'The Establishment of literary journals', it acknowledged, 'has certainly been an event of the greatest consequence in the republic of letters'. Journals had 'been the means of diffusing knowledge far and wide, and of kindling a love of learning, where the seeds of genius would otherwise, in all likelihood, have perished in wretched torpidity'. Increasingly, however, these benefits were being overshadowed by 'flagrant abuses which have disgraced the monthly reports of literature', including, 'without a single exception', the charge of 'being tinctured with a party spirit'. Some reviewers, the letter warned, 'instead of being impartial reporters, are contending amongst themselves with all the ardour and petulance of professed disputants' (6 (1798): 101). Their impartial role forgotten, critics had become equivalent to the gladiators and circus entertainers whose increasing popularity was, for many historians, an index of the decline of Rome.

The real victims, critics agreed, were those authors and readers who retained their respect for the true nature of literature. Reviewers enjoyed the double advantage over authors of being able to shoot their poisoned darts from the shadows of anonymity, and being able to communicate to a much larger audience than the author could ever hope to reach.[111] And the public, discouraged from forming its own opinions, was instead being told what to think. The *Analytical Review*, in the preface to its opening number, warned that

Reviewers have engaged in *wars* with authors; and men without a name, from the shade of obscurity in which they were concealed, have ventured to abuse at random the first literary characters. In many cases they have entirely lost sight of that modesty, which ought perhaps to accompany him, who being a private individual, presumes to speak to the public at large, and have set themselves up as a kind of oracles, and distributed from their dark thrones, decisions to regulate the ideas and sentiments of the literary world ... Mysterious transactions have taken place between Authors or Booksellers and Reviewers, and the respectable part of the public, suspecting that there was more of this dishonourable business done than really was the case, have lost their confidence in such Critics; and thus the character and reputation of the journals have been injured and degraded. (1 (1788): ii)

The letter to the *Monthly Magazine* identified the same groups as the victims of this new breed of cultural tyranny. The author suffered 'the misfortune of having his arguments misrepresented; and his whole treatise condemned in an extensive publication ... by a combatant who is sheltered under an impervious veil ... The public also are very unfairly dealt with by this mode of conduct; for the right of judgement is hereby taken out of their hands' (6 (1798): 101–2).

The image of the critic as a cultural middleman, organizing and condensing literature so that readers might decide for themselves, was premised on a binary opposition that is easily deconstructed. Description, however apparently neutral, is always prescriptive, and part of the critic's avowed task was selecting those pieces of literature that were good enough to warrant having an oppor-

tunity to be judged by the public at all. Nor were critics timorous
about asserting their opinions in absolute terms. None the less,
on however rhetorical a level, it remained important that the
reviewer accept that the final assessment of literary merit lay not
with the critic himself but with what the *Monthly Review* called 'the
August assembly and tribunal of the public' (1 (1790): 424). As
the *Analytical* put it, the 'GRAND ORIGINAL END' of reviewing was to
enable 'the public . . . to judge of a book for themselves' (1 (1788):
iii). Instead, inflamed by party spirit, and encouraged by an undis-
cerning reading public, reviewers had become intellectual gladiators promoting their own particular agendas.

Journals which offered these opinions were far from announcing
their own obsolescence. If the role of periodicals was to assert the
importance of correct taste within the literary republic, and, by
doing so, halting or even reversing those negative cultural developments which had cast the role of literature into question, this task
was doubled by the even more heroic aim of reforming the periodical press itself – the good sheriff who must put the bad sheriff
in his place before he can get on with cleaning up the republic.
Nevertheless, however eager particular journals and critics may
have been to exempt themselves from this narrative of historical
decline, the frequency with which these prognostications recurred
called the Enlightenment ideal of literature as a disinterested
means of promoting the diffusion of knowledge into serious
question.

'Wars with authors . . . [launched] from the shade of obscurity';
'mysterious transactions . . . between Authors or Booksellers and
Reviewers'; arbitrary rulings of a 'secret tribunal'; assailants protected by 'an impervious veil'; the calculated power of 'a bold and
direct falsehood' – this is the shadowy rhetoric of cloak-and-dagger
thrillers, not the language of rational demystification. What
emerges out of these suspicions and denunciations is the ghostly
figure of the Enlightenment as the *unheimlich* itself, a force which
dislocates its faith in the power of literature to ensure the progress
of learning by splitting to reveal the monstrous side of its own
fantasy of 'improvement'.

In many ways, it is a story that echoes John Robison's warning
about the Illuminati in *Proofs of a Conspiracy* (1798). The professed
goals of the Enlightenment reformers were inspired by nothing
less than a fantasy of perfect transparency: aligning morality and

power through the dissemination of knowledge, so that the interests of the individual would be reflected in prevailing standards of public opinion, which would in turn be reflected in both the policies of the state and the relations between individuals. Secrecy was traditionally associated with the arbitrary power of government by domination, a system of rule that relied upon the ignorance of its subjects because it tended to impose itself on, rather than reflect, the popular will. The Enlightenment opposed itself to the 'entire catalogue of secret practices first inaugurated by Machiavelli that were to secure domination over the immature people. The principle of publicity was later held up in opposition to the practice of secrets of state.'[112] This critique of political tyranny was frequently extended to the realm of personal experience. In her novel *Secrecy*, in which the reformist author Eliza Fenwick explored the difficult relationship between love and reason within the literary conventions of the gothic romance, secrecy is consistently identified as the greatest obstacle to a truly virtuous society. Forced to adapt her struggle to her adversaries' immoral terms, the novel's heroine, Caroline Ashburn, realizes too late that she has made a 'fatal mistake' in assuming that 'secrecy could repair the inability of reason' (336).

For many, however, the dream of literature as a public sphere, governed by reason and contributing to the good of all, had become a myth that concealed the ubiquity of conspiracies and irrational vendettas within the republic of letters. Print culture, like the revolution in France, had tilted over into the nightmarish vision of its own dark double – a series of endlessly accelerating, self-consuming processes of technological innovation and proliferation, embraced by a reading public that respected neither truth nor literary merit. Reviews, which were supposed to address these problems, only accentuated them. The republic of letters was built on an individualist emphasis on the sovereignty of reason, but reason, and with it the public importance of authors, was increasingly seen to have been eroded by the popularity of literature.

Like Fox's obituary for the press in his letter to Joseph Johnson (which we saw at the end of chapter 1), these laments for the death of literature were premature. The same worries about literary overproduction and the threat it posed to authorial distinction, and the same tendency of reviews to offer themselves as solutions to these problems, continued to be heard decades later. In 1820, the *Retrospective Review* placed a familiar stress on the double-edged significance of libraries which,

while they are proud monuments of the ingenuity and all-reaching, all-fathoming mind of men; yet must strike the heart of the student that enters them with despair, should he aim at attaining universal knowledge through the medium of books ... The knowledge of their external qualities, and the adventitious circumstances attending their formation or history, has become a science – professors devote their lives to it, with an enthusiasm not unworthy of a higher calling – they have earned the name of *bibliomaniacs*. (1 (1820): vii–viii)

The refusal to recognize that systems of bibliographical organization only highlighted the impossibility of assimilating new forms of knowledge converted the belief in the adequacy of these rational processes into a dangerous irrationality, a *mania* that was the opposite of scientific rigour. Hazlitt concluded his celebration of the liberating powers of literature as a force capable of storming the best defences of the feudal baron with a similarly apocalyptic vision:

Formerly, neither the vassal nor his lord could read or write, and knew nothing but what they suffered or inflicted: now the meanest mechanic can both read and write, and the only danger seems to be that every one, high and low, rich and poor, should turn author, and the whole world be converted into waste paper. (17 (1828): 327)

Nor were these worries about the general dangers of cultural decline free of occupational self-interest. Critics continued to link the problem of excess to the issue of authorial distinction. A correspondent to *Blackwood's* worried that '[a]uthorship, formerly a rare and envied distinction, is now so common as to lift a man (I should say a person, for it is now as much a female as a male quality) but little above the mass of men around him' (1 (1817): 455). In the first of his lectures on Milton and Shakespeare in 1811 and 1812, Coleridge made the same point, that the popularity of literature had steadily undermined, rather than reinforced, authors' social distinction:

In older times writers were looked up to almost as intermediate beings, between angels and men; afterwards they were regarded as venerable and, perhaps, inspired teachers; subsequently they descended to the level of learned and instructive friends; but in modern days they are deemed culprits more than benefactors ... If a person be now seen reading a new book, the most usual question is – 'What trash have you there?' I admit that there is some reason for this difference in the estimate; for in these times, if a man fail as a tailor, or a shoemaker, and can read and write correctly (for spelling is still of some consequence) he becomes an author. (*Lectures*, 35–6)

For conservative journals and writers such as *Blackwood's* and, by 1811, Coleridge, the dangers of these popularizing trends were obvious enough. So pressing were these anxieties, however, that they were not confined to conservatives alone. Their distorting influence is perhaps most clearly expressed in William Hazlitt's frequently noted self-contradictions: a reformer in politics and a high Tory in culture.[113] 'Literature', suggested Hazlitt,

formerly was a sweet Hermitress, who fed on the pure breath of Fame, in silence and in solitude; far from the madding strife, in sylvan shade or cloistered hall, she trimmed her lamp or turned her hourglass, pale with studious care ... Modern literature, on the contrary, is a gay Coquette, fluttering, fickle, vain; followed by a train of flatterers; besieged by a crowd of pretenders; courted, she courts again; receives delicious praise, and dispenses it; is impatient for applause; pants for the breath of popularity; renounces eternal fame for a newspaper puff ... is the subject of polite conversation; the darling of private parties; the go-between in politics; the directress of fashion; the polisher of manners ... glitters, flutters, buzzes, spawns, dies, – and is forgotten! (16 (1823): 219)

Just as images of women were used throughout the eighteenth century as a means of articulating fears about the dangerous instability of a commercial economy, so for Hazlitt was the split image of the virtuous and the fallen woman attractive as a means of expressing anxieties about a capriciousness that was wholly at odds with literature's more distinguished role. As reading and writing were becoming fashionable, literature was being caught up within an endless and bewildering nexus of exchanges which effectively uprooted it from any certainty of inherent value. All of which only increased the allure of a dream of cultural stability which found expression in Hazlitt's conflicted image of an impossibly pure, and flagrantly debased, femininity. Victor Frankenstein's warning about the dangers of unlimited enquiry might be applied not only to individual writers but to the energies of an entire intellectual community, and not merely to 'scientific knowledge' but to the totalizing dream of the scientificity of all knowledge.[114] However perfect in each of its separate departments, literature was beginning to seem almost monstrous. Instead of transforming society by promoting the diffusion of rational ideas, it was in danger of smothering the world with waste paper. Authors, like Frankenstein himself, were at risk of being overwhelmed by their own creation.

Undaunted, journals continued to offer themselves as an important antidote by providing what the *Retrospective Review* called 'a bird's-eye view of the rise and progress of our literature' (1 (1820): xii). Like its predecessors, the *Retrospective* aspired to be a form of literature whose focus would be 'the history of literature' (viii). Equally familiarly, it highlighted the heroic nature of this ambition to save literature from its own excesses by emphasizing the extent to which other journals, having made the same claim, had already been corrupted:

Reviews have sprung up as rapidly, and as well armed, as the fabled warriors from the teeth sown by Cadmus, to stand in the gap in the hour of need; but it has been 'whispered in the state', that, like the same sons of the earth, these self-elected champions, neglecting the public weal, have turned their arms against each other – that having cleared a ring for themselves under the false pretext of a public cause, they have ceased to exhibit themselves in any other character than that of intellectual gladiators; with literature for an arena – the public for spectators – and weapons poisoned with party malice and personal slander. (i)

There are few more graphic accounts of the fragmentation of the bourgeois public sphere: the *usefulness* of print culture had been reduced to entertainment value, the important role of authors transformed into a carnivalesque parody of itself. This ideal of literature as an information revolution unravelled at a more gradual pace than did the more explicitly political struggle which was the subject of chapter 1. The two historical processes intersected, however, in their related fears about the dangers which growing readerships posed to different forms of authority – the power of the state or the status of the author. Their intersection highlights the political nature of debates about literature in the period, and the *literariness* of political debates conducted in print by authors who were also preoccupied with threats to their own professional distinction in 'this scribbling age, when every man who can write composes a pamphlet, and every journeyman bookseller erects himself into a publisher' (*GM* 62 (1792): 934). These related excesses and anxieties, originating in the political and cultural spheres, helped to intensify the reaction against the claims of emergent counterpublics and, as I shall argue in my conclusion, to shape the beginnings of our own canonical assumptions about the nature of literary studies.

PART TWO

Marginalia

Swinish multitudes

Two letters appeared in the November 1797 and January 1798 editions of the *Gentleman's Magazine*, signed with the pen-name Eusebius. They highlighted the dangers of the wrong sort of literature falling into the hands of young women, in the first letter, and the labouring classes, in the second. Together they suggest the growing anxieties we have already encountered about literature as a sphere for the exchange of ideas and as a means for the diffusion of knowledge. To be published was to be placed before the public, which would act as the arbiter of a work's success or failure, but paradoxically, this heightened rather than eradicated the task of ensuring proper taste on the part of those who were to act in this role as arbiters. 'Of all reading, that of novels is the most frivolous, and frequently the most pernicious', Eusebius warned:

Many of them suggest false notions of life, inflame the imagination, deprave the judgement, and vitiate the heart. A lady, whose mind is not engaged in more useful, or capable of more rational, employment, sends her servant to the Circulating Library; and he returns loaded with volumes, containing pathetic tales of love and madness; tales, which fill her head with the most ridiculous chimeras; with romantic scenes of gallantry; with an admiration of young rakes of spirit; with dreams of conquests, amorous interviews, and matrimonial excursions . . .

A young woman, who employs her time in reading novels, will never find amusement in any other sort of books. Her mind will be soon debauched by licentious description, and lascivious images; and she will, consequently, remain the same frivolous and insignificant creature through life; her mind will become a magazine of trifles and follies, or rather impure and wanton ideas. Her favourite novels will never teach her the social virtues, the qualifications of domestic life, the principles of her native language, history, geography, morality, the precepts of Christianity, or any other useful science. (67 (1797): 912)

The moral permissiveness encouraged by novels and the dangerous instabilities of femininity are seen, in Eusebius's letter, to be
mutually reinforcing. Novels are hazardous because they encourage those defects which are already present in women's character;
women are naturally attracted to novels because these books represent all that is most frivolous in the world of literature. But
novels and women are also linked in a more unconscious manner,
because women, according to these sorts of representations,
seemed to *resemble* novels – unworthy intruders in the republic of
letters more eager to attract attention than to offer any serious
or lasting contribution to rational debate. Novels, like Hazlitt's
image of literature as a fallen woman, travelled everywhere, never
staying in one place for long, eager for attention, falling into all
the wrong hands, for all the wrong reasons.

   In the second letter, Eusebius was concerned with the question
of the education of the lower orders, though this time the issue
was not so much what the lower orders should read as the debat-
able wisdom of encouraging them to read at all. Highly question-
able in this regard was the work of the Reforming Societies, whose
collective purpose, Eusebius suggested with more than a hint of
irony, was one 'of *illuminating* the common people of England, for
rendering them capable of reading their *edifying* publications, and
opening their eyes to the *glorious* advantages of liberty and equality', the results of which were only too clear:

It is a well-attested fact, that no less than 400 copies of Paine's Age of
Reason were, on one market day, distributed, *gratis*, among the ordinary
farmers, servants, and labourers, at York, in a cheap and commodious
edition, in order to disseminate its principles, and extend its *illuminating*
influence among the vulgar. Those, who have received a tincture of scholarship at a Sunday-school, without any regular discipline for the rest of
the week, will be proper subjects for their purpose, and no doubt will be
the first to derive instruction from the luminous pages of this precious
reformer. It would have been useless, it would have been throwing their
pearls before swine, to have *stuffed* these edifying publications into the
pockets of illiterate rusticks . . .
   Eusebius is no enemy to instruction; but he still insists, that industry
in the lowest classes of society is better than scholarship; and that to
give them the latter without the former, is to put swords into their hands,
which may be instrumental to their own destruction. (68 (1798): 32–4)

In a sense, the problem here was exactly the opposite of the case
of the women novel readers. Eusebius's worry was not that the

lowest classes might resort to literature as a distraction from their worldly cares, but that they might lay claim to the faculty of reason and, not recognizing that their own limited understandings ought to disqualify them, might presume to participate in the public exchange of ideas about questions bearing on the general good.[1] In both cases, what worried Eusebius was the power of literature to encourage 'false notions of life' amongst readers whose imaginations were too easily inflamed and whose powers of reason were too stunted for them to be able to detect the errors of wilfully misleading publications such as romantic novels and Paine's *Age of Reason*. The two letters reflect the degree to which the political and cultural concerns explored in chapters 1 and 2 converged in a nervousness about the dangers of an unrestricted reading public which, in turn, echoed larger liberal-democratic anxieties about the extent and nature of the populace that qualified for political participation.[2] Unlike those men who were intelligent enough to debate issues of general importance without falling sway to intoxicating visions of impossible social liberty, women and the lower orders could not be trusted to exchange ideas rationally. They were each, in their own way, more interested in being deluded.

The problem with the Enlightenment dream of 'improvement', which had at its heart a kind of missionary zeal, was that it presupposed extending the benefits of reading to those people who, because they were not already improved, could not be expected to understand the proper reasons for reading in the first place. Women, the lower orders, and that anomalous group, colonial subjects, constituted the beyond of the republic of letters – social domains which could not be trusted with the cultural authority that ought to accrue to an informed reading and writing public. To the extent that their ignorance posed a threat to social stability, many commentators (but not Eusebius) agreed that these subordinate groups required proper education in order to be rendered useful. But although they required this education as an antidote to their ignorance, they also threatened to contaminate the prestige of learning itself: in other words, they required the attention of cultural authorities, but not in order that they might be invested with any authority as a consequence of that attention.

Having encountered these sorts of representations of subaltern readerships in the debates between dominant reformist and conservative writers, I want to turn to these border areas in order to develop a clearer sense of the developments which were so threatening to authors who, in one way or another, identified themselves as defenders of the republic of letters. The anxieties of conservative critics bear witness to the extent to which these aspirants' hybrid social identities – able to read but not fit to influence public opinion, or in the case of Orientalists, cultural middlemen introducing the irrational beauties of Eastern literature to English readers – unsettled the narratives that helped to define the social geography of the republic of letters. But despite the denunciations of their antagonists, the threat that these emergent readerships posed to the social coherence of the literary republic was not always rooted in a repudiation of the importance of discursive exchange. Their insistence on the legitimacy of their own access to literary authority echoed rather than contradicted the claims of those whose position they were seen most to undermine. And it was precisely this resemblance, as much as any difference, which made their denunciation all the more urgent. As Jon Klancher puts it, 'the radical public was not only a demonstrable audience in the late eighteenth and early nineteenth century: it was also something irritatingly lodged inside middle-class consciousness itself'.[3]

The real problem for Enlightenment reformers, which was the opposite of worries about the ill-qualified nature of new reading audiences, was that too great an 'improvement' of the disenfranchised threatened the privileged stature of those whose social importance was attached to this role of improving others. Where 'new' readerships were denounced for their irrational predispositions, it was often, ironically, a response to the opposite threat: that subaltern groups were laying claims to the power of reason and the authority of the reading public which mimicked rather than opposed the claims of those who already occupied an established place within the social and literary hierarchies.

These dynamics have been foregrounded by critics who have modified Jurgen Habermas's historical account of the universality of the public sphere by focusing on what Craig Calhoun describes as 'multiple, sometimes overlapping or contending, public spheres'.[4] Anxieties about the misuse of literature in the hands of various subaltern groups suggests that the relationship between these publics was contestatory rather than supplementary; the rhetoric of universality was premised on a denial, rather than an embrace, of these multiplicities. By focusing our attention on these various publics, and on the often turbulent relationships between them, critics have helped to situate our understanding of the bourgeois public sphere within what Geoff Eley describes as 'the *wider* public domain, where authority is not only constituted as rational and legitimate but its terms may also be contested and modified (and occasionally overthrown) by society's subaltern groups'.[5]

Jean Bethke Elshtain argues in *Public Man, Private Woman* that 'the terms public and private', which structured these debates, 'are evanescent notions' that are best approached not as predetermined categories but as evidence of a heterogeneous process of categorization which is itself the scene of a political struggle for symbolic capital (4). Far from being invested with innate meaning, such terms are elements of a semiotics of culture which helps to determine both the various codes of social distinction and the limits within which different forms of agency become possible within any historical moment. Their changing definitions constitute the ideological landscape within which different discursive exchanges are negotiated, but their definitions also represent one important focus of these debates. The exclusions which these categories reinforced could not, therefore, prevent the growth of alternative public spheres which exposed the limits of the bourgeois sphere's claims to universality.

In offering readings of the ways these hybrid literary constituencies echoed the very narratives they seemed most to threaten, I want to use a distinction made by Peter Stallybrass and Allon White in *The Politics and Poetics of Transgression* between 'two quite distinct kinds of "grotesque"' (193). Reading Pierre Bourdieu's analysis of the different sites of contestation for symbolic capital against Mikhail Bakhtin's theory of the grotesque, they argue that various processes of hybridization inherent in bourgeois society produced 'new combinations and strange instabilities in a given semiotic system' which exceeded the traditional oppositions of polite/vulgar, high/low, or culture/anarchy. More threatening than the subordinate term in each of these pairs were those social developments which threatened the distinctions altogether. They differentiate between 'the grotesque as the "Other"' of the defining group or self, and the grotesque as a boundary phenomenon of hybridization or inmixing, in which self and other become enmeshed in an inclusive, heterogeneous, dangerously unstable zone' (ibid).

The universality of bourgeois self-representations presupposed the fiction of a single reading public encompassing all rational individuals. But the democratization of reading did not just expand the reading public, it fractured it into multiple overlapping publics with competing priorities, points of consensus, and normative assumptions. Reason, far from operating as a consolidating dream of a discursive position beyond social difference (as accounts of literature as a public sphere suggested), had become an important site of contestation – 'a dangerously unstable zone' – in itself. What was particularly troubling about this was that it exposed implicit tensions in the expansionary logic that underpinned the Enlightenment shift towards a market-determined reading public. It was the fulfilment, rather than the betrayal, of the educational impulse inherent in this progressive ethos.

More unsettling still, for those who found these developments troubling, was the ease with which growing numbers of people were becoming involved, not just as readers, but as authors. And like the growth of the reading public, the increasingly easy transition from reading to writing was all the more threatening because it represented an extension of, rather than a departure from, the Enlightenment belief that reading was educational, not simply because it gave people access to more information, but also because it developed people into better, more actively critical readers. Putting this sort of response into writing was simply a further step in the evolution of a discriminating mind. This multiplication of literary functions was already prevalent in a less threatening form in the attempts of literary journals to create the impression of a single community of readers and writers by including extended 'Letters to the Editor' sections. Since at least the days when the *Spectator* had invited its readers to deposit their letters through the jaws of a lion's head attached to the west side of Button's Coffee House, literature had been envisioned as a communicative process fusing readers and writers together in an extended and ongoing dialogue.[6] What was most unsettling about the developments of the 1790s, therefore, was that in some ways, there was nothing new about them.

The claims of women and the lower orders, and the problematic relationship between Oriental literature and the politics of empire, helped to expose tensions that had always been rooted in the definition of literature as a public sphere with universalizing ambitions but highly selective assumptions. They did so because they straddled the boundaries which assured the social distinction of authors at a time when this distinction was already under threat from the various perceptions of accelerating cultural erosion that we have examined above. Political tensions were mediated by debates about literature, but these debates were in turn mediated by more general cultural anxieties about fashion, commerce, literary overproduction, and so on. Claims in the period about the social limits of reason have to be read as the product of a dense and shifting network of transferences and projections that were rooted in the problematic status of the professional author.

By insisting on their right to a full share in the blessings of the Enlightenment, the emergent subaltern publics helped to expose the limitations of many reformers' ideas about the democratic potential of the diffusion of knowledge. For this they were demonized in their own time, and too often subjected to what E. P. Thompson has described as 'the enormous condescension' of critics who remain content to treat them as a colourful prehistory which, perhaps regretfully, but ultimately necessarily, had to be left behind in the development of the poetic genius of a few individuals whose literary achievements could themselves be assumed to embody the spirit of the age.[7] It is to these three different regions, lying along the edges and troubling the security of the republic of letters, that I now want to turn; it is here, as much as anywhere else, that our received assumptions about the nature of literature have their roots.

CHAPTER THREE

The poorer sort

When it was impossible to prevent our reading something, the fear of the progress of knowledge and a *Reading Public* . . . made the Church and State . . . anxious to provide us with that sort of food for our stomachs, which they thought best.
William Hazlitt, 'What is the People?'

CAREFUL SAVING MORAL MEN AND WOMEN

The panes obscur'd by half a century's smoke:
There stands the bench at which his life is spent,
Worn, groov'd, and bor'd, and worm devour'd, and bent,
Where daily, undisturb'd by foes or friends,
In one unvaried attitude he bends . . .

Such is his fate – and yet you might descry
A latent spark of meaning in his eye.
– That crowded shelf, beside his bench, contains
One old, worn, volume that employs his brains:
With algebraic lore its page is spread,
where *a* and *b* contend with *x* and *z:*
Sold by some *student* from an Oxford hall,
– Bought by the pound upon a broker's stall.
On this it is his sole delight to pore,
Early and late, when working time is o'er:
But oft he stops, bewilder'd and perplex'd,
At some hard problem in the learned text;
Pressing his hand upon his puzzled brain,
At what the dullest school-boy could explain.

From needful sleep the precious hour he saves,
To give his thirsty mind the stream it craves:
There, with his slender rush beside him plac'd,
He drinks the knowledge in with greedy haste.[1]

Encountered today, readers might react against the sentimentality of Jane Taylor's portrait of this self-improving underdog, as determined to educate himself as he was horribly limited in his means for doing so. It was, however, a story which many working-class advocates were eager to tell about themselves. Suffering from enormous disadvantages, with little opportunity or obvious incentive to develop their reading skills, these self-taught authors implied that their achievements ought to be regarded as heroic rather than threatening. In turn, they also suggested, this heroism made them more, rather than less, qualified to become members of the reading public – that 'informal Congress' whose practices were so closely connected with the Enlightenment dream of liberty.

This version of a well-behaved working class, intent solely on improving their collective lot by embracing the reformist power of an extended rational debate in print, does not square with the more unruly version of the radical and ultra-radical tradition presented by critics such as Ian McCalman, Jon Klancher, E. P. Thompson, Marcus Wood, and David Worrall, but this contradiction is precisely my point. The radical movement was unruly both in its potentially revolutionary attitudes towards authority, and in terms of its internal divisions over the issues of the ultimate goals and the acceptable strategies of the movement. It was partly in order to contain the political threats posed by these tensions that activists and writers such as Francis Place, Thomas Hardy, and John Thelwall took pains to insist on their own rational commitment to public debate. Framing a study of their interventions within this prior recognition of the potential unruliness of the radical movement locates these individuals at the *polite* end of the reform movement – seeking change through debate – but it also highlights the performative nature of their narratives. Their commitment to the rationalist creed of the Enlightenment public sphere suggests a more fundamental awareness of how much was at stake in terms of political strategy in being able to comply, and to be seen to comply, with its main characteristics. Like professional authors, who were all the more insistent upon constructions of the author as a servant of public virtue because of the extent of the evidence that the literary industry was driven by the dictates of fashion, plebeian leaders insisted on the fiction of a polite homogeneous class as a way of containing problems created by alternative impressions.

In his autobiography, the London Corresponding Society activist Francis Place recalled his dedication to learning in a passage that is strikingly similar to Taylor's 'pale mechanic':

> I used to plod at the French Grammar as I sat at my work, the book being fixed before me I was diligent also in learning all I could after I left off working at night . . . I usually when I had done with my french, read some book every night and having left the Corresponding Society I never went from home in the evening I always learned and read for three hours and sometimes longer.[2]

In his 1801 *Memoirs* (written in the third person) John Thelwall emphasized that, like Place, he had spent 'much of that time which ought to have been devoted to business, in the perusal of such books as the neighbouring circulating library could furnish' (vi). Still unsatisfied with the amount of time that he could devote to study, 'he even carried a wax taper in his pocket, that he might read as he went along the streets by night' (ix). The *Memoirs* (1792) of the shoemaker-turned-bookseller James Lackington recalled that when his mother became too poor for him to continue his schooling, he forgot how to read. Encouraged by his subsequent conversion to Methodism, however, he started reading again, 'ten chapters of the bible nightly; Mr Wesley's Tracts, Sermons, etc' (62). Like Place and Thelwall, he was forced to accommodate his reading to a work schedule which, as an apprentice shoemaker, left little time for self-improvement: 'I had such good eyes, that I often read by the light of the moon, as my master would not permit me to take a candle into my room, and that prohibition I looked upon as a kind of persecution' (62–3). For both himself and Mr Jones, a friend who acted as his 'secretary', intellectual needs supplanted all but the most necessary physical ones: 'so anxious were we to read a great deal, that we allowed ourselves but about three hours sleep in twenty-four' (99). Lackington told of a friend with a similar history, Ralph Tinley: 'Those hours which he could spare from a proper attention to the duties of a husband and a father, and manual labour as a shoemaker, were incessantly employed in the improvement of his mind in various branches of science; in many of which he attained a proficiency, totally divested of that affectation of superiority which little minds assume' (247).

Turning conservative critics' fears about the dangers of small pamphlets circulating throughout a swollen reading public back against them, Thomas Hardy, the founder of the LCS, insisted that the demand for shorter works by the leading advocates of the American Revolution had been both a natural consequence of social inequality, and a desirable way of diffusing knowledge amongst 'the poor and middling classes of the people':

From the small tracts and pamphlets, written by these *really* great men, much political information was diffused through the nation, at that period, by their benevolent exertions; the beneficial effects of which are felt to the present day. The sphere of life in which I was necessarily placed, allowed me no time to read long books; therefore, those smaller ones were preferred, being within the compass of my ability to purchase, and time to peruse, and, I believe, they are the most useful to any class of readers.

Moving beyond these memories of his own development, Hardy extended this recognition of the importance of short political texts to others who, like him, lacked the time or money for longer works. '[P]olitical knowledge was diffused generally throughout the nation', he recalled, 'by means of small Tracts, which were well adapted for giving information to persons of every capacity, and also by political discussions and conversations in the various meetings'.[3]

Alan Richardson's study of reformers' autobiographies as a literary genre is instructive for its attention to the interfusion of what Richardson calls 'a proto-Victorian, self-help ideology' with other, more communitarian concerns.[4] It is precisely this tension between collective struggle and personal 'egotism' that Hardy was trying to contain when, like Thelwall, he chose to write his *Memoir* 'in the third, rather than in the first person' in order to obviate 'the necessity of calling the great *I* so repeatedly to my assistance'.[5] The textual awkwardness which sometimes resulted may suggest that these tensions could only be contained at the price of considerable personal alienation, but Hardy's comments also indicate precisely how aware he was of just what was at stake in these stylistic complexities. Nor should we forget that these literary struggles, which fused together complex debates about political and literary representation, were describing a period when, as Mary Wollstonecraft discovered in her *Letters from Sweden, Norway, and Denmark* (1796), it was not always possible to 'avoid being continually the first person – "the little hero of each tale" '.[6]

Far from denying their adverse backgrounds, these self-taught activists tended to emphasize the unsteady nature of their intellectual progress. Lackington recalled, of his and Jones's efforts:

I made the most of my little stock of literature and strongly recommended the purchasing of Books to Mr Jones. But so ignorant were we on the subject, that neither of us knew what books were fit for our perusal, nor what to enquire for, as we had scarce ever heard or seen even any *title pages*, except a few of the religious sort, which at that time we had no relish for. So that we were at a loss how to encrease our small stock of science. And here I cannot help thinking that had Fortune thrown proper books in our way, we should have imbibed a just taste for literature, and soon made some tolerable progress; but such was our obscurity, that it was next to impossible for us ever to emerge from it.

Like Lackington, Place remembered that his 'reading was of course devoid of method, and very desultory'.[7] Their uncertainty about what to read confirmed many critics' worries that the ignorance of this new readership deprived them of the ability to recognize the full potential which literature ought to offer. Implicit in this worry, however, was a conflation of the ignorance of these readers about what to read, with a mistaken idea about *why* they were reading, which, in turn, was assumed to reflect a corresponding confusion about the relationship between the reading public and various forms of social and political authority.

It was precisely this confusion between two very different assumptions that authors such as Thelwall, Place, and Lackington were eager to contest. At the same time as they foregrounded the extent of their initial disorientation within the labyrinthine world of literature, they made it clear that their reasons for reading coincided with the most established ideas about the social role of literature. Place carefully specified that, even in his most uninformed days as a reader, he was interested in 'useful books, not Novels'. He gave as some examples a list of many of what were widely recognized as the most important areas of literature (including 'good' novels):

the histories of Greece and Rome, and some translated works of Greek and Roman writers. Hume Smollett, Fieldings novels and Robertsons works, some of Humes Essays, some Translations from french writers, and much on geography – some books on Anatomy and Surgery, some relating to Science and the Arts, and many Magazines. I had worked all the Problems in the Introduction to Guthries Geography, and had made some small progress in Geometry. I now read Blackstone, Hale's Common Law, several other Law Books, and much Biography.[8]

Reflecting on his efforts to read his own life as a text, Thomas Hardy similarly insisted that the 'life of a plain industrious citizen affords nothing of the light or the ludicrous circumstances which compose a great part of the frivolous reading of the present day'.[9]

Instead of confirming the anxieties of critics such as Mathias and Eusebius about new readerships, Hardy, Place, and Lackington implied that adverse circumstances highlighted rather than diminished the seriousness of their reasons for reading. If this was contrary to their critics' opinions, so too was the second and related implication that it was not the uneducated poor but the privileged minority – Taylor's 'some *student* from an Oxford hall' – who were most likely to be frivolous in their commitment to learning. It was an argument which subtly reversed the entrenched distinction between the polite and the vulgar: not only had they turned author, Hardy, Place and Lackington implied, they had done so in order to highlight both the obstacles they had had to overcome and the larger material success which had been the fruit of their obsession with self-improvement. All three men had, in their ways, joined the ranks of the 'polite'. But rather than disqualifying them from arguments which they may have wanted to make on behalf of the lower classes, they argued that this rise in social status was inseparable from a thirst for reading that was itself characteristic of the dignity of their earlier peers.

The case that Place, Lackington, and Hardy made for the lower classes based on their own personal successes implied an understanding of the proper role of literature as a medium for the diffusion of ideas, rather than sedition, but this did not mean that these authors were apolitical. In part, this conviction was due to a shared recognition of the multiple social forces which opposed their desire for improvement. Critics who mistrusted the motivations of working-class readers were, all three pointed out, as great a barrier to their improvement as was the lack of either leisure time or prior knowledge about which books most suited this purpose. Lackington began his autobiography with a triple dedication: to the public, to 'Respectable BOOKSELLERS', and to 'those sordid and malevolent BOOKSELLERS' who resisted the expansion of the privileges of education beyond the polite classes. To this third category, Lackington promised, in a deliberately vulgar

style, 'I'll give every one a smart lash in my way'. In the preface
to his second edition, he carried on his confrontation with these
misers of the Enlightenment:

The first edition of my memoirs was no sooner published, than my old
envious friends, mentioned in the Third Class of my Dedication, found
out that it was 'd—n'd stuff; d—n'd low!' the production of a *cobbler*, and
only fit to amuse that honourable fraternity; or to line their garrets and
stalls.[10]

Far from entering a democratic world in which individuals were
estimated on the basis of personal ability according to the meritocratic instincts of the market, Lackington discovered that the general practices of the book trade were dedicated to the conservation
of knowledge amongst a privileged elite, rather than to ensuring
its diffusion throughout society. Invited to private trade sales
where 'seventy or eighty thousand volumes [were] sold after dinner', he was 'very much surprized to learn, that it was common
for such as purchased remainders, to *destroy* one half or three
fourths of such books, and to charge the full publication price, or
nearly that, for such as they kept on hand'.[11] This artificial
inflation of book prices was reinforced by banishing from the trade
sales anyone who was known to sell articles under the publication
price. Contrary to the radically democratic implications suggested
by the rhetoric of the marketplace, the book trade continued to
operate as a closed association of entrenched interests determined
to preserve existing conditions by artificially limiting the diffusion
of knowledge. Far from living up to its democratic reputation as
the impartial arbiter of individual merit, the book trade functioned as an important site of contestation in the struggle to re-
imagine the power of literature within new readerships for whom
books were generally too expensive. Convinced that this oligar-
chical approach was self-defeating, Lackington became a retailer
of remaindered books, selling 'them off at half, or a quarter of the
publication prices', and in doing so, preserving and distributing
'many hundred thousand volumes' which would otherwise have
been destroyed.[12]

   Nor was this determination to arrest the spread of learning limited to the book trade. It was embedded in the attitudes of people
of all ranks to their social inferiors. To be better read than someone who was materially better off was a kind of rebellion, a wilful

act of insubordination which threatened the established hierarchy of class privilege by confusing different types of symbolic and financial capital. Writing in 1824, Place recalled 'the time when to be able to read and to indulge in reading, would if known to a master tradesman, have been so serious an objection to a journeyman, that he would scarcely have expected to obtain employment'. This prejudice was doubled at a higher level by the attitudes of wealthy customers to master tradesmen:

Had these persons been told that I never read a book, that I was ignorant of every thing but my business, that I sotted in a public house, they would not have made the least object to me. I should have been a 'fellow' beneath them, and they would have patronized me; but, – to accumulate books and to be supposed to know something of their contents, to seek for friends, too, among literary and scientific men, was putting myself on an equality with themselves, if not indeed assuming a superiority; was an abominable offence in a tailor, if not a crime, which deserved punishment, had it been known to all my customers in the few years from 1810 to 1817 – that I had accumulated a considerable library in which I spent all the leisure time I could spare, had the many things I was engaged in during this period, and the men with whom I associated been known, half of them at the least would have left me, and these too by far the most valuable customers individually.[13]

Instead of reinforcing the normative implications about moral differences between the polite and vulgar classes, Place's experiences with the well-to-do seemed to offer proof of the opposite: what was least tolerable about 'the vulgar' was not their vulgarity, but that they sometimes behaved in ways which mimicked those virtues which were assumed to distinguish the polite classes. Worse than any type of ignorance or vice was the aspiration of a member of the lower classes to an enlightened mind and 'proper' use of personal wealth and leisure time. When they should have been living it up like their irresponsible peers, they sometimes insisted on laying hold of those forms of symbolic capital which ought to have been the exclusive property of their betters, by accumulating libraries and becoming well read.

Part of the cultural authority which accrued to those who excelled in the republic of letters devolved from the idea that it was based on merit and a sense of commitment to the general good. But the prejudices encountered by Lackington and Place suggested that this myth of democratic opportunity was already wholly subject to existing class barriers. In turn, these contradictions were perpetuated by wider cultural assumptions which distinguished between the polite and the vulgar along the lines of 'accurate judgement and elegant taste', and 'a habit of correctness and elegance of expression' (*AR* 22 (1795): 450, 349). By 'the epithet polite', the *Analytical Review* emphasized in its review of Cumberland's *The Observer*, it meant the absence of 'any vulgar expressions or plebian sentiments' (9 (1791): 137). Maria, the heroine of Wollstonecraft's novel of the same name, whose sentiments had been raised 'superior to [her] station' by the company of her master's literary friends, testifies to her feelings of disgust 'in viewing the squalid inhabitants of some of the lanes and back streets of the metropolis, mortified at being compelled to consider them as my fellow-creatures, as if an ape had claimed kindred with me'.[14]

Aware of the limiting effects which these distinctions placed on the social and political aspirations of the lower classes, authors such as Place, Thelwall, Hardy, and Lackington explicitly extended their radical Enlightenment vision to the inhabitants of the lanes and back streets, a group which Place referred to as 'the careful saving moral men and women who have set their hearts on bettering their condition and have toiled day and night in the hope of accomplishing their purpose'.[15] Lulled into a kind of complacency by his earlier genteel aspirations, Thelwall recalled the shock of adapting to a lower social status after the death of his father had ended his expectations of becoming 'an historical painter':

Tho much more gross in their exterior, and far less polished in their language and manners, he was far from finding these men more essentially ignorant than the class with which he had hitherto been familiar. For Condition, so decisive as to the deportment of individuals, does not, by the same scale, dispense intelligence. On the contrary, it will, perhaps, be found, upon accurate investigation, that the manufacturing and working classes, in large towns and populous neighbourhoods, (those, at least, whose vocations are of a gregarious and somewhat sedentary nature) are much better informed than the thriving shopkeepers of our trading towns and cities.[16]

The working classes were more enquiring than their more prosperous social counterparts for reasons which perfectly accorded with traditional Enlightenment ideas about the importance of intellectual debate. Despite their poverty, working conditions tended to generate communities whose exchanges of opinion and information facilitated the development of knowledge more easily than did the relative isolation of 'thriving shopkeepers'.

Lackington both identified a growing disposition amongst the lower classes towards reading, and as he had done in his relationship with 'Mr Jones', congratulated himself on having 'been highly instrumental in diffusing that general desire for READING, now so prevalent among the inferior orders of society'. Once in operation, the book trade made possible a spontaneous set of exchanges between authors and readers, but this set of conditions was not itself automatic. By proving to other booksellers that 'SMALL PROFITS DO GREAT THINGS' (as Lackington had emblazoned on his carriage), he could take pride in having helped to break down those social barriers which the book trade, far from destroying, had reinforced. These changes in reading habits amongst the lower classes, with the moral transformation they implied, was a favourite theme of his autobiography:

The poorer sort of farmers, and even the poor country people in general, who before that period spent their winter evenings in relating stories of witches, hobgoblins, &c. now shorten the winter nights by hearing their sons and daughters read tales, romances, &c. and on entering their houses, you may see Tom Jones, Roderic Random, and other entertaining books, stuck up on their bacon-racks, &c. If *John* goes to town with a load of hay, he is charged to be sure not to forget to bring home 'Peregrine Pickle's Adventures;' and when *Dolly* is sent to market to sell her eggs, she is commissioned to purchase 'The History of Pamela Andrews'. In short all ranks and degrees now READ.[17]

Place agreed with Lackington's suggestion that the act of giving these people the sort of education which would dispose them towards a love of literature, with the reformation in their moral character that would inevitably follow, was both a laudable goal and an historical fact: 'we are a much better people now than we were then, better instructed, more sincere and kind hearted, less gross and brutal, and have fewer of the concomitant vices of a less civilized state'. Both accounts reproduce the more general reformist belief in a teleology of historical progress in the particular spectre of the improvement of the lower orders.[18]

These developments, as real as they were, Place argued, accentuated rather than diminished the need for encouraging reforms. The steadfastness with which such people dealt with the crippling

effects of their daily routines was a sign, not of their disqualifi-
cation from the reading public because they were incapable of
thinking about general rather than particular issues, but of a
moral integrity which made the goal of their eventual inclusion
all the more important:

I have seen a vast many such, who when the evil day has come upon
them, have kept on working steadily but hopelessly more like horses in
a mill, or mere machines than human beings, their feelings blunted, poor
stultified moving animals, working on yet unable to support their families in any thing like comfort, frequently wanting the common necessaries
of life, yet never giving up until 'misery has eaten them to the bone',
none knowing none caring for them, no one to administer a word of
comfort, or if an occasion occurred which might be of service to them,
none to rouse them to take advantage of it.[19]

Classical republicanism's equation of the moral worth of the patriotic citizen with the leisure time necessary to be able to think
broadly about general issues, denigrated those whose routines
reduced them to a narrowness of vision and purpose. Place, on the
other hand, insisted that the very willingness to continue in these
routines on behalf of themselves and their families was as great a
sign of moral integrity as was the possession of those privileges
which underpinned the possibility of disinterested contemplation.
Without rejecting the claims of the middle class to a form of political empowerment linked to their enthusiasm for literature, Place
argued passionately that this yearning for improvement as a result
of the diffusion of knowledge generally excluded a part of society
which, in the few times that it was remembered, was represented
in negative terms that were wholly inaccurate:

All above them in circumstances, calumniating them, classing them with
the dissolute, the profligate, and the dishonest, from whom the character
of the whole of the working people is taken. Yet I have witnessed in this
class of persons, so dispised so unjustly judged of by their betters, virtues
which I have not seen, to the same extent as to means, among any other
description of the people. Justice will never perhaps be done to them
because they may never be understood, because it is not the habit for
men to care for others beneath them in rank, and because they who
employ them will probably never fail to look grudgingly on the pay they
are compelled to give them for their services, the very notion of which
produces an inward hatred of them, a feeling so common that it is visible
in the countenance and manners in nearly every one who has to pay
either journeymen, labourers, or servants.[20]

Contrary to Enlightenment ideas about literature as a sphere facilitating unrestricted discursive exchange, the issue of who told whose stories, which was fundamental to questions of social justice, was bound up with existing asymmetries of power.[21] The most destitute would be wrongly remembered because their story would continue to be told by others who mistook the moral courage of their determination to endure grinding routines for an unreflective stupidity. The *Analytical Review* could suggest that 'the adult poor are in general notorious in ignorance and stupidity', but Place challenged the standards of judgement which could mistakenly identify these people, who possessed greater virtues in proportion to their means than anyone else in society, as stupid, or what was still worse, as a threat to the nation (7 (1790): 222). From Place's perspective, the dismissiveness of the *Analytical* said more about the patronizing attitudes of the middle classes than about the poor themselves.

Like Burke, but from the opposite political extreme, Place rejected claims for the republic of letters as an open sphere of unlimited debate leading to generalized social progress. The principle of disinterestedness was laudable, but in practice democratic ideas about literature concealed a bias which reinforced rather than displaced entrenched assumptions about the lower orders. Knowledge could never be so easily separated from power as utopian visions of the public sphere supposed. Far from being universal, the emphasis of many reformers on accessibility extended only to those who were already empowered enough to participate in the debates within the literary community, if not in the formal political process itself. As we have seen, the point was frequently repeated that the accessible language and low cost of reformist writings, designed to capture the attention of the disenfranchised, was more of a crime than the seditious ideas they contained. If the definition of those who qualified to participate within the public sphere replicated the existing class structure without any justification for doing so beyond what Place had denounced as misrepresentations of the lower orders, then the myth of the public sphere only reified the political contradictions it claimed to transcend.

Those whose lives had been edited out of dominant versions of history failed to be represented in debates within the public sphere because they had been so thoroughly marginalized. History had simply left them out. Nor, Place insisted, was this simply a matter of innocent oversight. But whereas Burke emphasized a conspiracy of 'the political Men of Letters' to reshape the socio-political hierarchy in their own image, Place identified the generalized bigotry of the 'polite classes' in their dealings with social inferiors. The moral syntax, he argued, had in some important ways been inverted: the 'vulgar' were often morally superior, while the disdain of their social superiors was itself a kind of vulgarity. And, he insisted, this bigotry, far from being a sign of absolute difference, was rooted in a denial by the privileged classes of a complicity based on mutual dependence. The inseparability of high and low, polite and vulgar, gentry and working class, producers and consumers, rather than the barriers which divided them, explained this resistance to the aspirations of the lower classes.

Reflecting on the related equation between the educational opportunities of the polite classes, the capacity for disinterested conduct, and eligibility for political participation, Hardy insisted on a similar reversal in the moral syntax of class difference:

It is strange that men who are supposed to possess superior talents, education, and discernment, and who are also rulers and legislators, should suffer their evil passions to lead them, to say the least of it, into such gross errors. But what will corrupt and wicked men not do, in certain situations, to retain their assumed power, and to secure to themselves the wages of iniquity?[22]

The privileges which underpinned this assumed concern for the general good were ultimately a consequence of the very social inequalities they were supposed to transcend. Because the pose of disinterested concern could never finally escape this connection, it necessarily remained a fiction that disguised the selfishness which shaped official political conduct. The only individuals capable of acting with genuine disinterestedness, this logic also implied, were those reformers who lacked the vested interests which inevitably corrupted their superiors.

In his reconsideration of his own historical account of the universality of the bourgeois public sphere, Habermas has emphasized the culturally differential nature of the ideology of publicity. Recognizing that universality was defined precisely in terms of those social elements which remained outside it, Habermas argues that '[b]oth women and the other groups were denied equal active participation in the formation of political opinion . . . [But] unlike the exclusion of underprivileged men, the exclusion of women had structuring significance'.[23] I have no quarrel with the first half of Habermas's claim, but the arguments of radicals such as Place, and the distinctions informing the various charges of seditious libel (price, length, style) suggest that class differences were fundamental, rather than accidental, to the definition of publicity. Habermas's willingness to recognize the class exclusions which characterized the bourgeois public sphere without attributing a 'structuring significance' to these exclusions suggests how enduring the problems inherent in these constructions of reason as the basis for public virtue remain. To be rational was to be manly, but to be manly was to occupy a social station above that of manual labour.

A MIGHTY LEVER

The aspirations of the newly extended reading public did not go unnoticed amongst those who remained unsympathetic. Conservative critics, including the prosecution in Thomas Hardy's, John Horne Tooke's, and John Thelwall's 1794 treason trials, frequently argued that the reform societies' commitment to the legitimate force of ideas was based on the societies' calculation that the ideas they supported could never be widely enough embraced to have any real effect. Angered, those who had been led to believe that these reforms were possible would become a ready instrument in the societies' undisclosed goal of fomenting revolution. It was a masterly plan which not only masked itself with the legitimating rhetoric of ideas rather than actions, but even used this rhetoric to provoke the uneducated into the most rash course of action conceivable. In a pamphlet entitled *Letters of the Ghost of Alfred addressed to the Hon. Thomas Erskine and the Hon. Charles James Fox on the occasion of the state trials at the close of the year 1794 and the beginning of the year 1795* (1798), John Bowles acknowledged that the LCS had played no part in the supposed attempted assassination of the king in October 1795, but this was not, he added, because of any law-abiding intentions. On the contrary, Bowles argued that 'these Conspirators are fully aware' that in order to achieve *total* revolution,

they want nothing but an uninterrupted access to the public mind. If they could, by an unlimited licence in speech and writing, obtain permission to utter whatever sentiments, to promulgate whatever opinions, and to inculcate whatever principles they please, upon all subjects relating to any respect of Government, they are morally certain of being able, by degrees, to poison the minds, to excite the passions, of the mass of the People, to such a degree, that it would become impossible to restrain the exercise of the *'sacred right of insurrection'*. (105)

Such a situation, Bowles argued, eliminated the distinction between rational debate and violent insurrection which arguments for the public sphere depended on. Because incitements to violence would only lead to premature and therefore limited insurrection, these conspirators insistently declared their attachment to peaceful means of free discussion, believing that this would in itself be enough to achieve complete social upheaval:

they artfully profess to confine all their pretensions to the sacred right of free discussion; and they disclaim, in the most solemn manner, all recourse to other means. This is all they appear to require, and, indeed, all they actually want, in order to enable them to effectuate their designs. They well know ... that discussion, in the unlimited sense in which they claim the right, and in the excess to which they mean to carry it, is a powerful engine for the subversion of Government – a mighty Lever, sufficient, if judiciously applied, to overturn the Social Order of the Whole World. (106–7)

When the lower orders insisted on their right to participate in rational debates about issues of government, they really meant that they wanted to provoke revolution – a deception which disrupted the equation between the inclusive ideal of rational debate and the hope of genuine social progress. Nor, Bowles emphasized, were the leaders of groups such as the LCS even confused about this. They were fully aware that the more they called for peaceful discussion, the greater would be the violence that resulted. He reprinted remarks by Thelwall – whom he referred to as 'the Lecturer, who makes a livelihood by the sale of his Seditious Poison' – about the importance of engaging in 'free discussion' rather than 'open force' as proof of the true extent of this conspiracy (106).

  This charge was echoed more abstractly in denunciations of the forced spread of radical texts as a violation of the normal circulation of literature amongst readers whose interest in these debates ought to manifest itself in their own initiatives to select reading materials. Vicesimus Knox observed in 1793 that 'books adapted to the capacity of the lowest of the people, on political and all other subjects, are *industriously obtruded* on their notice'.

Eusebius warned 'that no less than 400 copies of Paine's *Age of Reason* were ... *stuffed* ... into the pockets of illiterate rusticks'. Hannah More complained, even more dramatically, that reformers 'carried their exertions so far as to load asses with their pernicious pamphlets and to get them dropped, not only in cottages, and in highways, but into mines and coal-pits'. William Hamilton Reid, in his exposé of the LCS, noted in a similar spirit that 'the evil complained of was *obtruded* by a certain society, assisted by the politics of the moment'.[24] As I noted earlier, the counsel for the prosecution made the same point in the trial of *Rights of Man* when he warned that he had decided to prosecute after becoming aware that 'it was either totally or partially thrust into the hands of all persons in this country, of subjects of every description; when I found that even children's sweetmeats were wrapped up with parts of this, and delivered into their hands, in the hope that they would read it'.[25]

This denunciation of the forced circulation of texts was all the more effective because it suggested a deliberate and threatening bastardization of what was, as Jon Klancher explores in his study of Arthur Young's *Travels in France*, the sacred concept of 'circulation' within late eighteenth-century ideas about cultural production.[26] As such it could be denounced as dissemination, the negative opposite to the more healthy ideal of circulation as a series of 'natural' exchanges that coincided on a symbolic level with the inexorable logic of the market: 'To circulate is to follow a path, however circuitous or labyrinthine its windings, along an ordered itinerary; in this motion, a cultural profit accrues ... But to "disseminate" is to flood through the interstices of the social network.'[27] Because dissemination implies a surplus that threatens to negate the inherent value of those productive literary exchanges that enrich the minds of a nation, it can be conceived only as a series of violations that parody the natural state of print culture: a page from *Rights of Man* used as a wrapper for a child's sweetmeats, for example.

The pejorative nature of the insinuation that, without the efforts of the proselytizers of discontent, the lower orders could not possibly be interested in publications addressing political issues, was not lost on Thomas Erskine, nor on Thomas Spence, who quoted Erskine's response in a serialized account of the trial in his journal *Pig's Meat; or, Lessons for the Swinish Multitude*:

The First Part of the Rights of Man, Mr Attorney General tells you, he did not prosecute, although it was in circulation through the country for a year and a half together, because it seems it circulated only amongst what he stiles the judicious part of the public, who possessed in their capacities and experience an antidote to the poison; but with regard to the Second Part now before you, its circulation has been forced into every corner of society; had been printed and reprinted for cheapness even upon whited brown paper, and had crept into the nurseries of children, as a wrapper for their sweetmeats. (1 (1793): 173–4)

For Paine's sympathizers, these sorts of comments were merely another symptom of the patronizing attitude of the polite classes, who thought of the lower orders as children, unable to read in a critical spirit, and therefore at the mercy of whatever literature was forced upon them. The metalogic behind the inclusion of the trial in *Pig's Meat* was that, so forcefully did the implications of the prosecution's arguments bear out Paine's social criticisms, they could themselves become part of the radical literature that was circulating unnaturally, outside the bounds of the polite readership, amongst a class of readers who threatened to untie the assumed connection between literature, knowledge, and social progress.

The radical press simultaneously questioned the exclusionary effects of traditional interpretations of the public sphere and exploited the democratic implications these interpretations none the less contained. Spence's *Pig's Meat*, published in weekly penny numbers, combined biblical passages and readings from significant writers on the importance of the liberty of the press and the political authority of 'the people'.[28] It offered a collection of passages from both the populist chapbook tradition and the great Whig canon, anthologizing a range of authors and sources which included Shakespeare, Goldsmith, Barlow, Cromwell, Harrington, Milton, Hume, Locke, Berkeley, Swift, Tacitus, D'Alembert, Paine, Richard Price, Priestley, Dr Johnson's *Dictionary*, Erskine's trial speeches, the *Analytical*'s review of *Rights of Man*, and segments of the new French Constitution. These passages were combined with satirical pieces and songs written to the tunes of 'Hearts of Oak', 'Derry, down, down', 'Rule Britannia', and 'God Save the King'. All of this had been collected, the magazine announced, 'by the Poor Man's Advocate, in the Course of his Reading for more than Twenty Years' (1 (1793): 1). It was intended 'to promote among

the Labouring Part of Mankind Ideas of their Station, of their
Importance, and of their Rights' and to convince them 'That their
forlorn Condition has not been entirely overlooked and forgotten,
nor their just Cause unpleaded, neither by their Maker, nor by
the best and most enlightened of Men in all Ages' (1). It included
a question-and-answer version of *Rights of Man* and a serialized
account of Erskine's defence speech in the trial for part 2 of *Rights
of Man*, all substantiating what Spence reprinted as the central
point of the defence:

Every man, not intending to mislead and to confound, but seeking to
enlighten others with what his own reason and conscience, however
erroneously, dictate to him as truth, may address himself to the universal
reason of a whole nation, either upon the subject of governments in
general, or upon that of his own particular country. (168)

When Spence printed the jury's verdict, 'GUILTY!!!!!!!' it was clear
that was what being indicted was not Paine but the democratic
myth of the republic of letters (2 (1794): 274). After Erskine successfully defended the *Morning Chronicle* for printing a paid notice
inserted by the Society for Political Information in Derby, Spence
included, under the title 'A LESSON FOR DARING PUBLISHERS', a reproduction of the notice itself, prefaced by a statement that it was
'inserted in this Publication as a Specimen of what the FREEBORN
SONS OF OLD ENGLAND may no longer publish with Safety' (1 (1793):
229–30).

If periodicals aspired to reproduce on a textual level the
impression of coffee-house culture as a universally available public
space, the dialogical richness of radical pamphlets such as *Pig's
Meat* might be said to reproduce the radical tradition of tavern
debating, filled with political argument, wild toasts and songs, and
barbed humour.[29] Nothing was exempt from Spence's satirical eye.
Customs and institutions which posed as sacred were exposed for
hypocrisies underlaid by various forms of self-interest. Under the
heading

> Glorious News for Church and – Rioters!
> The Church is not in danger – it is only to be sold!!

Spence reprinted two advertisements, ostensibly from the *Morning
Chronicle*, advertising the upcoming sale of parishes (1 (1793):
193). As Klancher has noted about the 'riotousness of the radical
text', radical writers quoted, parodied, compiled, and ridiculed in

a carnivalesque mix of warring contexts, levelling political hierarchies through literary strategies that juxtaposed and interfused
apparently distinct levels of social and political concern.[30] In offering so richly dialogical a product, Spence succeeded in politicizing
what Susan Pedersen describes as 'the antiauthoritarian, subversive, "world-turned-upside down" aspect' of chapbook literature,
which tended to remain 'sceptical of natural laws, social order,
and religious duty' without extending this anarchic spirit to any
real form of political commentary.[31] The plurality of voices within
these texts mirrored the demands of radical reformers for a more
inclusive social vision which did not require their reformation
according to others' ideas about improvement as the price of their
admission into the privileged confines of the reading public.

It need hardly be said that Spence did not escape the jealous
eye of government. After he was imprisoned in Newgate without
trial from 17 May to 22 December 1794, he resumed his magazine, this time referring to himself as 'the Poor Man's Advocate
(an old persecuted Veteran in the cause of Freedom) in the
Course of his Reading for more than Twenty years' (3 (1794): 1).
Carrying his intertextual strategies to a new level, Spence
reprinted his own letter, which had been included in the *Morning
Post* on 18 December 1794 (the same day the last of the twelve
treason prisoners were released), highlighting his continued
detention and the desperate effects it was having on his shop. By
intermixing respected sources with satirical pieces, and by including personal letters which advertised his own inscription within
the struggle to redefine the intersection of literature and politics,
Spence simultaneously exploited the most radical possibilities
inherent in the reformist idea of the republic of letters and
exposed the ultimate conservatism of those ideas as they were
conventionally formulated. In doing so, he helped to revolutionize
the idea of audience, flooding 'through the interstices of the social
network' by confusing the high and the low, the polite and the
vulgar, and the serious and the seditious, through both his choice
of selections and his methods of presentation.

Reports of 'arming and drilling in his shop' suggest that
Spence did not limit his revolutionary commitments to literary
style.[32] But despite his belief in the strategic potential of violent
insurrection, Spence was too aware of the discursive power of
the Enlightenment ideal of print culture to remain indifferent

to it. Instead, on trial for his *The Restorer of Society to its Natural State*, he embraced it in millennial terms which highlighted his radical commitments:

I have all my Life thought that the State of Society was capable of much Amendment, and hoped by the Progress of Reason aided by the Art of Printing that such a State of Justice and Felicity would at Length take place in the Earth as in some measure to answer the figurative descriptions of the Millennium, New Jerusalem, or future golden Age. ('Trial' (1803): 35)

In court as in print, Spence remained a *provocateur*. His shift from Enlightenment optimism to millennial prophecy suggested the revolutionary commitments which supplemented his considerable literary efforts without abandoning his declaration of faith in the political importance of print culture. To embrace a utopian ideal of the power of reason was to situate oneself at the unstable intersection of Enlightenment thought and enthusiastic fervour.[33]

Daniel Isaac Eaton, whose magazine *Politics for the People* offered a similar interfusion of 'high' and 'low' literary sources, adopted a satirical voice with the same radical effect as *Pig's Meat* in his pamphlet *The Pernicious Effects of the Art of Printing upon Society, Exposed* (1793). In it, Eaton traced the many blessings of the 'feudal system' in 'the Golden Age' when the social order was maintained by keeping 'the lower orders . . . in the most profound ignorance' (6, 3). Rulers were free to engage in war knowing that they could rely on the unquestioning support of subjects who, content with their station, enjoyed a situation that 'was equal, if not preferable, to that of the slaves in our West-India islands – notwithstanding the friends of the slave-trade have lately represented the condition of the negroes to be so very enviable' (7). Noting that the advantages of this social order were too numerous to be catalogued within the limits of his essay, Eaton concluded his ode to this feudal Golden Age with a lament for the passing of the *ancien régime*:

what will my reader think, when I inform him, that the late government of France was feudal in the extreme; how will he pity and deplore the madness and folly of that deluded nation – no longer blessed with a king, nobles, or priests, but left, like a ship in a storm, without a pilot, to their own guidance – with hands uplifted he will exclaim, 'What will become of them!' (8)

If Eaton's mock reverence for this feudal past caricatured Burke's nostalgia for a lost chivalric order in the *Reflections*, the exaggerated horror with which he then proceeded to catalogue the evils stemming from the rise of print ridiculed the severity of the reaction – shaped chiefly by Burke – against the demands of British reformers. With the advent of printing 'as the medium of diffusing sentiments &c' (8), Eaton argued, the task of governing with unquestioned authority had become virtually impossible:

The lower orders begin to have ideas of rights, as men – to think that one man is as good as another – that society is at present founded upon false principles ... that laws should be the same to all; and that the rich have no right to dictate to the poor what sentiments they shall adopt on any subject – or in any wise prevent investigation and inquiry. This, with a great deal more stuff is called the rights of man – blessed fruits of the art of Printing – the scum of the earth, the swinish multitude, talking of their rights! and insolently claiming, nay almost demanding, that political liberty shall be the same to all ... what audacity! (9)

To make matters worse, he continued, 'infatuated' women had seized on the press, 'that fruitful mother of mischief', to carry out an equally mistaken campaign for the 'Rights of Women' (9). Eaton concluded by applauding 'the late tax upon paper' as an effort to impede this 'diffusion of knowledge and science' (14–15).[34] But, he insisted, this in itself would not be enough. A more prudent plan would be to

Let all Printing-presses be committed to the flames – all letter foundries be destroyed – schools and seminaries abolished – dissenters of every denominations [*sic*] double and treble taxed – all discourse upon government and religion prohibited – political clubs and associations of every kind suppressed, excepting those formed for the express purpose of supporting government; and lastly, issue a proclamation against reading, and burn all private libraries. (15)

Eaton's satiric intensity might seem to us today to reflect a taste for absurd humour manipulated with shrewd comic effect. But it was also an insightful commentary on the intensity of the reaction against the idea of an unrestricted reading public engaged in critical debate about the issues of the day, which was denounced by critics such as Bowles as a certain prelude to revolution.[35] Eaton's point was that condemnations of the irrationality of plebeian claims to reason were themselves characterized by a spirit of irrationality which labelled any extension of the public sphere catastrophic. Loyalist critics may have insisted that reformers' interventions spelled the end to constructive debate, but, Eaton implied, this emotionally driven response had itself done far more to suppress the possibility of rational argument than anything the reformers had managed to accomplish.

Reform societies insisted that there was nothing new about their determination to promote the dissemination of radical literature. Many highly respectable intellectuals and statesmen, including Pitt, had joined an earlier movement for parliamentary reform, 'and with the founding in 1780 of the Society for Constitutional Information (SCI), it virtually began its own publishing industry, churning out great quantities of propaganda which circulated in every corner of the land'.[36] The foreign visitor C. P. Moritz marvelled, in 1782, at 'how the lowliest carter shows an interest in public affairs; how the smallest children enter into the spirit of the nation; how everyone feels himself to be a man and an Englishman – as good as his king and his king's minister'.[37] Reformers such as Pitt and Burke, from whom Erskine repeatedly quoted during his defences, may have changed their tune, but, defenders of the reform societies argued, these associations were doing nothing that had not been welcomed as patriotic in previous decades.

Mary Thale's account of the LCS confirms that, however much parliamentarians such as Pitt, Burke, and Dundas may have denounced the LCS as 'evil minded men who were inflaming the minds of the ignorant, secretly providing them with arms, [and] seditiously plotting to destroy the government',[38] the Society's strategic priorities remained consistent with the earlier reform movement, which had been active at a time when, like the 1790s, 'politics were the general topics of conversation in almost every company'.[39] Insisting on the legitimacy of their educational strategy, Hardy claimed that the 'London Corresponding Society did more in the eight or nine years of its existence, to diffuse political knowledge among the people of Great Britain and Ireland than all that had ever been done before'. Because they recognized that 'the greatest obstacle to obtaining redress' was not a corrupt government, which would inevitably give way to an enlightened reading public, but the *gross ignorance, and prejudice*, in the bulk of the nation', they aimed at 'dispelling that ignorance, and prejudice, as far as possible . . . by means of the printing press'.[40]

They may have thought highly of the French example of political reform, but leading members of the LCS such as Hardy, Place, Thelwall, and Maurice Margarot stressed the importance of pursuing these ends by shaping popular opinion. Their *Congratulatory Address to the National Convention in France* explicitly juxtaposed 'the conjoint reign of ignorance and despotism' with the 'rapid progress' that 'information' was making in its circulation throughout the English populace.[41] The use of LCS meetings to read and discuss political pamphlets was doubled by their massive publication and circulation of political tracts such as Paine's *Rights of Man* and *Age of Reason*, William Frend's *Peace and Union*, and the seventeenth-century treatise on juries, *The Englishman's Right*. The Society also published a series of their own pamphlets as well as two periodicals, *The Politician* and *The Moral and Political Magazine of the London Corresponding Society*.[42] The reform movement may not have achieved any immediate victories, Hardy allowed during a speech given at the 1830 Anniversary Dinner marking his acquittal, but by encouraging 'people to think, to read, to reason, who had not before given politics a thought', it had initiated a process which had been 'rapidly increasing' in the following decades.[43]

In his defence of Hardy in 1794, Erskine insisted that for the LCS, as for earlier reform organizations, it was never a question of using force but rather 'a design to undermine monarchy by changes wrought through public opinion, enlarging gradually into universal will'.[44] He maintained that even according to the evidence presented by the prosecution, both the LCS and the SCI were overwhelmingly committed to solid Enlightenment beliefs about the reformist power of ideas developed through the medium of print culture. In a letter stating their reasons for forming into a club, the LCS emphasized its determination 'to render assistance to their fellow-citizens in this neighbourhood, and in parts more remote . . . until the whole nation be sufficiently enlightened and united in the same cause, which cannot fail of being the case, wherever the most excellent works of Mr Thomas Paine find residence'. A letter from the Revolution and Constitutional Societies at Norwich similarly stated 'that Mr Paine's books were to be the medium, through which the prejudices that had grown up under the British government were to be got rid of'. This sentiment was repeated in a letter, also included in the prosecution's evidence, from the Sheffield Society of the Friends of the People to the LCS:

I am directed by this Society to inform you, that it is with infinite satis-
faction they receive the information, that your firm and laudable endeavours are directed to that effectual and necessary purpose, of opening
and enlightening the public mind, and disseminating useful knowledge
amongst the general mass of the people.[45]

Any reasonable interpretation of passages such as these, Erskine
argued, proved that the societies were in fact committed to an
approach that perfectly reflected the most conventional Enlightenment beliefs about the force of ideas diffused through a reading
community. Although Godwin would condemn the LCS for not
properly appreciating the difference between ideas and actions,
Erskine maintained that their writings indicated a perfect coinci-
dence with Godwin's opinions about the power of enlightened
public opinion. In the 1830 Anniversary Dinner speech, Hardy
reflected on the prosecution's display of a group of weapons that
were supposedly proof of his violent agenda in terms which
reinforced Erskine's earlier emphasis on the Society's fidelity to
responsible Enlightenment priorities:

The London Corresponding Society, as a Society, never did give any countenance to the use of such instruments. Their instruments were of another
and more rational kind; truth, and reason, with the copious use of the
press, were the instruments with which the Society commenced, and
which it continued to exercise, with great success.[46]

That the prosecution (and Godwin) could misinterpret this point,
which manifested itself so clearly throughout its own evidence,
only indicated the extent to which entrenched assumptions about
the freedom of the press reproduced the class biases to which this
freedom was ostensibly opposed.

The Society's emphasis on 'Members Unlimited', a topic which
forms the focus of the opening pages of Thompson's *The Making of
the English Working Class*, testifies to an awareness within plebeian
society of the issue of publicity as historians of the bourgeois
public sphere such as Baker, Eley, Fraser, and Habermas have
since described it. Perfectly anticipating the language of these
critical debates, Hardy insisted that the primary object of 'the
Society ... was publicity, the more public [they became] the better'. Even the name, the London Corresponding Society, which
suggested their intention of 'corresponding with other Societies
that might be formed, having the same object in view', evoked

the communicative ideal which informed phrases such as 'men of letters' and 'the republic of letters'.[47] Employing the same metaphor that Godwin and Mathias had used to define literature, Hardy recalled that 'that powerful engine, the printing press', had constituted one of the most significant sites of political struggle between 'the friends of liberty, and the supporters of arbitrary power'.[48]

Thompson has argued that the revolutionary element of the English Jacobin tradition was always balanced by an alternative stress on the importance 'of self-education and of the rational criticism of political and religious institutions'. John Dinwiddy similarly suggests that the LCS's quest for a 'Revolution in the Minds of [the] Nation' focused on the cultivation of literature as a fund of public knowledge.[49] This is not to discount the pressure that existed within the reform societies for more extreme forms of intervention. But as Thompson and Dinwiddy argue, it is important that our recollection of denunciations of the LCS as an unruly proto-revolutionary body not overshadow its own insistence on the power of print culture.

In a published version of a speech given at a mass meeting organized by the LCS on 12 November 1795, John Thelwall echoed Erskine's defence of the Society, 'whose professed and real object', he insisted, was 'to preserve tranquillity by disseminating information; and to promote the Cause of Liberty by a firm and temperate exposition of the invasions of tyrannical corruption, and the consequent miseries of an oppressed and overburdened people'.[50] Far from seeking to overturn the government, he argued, the reform societies were the surest defence of it, since 'the vital energies of the British Constitution consist in the liberties of *Speech, and of the Press*'. He had made the same point at a previous meeting seventeen days earlier. Distinguishing his own efforts from the negative example of the French Revolution's excesses, Thelwall insisted that 'the way to attain liberty . . . is not by being mad and desperate; but by calmly exerting your intellect in acquiring a just knowledge of the nature and causes of your oppressions'.[51] 'Let us cultivate reason', he urged the crowd, 'and if violence comes, let it come from our oppressors; and that, in so barefaced and unprovoked a way, that all men shall be compelled to cry out against them'.[52] The cautionary note might well have had an implied threat, but the threat of violence was to originate with the state, rather than with a popular movement disgruntled by the failure of their efforts to achieve their goals through rational debate.[53]

These populist exertions constituted an important English liberty, but they were also being exercised in the hope of achieving further liberties which could only be realized by removing existing oppressions. There could be no solution to oppression which was not also a triumph of justice. And justice, Thelwall emphasized, using the biblical metaphor of the axe laid to the root that Paine had popularized in *Rights of Man*, was secured by the free discussion of principles of right and wrong rather than by rash behaviour:

Be assured then, it is by the discussion of principle alone, by laying the axe of reason to the root of the tree of corruption, that the blasting foliage of luxury, and the poisonous fruit of oppression can be destroyed.

The current situation was in many ways getting worse, he admitted, but this increased the importance of recognizing that 'the only way to amend it is by exerting our faculties in discussing the principles of right and wrong: for when men come to free discussion, when justice and injustice, truth and falsehood are painted in proper colours, all men will love that which is right, and hate that which is wrong'.[54] It was a classic version of the reformist dream of the public sphere as an engine of non-violent social change. Set within the context of a mass movement, however, it was condemned as a strategy aimed at inciting violence.

Whereas conservative critics (and Godwin) opposed mass meetings and political societies because they diminished the rational capacity of the individual, Thelwall celebrated the LCS's meetings, not as a threatening show of strength but as evidence of 'the omnipotent voice of public reason'.[55] Godwin's may well have been a vision of a public composed of very private individuals communicating through print, but it none the less anticipated a growing concert of opinion as truth asserted itself. Mass meetings, Thelwall implied, were simply proof of this stage of the convergence of the ideas of separate individuals. The Gordon Riots had confirmed the mischief which could result if the leaders of such meetings abused their authority, just as the power of literature could itself be abused if authors wrote from mischievous purposes, but this did not imply that meetings could not also be evidence of an enlightened public will. 'Keep clear then, citizens', he urged the crowd, 'of all tumultuary proceedings and violent resolutions; keep clear also of personal factions, groundless suspicions, rancour, animosity, and furious denunciation. Fix your attention on principles, not on men'.[56]

Thompson is right to note Thelwall's moral courage and theoretical acumen, but his sense of Thelwall's rejection of 'educational gradualism' – a policy Thompson identifies with Francis Place – in favour of 'an unlimited agitation', must be balanced against Thelwall's own emphasis on the necessity of an unlimited exchange of ideas if radical politics were to be pursued in the name of genuine liberty.[57] Thelwall's remarks need to be read as heavily coded political rhetoric designed to elicit particular responses on specific occasions. But even so, his commitment to 'principles' reflects a sophisticated sense of just how much was at stake in the attempt to appropriate Enlightenment concepts, embraced by middle-class reformers such as William Godwin, on behalf of social classes who, Godwin warned, were not presumed to be able to appreciate the difference between ideas and actions.

If Thompson underestimates Thelwall's commitment to an Enlightenment vision of reform, he is probably closer to the mark in his identification of Francis Place with that side of the radical reform movement which stressed educational approaches ahead of more activist forms of intervention. Writing his autobiography in 1824, Place chose to concentrate on the capacity of the LCS to achieve personal rather than political reform by stressing the seemingly apolitical lesson of the importance of self-improvement and the moral integrity of the individual:

The moral effects of the Society were considerable. It induced men to read books, instead of wasting their time in public houses, it taught them to respect themselves, and to desire to educate their children. It elevated them in their own opinions, It taught them the great moral lesson 'to bear and forbear'. The discussions in the divisions, in the Sunday evening readings, and in the small debating meetings, opened to them views which they had never before taken. They were compelled by these discussions to find reasons for their opinions, and to tolerate others.[58]

Political reform, Place implied, could only be realized as the indirect consequence of a previous transformation of those who believed in this goal – a reformation which would be characterized by this spirit of tolerance. Hardy mobilized a similar vocabulary of personal virtue when he insisted that the Society's constructive influence on its members could be seen 'in the continued respectability of their lives, in the morality of their conduct ... and in the elevated and opulent situations to which some have since attained in society'.[59] According to Place, the Society's meetings, in which there were 'readings, conversations, and discussions', had more the atmosphere of a graduate seminar than a centre for conspiracy:

> The usual mode of proceeding at these weekly meetings was this. The chairman, (each man was a chairman in rotation,) read from some book a chapter or part of a chapter, which as many as could read the chapter at their homes the book passing from one to the other had done and at the next meeting a portion of the chapter was again read and the persons present were invited to make remarks thereon. as many as chose did so, but without rising. Then another portion was read and a second invitation was given – then the remainder was read and a third invitation was given when they who had not before spoken were expected to say something. Then there was a general discussion. No one was permitted to speak more than once during the reading The same rule was observed in the general discussion, no one could speak a second time until every one who chose had spoken once, then any one might speak again, and so on till the subject was exhausted – these were very important meetings, and the best results to the parties followed.[60]

If the goal of parliamentary reform seems to have disappeared from these accounts, it is because the members of the LCS recognized (according to these versions of it, at least) that literature was the greatest engine of social transformation, and furthermore, they understood the limitations upon which this idea was premised. Instead of plotting insurrections, they concentrated on educating members in ways that would enable them to join that greatest of political forces, the reading public. It was a strategy designed to extend a claim to literature downwards to those people who were thought to be disqualified from it by their inability to participate in any disinterested way.

Not everyone believed this version of the story. The acquittals of Hardy, Horne Tooke, and Thelwall, and the cancellation of the remainder of the treason trials, did little to dampen the hostility felt by many towards the 'Jacobin threat' posed by the reform societies. The government's *Reports of the Committee of Secrecy* (1794 and 1799) stressed the commitment of particular individuals within the LCS to armed revolution, possibly assisted by a French invasion. This, in turn, seemed to be confirmed by news of the members' habit of referring to each other as 'Citizen'. William Hamilton Reid's *The Rise and Dissolution of the Infidel Societies in this Metropolis,* published in 1800, confirmed the fears of many critics that the leaders of the radical reform movement were interested in far more than constructive debate about general ideas. Referring to the works of 'Professor Robison and Abbé Barruel' (iii), Reid argued that the reformists were guilty of plotting a similar overthrow of the government by imposing 'uncontrolled experiments upon the lower orders of society in this country, among whom credulity is ever the strongest' (26). For critics of these societies, their Enlightenment pretences were either a sign of confusion or a deliberate conspiracy, or what was more likely, some combination of the two. However insistent Thelwall and Place may have been in their Enlightenment rhetoric, the image of a child's sweetmeat wrapped in a torn-out page of *Rights of Man* was, for many, a vivid expression of the dangers of mass societies committed to achieving political reform by preying on the minds of the innocent. Equally threatening in its own way, however, was the opposite possibility, that the radicals might genuinely have meant what they said about embracing these educational principles as a form of empowerment.

Fears for the security of the state had become inextricably enmeshed with a nervousness about the threat posed to authorial distinction by the prospect that working-class activists really *did* aspire to an equal share in the blessings of the Enlightenment, in what many conservatives fearfully regarded as a 'scribbling age, when every man who can write composes a pamphlet, and every journeyman bookseller erects himself into a publisher' (*GM* 62 (1792): 934). To the extent that plebeian aspirations clashed with these sorts of anxieties about the democratization of print culture, it was precisely *because* the rhetoric of radical reformers concentrated on storming the invisible walls of the republic of letters rather than the Houses of Parliament that it became quite so necessary to emphasize the irrationality of plebeian claims to the Enlightenment ideal of the transformative power of literature. Either way, with the advent of a reform movement on a mass scale, the prospect of open debate within print culture was being increasingly demonized as an inevitable prelude, rather than a healthy alternative, to violent insurrection.

CHAPTER FOUR

Masculine women

The circumstances of the times, aided by the natural curiosity of the human mind, will ensure an extensive circulation to these books. Yet we cannot help regretting, that these facts should be recorded by a female, who has been so deluded by a visionary phantom, as to forsake her friends and her country in pursuit of what she might have enjoyed at home without peril and with greater honour.

Review of Helen Maria Williams's *Letters Containing a Sketch of the Politics of France*, in the *British Critic*, November 1795

REVERENCING THE RIGHTS OF HUMANITY

I want to begin by reading two quotations against each other, the first from Mary Wollstonecraft's *A Vindication of the Rights of Woman* (1792), and the second a passage from a theatrical review in Leigh Hunt's *Reflector*, exactly two decades later. Together they reveal both the ambiguities and the anxieties generated by women's aspirations to participate in those fields of literary production that were traditionally reserved for men. In a footnote to *A Vindication of the Rights of Woman*, Wollstonecraft writes,

I have conversed, as man with man, with medical men on anatomical subjects; and compared the proportions of the human body with artists – yet such modesty did I meet with, that I was never reminded by word or look of my sex, of the absurd rules which make modesty a pharisaical cloak of weakness. And I am persuaded that in the pursuit of knowledge women would never be insulted by sensible men, and rarely by men of any description, if they did not by mock modesty remind them that they were women . . . Men are not always men in the company of women, nor would women always remember that they are women, if they were allowed to acquire more understanding.[1]

Whatever they might be when they are alone, in the company of women, men are not always men. In the pursuit of knowledge,

171

when they are not restricted by false modesty, men will forget
these distinctions and will respect women's right to interact 'as
man with man'. Nor, in Wollstonecraft's experience, do these
scenes of amnesia occur in those disciplines which are least
defined in terms of gender difference. Quite the opposite, they
occur during discussions about the medical and artistic study of
the human body: a site of knowledge that most commentators felt
was inappropriate for women, and which, at the very least, was
assumed to substantiate the differences between men and women.
Wollstonecraft, according to conventional ideas about female modesty, ought to be reminded that she is a woman by what she is
looking at, and by the fact that, as a woman, she ought not to be
looking at all. Her alternative position reflects her anti-
foundational sense of gender identity, but it also testifies to tensions created by her lack of access to an ungendered vocabulary
in a way that, as Carole Pateman notes, anticipates 'the final
words of Simone de Beauvoir's *The Second Sex*, where she states
that "men and women [must] unequivocally affirm their
brotherhood" '.[2]

In contrast with Wollstonecraft's position, which threatens not
only the opposition between man and woman but the connection
between the biological and the social, Leigh Hunt's thoughts on
Lady Macbeth reveal both a horror and a fascination with the
spectre of a manly woman:

We can read, with some patience, mixed with pity, of men who have
waded through bloodshed and perfidy to a throne, – of the ambition of
Richard, of Cromwell, and of Napoleon; but we are prejudiced, in the
first instance, against a woman of a masculine spirit; and this prejudice
is strengthened into disgust and detestation, when we see that spirit not
only daring to 'do all that may become a *man*', but even daring to 'do
more;' – when we see it struggling not only with female delicacy, but with
virtue and humanity, and burning to grasp at the worthless grandeur of
royalty, though at the expence of treachery, cruelty, and murder. Such,
however, is *Lady Macbeth;* and, being such, she no sooner sees the distant
vision of greatness opening upon her sight, than she prepares with determined alacrity to encounter the obstacles which her penetrating mind
foresaw would be opposed to her ambition: she invokes the 'spirits that
tend on mortal thought' to unsex her.[3]

In going beyond what a man ought to do, men are simply being
men, and their excesses can be encountered with patience and
with pity. Women, however, when they display a masculine spirit,

rebel against not only the social but the natural order as well. Recognizing in that order obstacles to her desires, the masculine woman will, like Lady Macbeth, invoke spirits to unsex her. She will need to forget that she is a woman, and if she can forget this well enough, she will not only commit those acts of violence which no woman would commit, but which no man ought to commit either. Confronted by women who go beyond the due limits of their sex – who, in effect, become unsexed – the viewer will feel threatened and will react with immediate prejudice; in going beyond themselves men are only acting like men, but if women go beyond themselves, then they cease to be women, and if women are no longer women, then men, who ought to be the opposite of women, begin to become unsexed themselves.

In chapter 3 I explored ways in which working-class activists responded to the contradictory assumption that reason – the ability to think objectively about things in a way that transcends the particular interests of any single class – was solely the property of the polite classes. I now want to turn to the ways that women writers engaged with similar reactions, which were also aroused by their claims to an equal capacity for rational (or 'masculine') thought. This line of inquiry intersects with a rapidly growing body of criticism that focuses on the ways that women writers exploited existing literary opportunities in order to promote the condition of women. By converting the romantic novel from a scene of seduction into a site of instruction,[4] or writing the gothic preoccupation with psychic and social entrapment as a meditation on subjectivity and domestic space,[5] novelists adapted the literary genre most associated with women readers as a means of addressing women's issues. Elsewhere, women writers exploited literary opportunities such as the more open genres of travel-writing,[6] the epistolary style,[7] the sympathetic and therefore 'feminine' aspects of educational writing[8] and the slave-trade debate,[9] and the banner of Christian evangelicalism,[10] as discursive strategies capable of undoing the double-bind between feminine softness and masculine purposefulness in the name of a non-threatening female activism.[11]

The broadly shared focus of these studies is the diverse ways that women writers implicitly revised, rather than directly challenged, established cultural assumptions by encoding subversive arguments about sexual politics within accepted literary genres and styles. My primary concern here is the other way around: the ways that women's participation in political debates impacted on ideas about literature. Ultimately, these different critical strategies merge in a shared sense of the profound interconnection of sexual politics mediated by literature and literary politics defined in gendered terms. Because of my particular path to this end, I am interested in women authors who explicitly confronted those asymmetries of power which inhered in the literary conventions of their day. Like working-class writers, their efforts were all the more disruptive because they were assimilationist rather than oppositional: their assertion of their legitimate access to masculine fields of intellectual inquiry threatened to undermine the gendered logic which made these boundaries (and, therefore, the codes of literary distinction that were rooted in them) possible. By insisting on the democratic logic of the Enlightenment's faith in the autonomy of the rational individual, they exposed the ethos of universality underpinning this faith as an ideology reflecting particular, rather than general, interests. In doing so they contributed to a wider crisis in literature that manifested itself in the backlash that was waged against both working-class and feminist radicals in the name of a besieged ideal of cultural propriety.

Because the attempt to resituate the dominant political debates of the period along the axis of gender was not inherently radical, I will offer an analysis of the differences between radical and conservative feminists, as well as outlining the ways in which this debate intersected with other cultural-political struggles.[12] Women writers from a variety of perspectives insisted on the importance of better education for women in order to improve their social opportunities, but as Alan Richardson notes, this shared concern was interpreted in widely different ways. For radical authors such as Catherine Macaulay, Mary Wollstonecraft, and Mary Hays, this amounted to a demand for women's right to an equal education – an interpretation that was rejected by their more conservative peers who retained a belief in distinct sexual identities and, therefore, in different educational and literary opportunities.

In 'Reform or Ruin: "A Revolution in Female Manners" ', Mitzi Myers emphasizes Wollstonecraft's and Hannah More's considerable degree of commonality, particularly in their refusal of women's frequently prescribed ornamental role, and in their focus on 'a pattern of female domestic heroism'.[13] This is true, Myers contends, not only because Wollstonecraft's arguments were in many ways more conservative, but also because More's message was more radical, than the 'clichés of bifurcation' which characterize much of the criticism would suggest (202). As important as Myers's argument is as a corrective to this too-easy polarization, though, it runs the risk of collapsing the positions of these often radically opposed thinkers together by reducing the conservatism of More's texts to so much camouflage – 'paid lip service' to dominant assumptions – beneath which there lurks the more radical message that is 'alive with submerged power' (209). Not for nothing did Richard Polwhele refer to More, who refused to read the *Vindication of the Rights of Woman*, as 'a character, in all points, diametrically opposite to Miss Wollstonecraft'.[14]

Rather than either opting for a bifurcated approach or insisting on their convergence, Richardson offers a triangulated model which distinguishes between the 'outspoken radicalism' of writers such as Catherine Macaulay, Wollstonecraft, and Mary Hays, 'the liberal compromises' of Maria Edgeworth and Anna Barbauld, 'and the deep-seated conservatism' of More and Sarah Trimmer. Nor is this sort of critical clarity a mere luxury of hindsight. As Richardson points out, many of these women were acutely aware of their ideological divergences. Barbauld rejected Edgeworth's proposal to co-edit 'a 'periodical paper' featuring the work of 'all the literary ladies of the present day' on the grounds of political differences: 'There is no bond of union among literary women, any more than among literary men ... Mrs Hannah More would not write along with you or me, and we should probably hesitate at joining Miss Hays, or if she were living, Mrs Godwin.'[15]

For radical feminists such as Macaulay, Wollstonecraft, Hays, and Mary Robinson (who published under the pseudonym Anne Frances Randall), the question of their access to masculine literary genres was important both as an end in itself, and as a potent means of redressing the wider asymmetries of power which sustained these inequalities. The provisional tolerance of many critics for women's writing, as long as it was consistent with the tender virtues of the amiable sex, denied women their full share of those political advantages which were to be gained from an appeal to a rights-based theory of social relations. Hays argued that critics who refused to recognize women as rational, and therefore morally independent, individuals reinforced this exclusion by insisting that women 'have nothing to expect when [their aspirations are] claimed as rights, to which claims [critics] constantly give the name of masculine, and unsufferable from women; but that they have every thing to hope for when entreated as favours'.[16]

These debates necessarily went far beyond issues related to literature but, even when not specifically focused on literary concerns, they were often mediated by questions about the relations between power and knowledge that were rooted in contemporary discussions about the role of print culture. This was true both because perceptions of the differences between various forms of literature corresponded to perceived differences of gender, and because activists such as Wollstonecraft blamed much of the subjugation of women on the pernicious effects of ideas reinforced by a male literary canon. If knowledge set people free, then the reverse was also true: the idea that femininity was incompatible with serious study perpetuated the subordination of women as unequal partners in the widely celebrated diffusion of knowledge. Because literature was both an engine of reform and a symbol of the progress which the reforming spirit had already achieved, the issue of women's access to the various fields of print culture raised much larger questions about whether women, like the lower orders, were to have an Enlightenment, and whether, by acting as agents rather than beneficiaries of that process, they would be allowed to define the nature of their 'improvement' for themselves.

By reading these disputes about the cultural location of women within the republic of letters in terms of the wider field of positive and negative pressures that haunted the ideal of literature as a public sphere, I want to complicate our understanding of the backlash against women such as Macaulay, Wollstonecraft, and Hays. Although broadly correct in their historical judgement, critics who equate the erasure of women from literary prominence with 'the remasculinization of literature' miss the point of many of the discursive complexities that characterized these debates.[17] Mary P. Ryan is right to argue that the 'converse gender logic' which equated women with feelings rather than with reason 'made "manliness" the standard of republican character and "effeminacy" the most debilitating political malady'.[18] But it is also true that, far from denying this value structure, radical feminist authors staged their claims for full literary status in terms of an appeal to reason as the basis of their contention that women were equally capable, and with absolute propriety, of 'masculine' behaviour.

The resistance to these demands had less to do with the 'remasculinization of literature' than with growing fears about the *de*masculinization of literature, or in other words, about the effeminacy of a cultural force whose manly firmness of purpose was plagued by spiralling levels of over-production and its increasingly fashionable status, on the one hand, and by critics' malevolence and the intrusions of party spirit, on the other. Rather than simply fostering a renewed insistence on the masculinity of *literature* (something which male and female critics agreed ought to be the case), these anxieties generated an increasingly rigid insistence on the unique masculinity of *men* and, therefore, on the distinctly feminine character of women.

For their detractors, women's claims to masculine virtue were not evidence of a capacity for sober reflection but a kind of 'Gallic frenzy';[19] they were characterized not by a steadiness of purpose that was the opposite of the dissipating effects of fashion, but by a love of masculine virtue *as* fashion, a misguided and unnatural enthusiasm which compounded excess with excess. The more loudly these women announced their equal capacity for rational enquiry, the greater they revealed their own irrationality. In the eyes of their detractors, women writers such as 'Wollstonecraft and Hays became both effeminately sentimental *and* indecorously masculine'.[20] Nor can these divisions be mapped onto other political divisions in any straightforward way. Joan Landes argues that '[c]onservatives and revolutionaries alike recoiled from the unnatural spectre of political women'.[21]

Central to all of this was the entanglement between three very different oppositions: biological difference (sex), culturally determined sexual difference (gender), and those characteristics denominated as masculine and feminine, which reflected but were not wholly tied to gender. Judith Butler has pointed out that the opposition between sex and gender is itself an anomalous one which rests upon the erroneous premise of some pre-ideological access to scientific understanding. None the less, on a discursive level the distinction was an important one. In many ways, the most significant debates about gender in the period were less about the deconstruction of the opposition between masculinity and femininity than about severing its connection with biological difference. Men were born men and women were born women, but, radical feminists argued, this did not necessarily preclude women from developing a masculine character. Nor was this necessarily a denial of women's identity because, within the anti-foundationalist approach of authors such as Wollstonecraft, it did not necessarily follow that biological differences between men and women ought to correspond to differences between 'masculine' and 'feminine' as personal characteristics. It was instead a matter of reimagining the points of connection between these oppositions. For their conservative counterparts, however, these various levels of physical and cultural difference were properly recognized as being strictly interconnected. Masculine virtue, far from describing a capacity for rational thought in any socially neutral way, highlighted a form of excellence that was the unique proclivity of men.

Rather than simply rejecting the gendered logic of these discriminations in favour of a more inclusive definition of the relation between literature and rational inquiry, many radical feminist authors sought to understand the problem in historical terms. 'It must be confessed', Macaulay allowed, 'that the virtues of the males among the species, though mixed and blended with a variety of vices and errors, have displayed a bolder and more consistent picture of excellence than female nature has hitherto done'. As a consequence of this, she concluded that 'when we compliment the appearance of a more than ordinary energy in the female mind, we call it masculine'.[22] Because men had manifested this 'excellence' more frequently than women, she continued, the term used to describe it had become sexually determined, and this remained the case even when it was used to describe women who displayed the same virtues. But this did not imply that women, when they were properly educated and placed in the appropriate social situations, were any less likely to demonstrate these characteristics than men. Nor did it imply that any new model of human behaviour was necessarily androcentric. Far from accepting Pope's dictum that '*a perfect woman's but a softer man*', Macaulay insisted that '*a perfect man is a woman formed after a coarser mould*' (ibid.). To make a problem historically intelligible was to begin to understand how it might be redressed.

Not all women were prepared to play so fast and loose with the issue of gender. Hannah More's *Essays on Various Subjects, Principally*

Designed for Young Ladies, originally published in 1777, went into its fifth edition in 1791, and for many readers the increasing cultural and political instabilities renewed the appeal of its message that 'the mind in each sex has some natural kind of bias, which constitutes a distinction of character, and that the happiness of both depends, in a great measure, on the preservation and observation of this distinction' (13). More was far from denying a social role to women, an exclusion which was, she explained, characteristic of 'Mahomet's Law' rather than of enlightened British culture, where, because 'there is as little despotism exercised over the minds, as over the persons of women, they have every liberty of choice, and every opportunity of improvement' (21). Women were free to choose, but this liberty of choice was best exercised in accordance with women's natural disposition:

She hopes they will not be offended if she has occasionally pointed out certain qualities, and suggested certain tempers, and dispositions, as *peculiarly feminine*; as well as hazarded some observations which naturally arose from the subject, on the different characters which mark the sexes. And here again she takes the liberty to repeat that these distinctions cannot be too nicely maintained. (2–3)

Women, like delicate 'porcelain' (3), were best kept in places 'of the greatest security' (4). Men, '[l]ike the stronger and more substantial wares', weathered life's strains better, and were 'formed for the more public exhibitions on the greater theatre of human life' (5). Given these overwhelming differences, More argued, surely it made better sense for women 'to succeed as women, than to fail as men' (14).[23]

Rather than suggesting that literature ought to be the prerogative of men, More argued that different types of literature were best adapted to each sex. In general, men thrived in areas such as science, and women in those genres which required 'lively imaginations, and those exquisite perceptions of the beautiful and defective, which come under the denomination of Taste' (6). Because the cultural geography of the republic of letters was various enough to suit both sexes, it was possible for women to fulfil themselves without trespassing into those more rugged regions best left to men:

pretensions to that strength of intellect, which is requisite to penetrate into the abstruser walks of literature, it is presumed they will readily relinquish. There are green pastures and pleasant vallies, where they may wander with safety to themselves, and delight to others. They may cultivate the flowers of imagination, and the valuable fruits of morals and criticism; but the steeps of Parnassus few, comparatively, have attempted to scale with success ... The lofty Epic, the pointed Satire, and the more daring and successful flights of the Tragic Muse, seem reserved for the bold adventurers of the other sex. (6–7)

The laws of genre and gender remained firmly bound together. What mattered most was to develop oneself in accordance with them. Echoing Burke, More suggested that the creative potential of men and women could be distinguished in terms of the difference between 'the sublime, the nervous, and the masculine', and 'the beautiful, the soft, and the delicate' (8). Women's particular strength lay in 'the boundless and aërial regions of romance', where 'Invention labours more, and judgement less' (11), and in '[t]hat species of knowledge, which appears to be the result of reflection rather than of science', and which is 'learned without the rules' (56–7).

For those women lacking literary inspiration, More insisted on the importance of reading as an antidote to a 'strong passion for promiscuous visiting, or dissipated society', or 'for gaming, dress, and public amusements' (23). By so applying themselves, women's minds were placed in 'a progressive state of improvement' that reconciled the blessings of the Enlightenment with an enthusiasm for domestic life (22). But this was only true as long as they pursued their education 'in the moderate degree in which ladies are supposed to use it' (24). They were better off for being well read, but only to the extent that their studies were 'intended to *adorn* their *leisure*, not to *employ* their *lives*' (133). Study was necessary to make women more agreeable companions rather than to give them professional aspirations.

Women, in other words, were very definitely to have an Enlightenment, but it was not to be the one men enjoyed. They were to be reformed by the progressive effects of print culture, but not in order that they might participate in those areas of literature for which nature had never intended them. Nor, More argued, should they confuse improvements which were a consequence of reading with an inappropriate demand for political rights based on a mistaken and unnatural sense of authority. The more reading developed women's understanding, the more they ought to be able to

appreciate the difference between masculine virtue, which manifested itself in 'the greater theatre of human life', and feminine
virtue, which displayed itself most perfectly in the sorts of sympathetic acts of personal encouragement or assistance that had
nothing to do with 'public exhibitions' (5). The distinction
between masculine and feminine virtue was as rigid as their connection to sexual difference was absolute.

Ironically, the *Monthly Review* blurred these distinctions when it
praised More's 'masculine mind', which, in defence 'of all that is
near, dear, and sacred . . . has towered, in dignified pre-eminence,
above her sex' (40 (1803): 107). Despite the phallic representation, the *Monthly's* tribute was not inspired by any suspicion of
More's desire to encroach upon those forms of writing and behaviour that were better left to men. Quite the opposite, More's mind
was masculine because of the sober reflection that characterized
her recognition of the inherent nature of femininity and her sense
of the importance of schooling the lower orders in ways which
ensured that they would remember that they *were* lower orders.
To the extent that she encouraged others to recognize the sorts
of distinctions which preserved the stature that ought to be
accorded to gentlemen – above the lower orders, fit for more challenging pursuits than women – More could be praised in a way
that erased the sexual specificity of the adjective 'masculine'.
Unlike some of her more notorious peers though, More was most
masculine at those times when she remembered what it meant to
be a woman.

The backhanded compliment paid by a correspondent of the
Gentleman's Magazine to Catherine Macaulay, which she reprinted
in the opening pages of her *Letters on Education*, was consistent with
the sort of opinions about the connection between literature and
sexual difference that More strongly advocated, and which Macaulay's efforts were dedicated to transforming: 'I have at last seen
Mrs Macaulay Graham's metaphysical performance. Her work is
really wonderful considering her sex; and in this I pay no ill compliment I hope to the ladies; for surely they themselves will generally acknowledge that their talents are not adapted to abstract
speculations' (vii). Inserted in her treatise, the letter both advertised Macaulay's achievements and emphasized the prejudices
which her educational commitments were determined to overturn.
Women *did* have a more difficult time excelling in these literary

fields, her use of the letter implied, but this was because of the resistance to the idea of women's intellectual equality rather than because of any natural inferiority.

Macaulay insisted, in direct contradiction with More, that 'there can be but one rule of moral excellence for beings made of the same materials, organized after the same manner, and subjected to similar laws of Nature' (204). Macaulay's educational energies were focused on developing 'a careless, modest beauty, grave, manly, noble, full of strength and majesty; and carrying about her an aegis sufficiently powerful to defend her against the sharpest arrow that ever was shot from Cupid's bow' (221). As far as Leigh Hunt's characterization of Lady Macbeth was concerned, the adjective 'modest' would sit uncomfortably alongside these other qualities: grave, manly, strong, majestic, and invulnerable to cupid's artillery. For Macaulay, though, this apparently unlikely combination was *precisely* the point. Those qualities conventionally described as 'manly' were sexually referential because men had in previous ages displayed them more frequently than women, but the terms could be equally extended to women who demonstrated similar traits.

For Wollstonecraft, Macaulay was in many ways the perfect embodiment of these masculine aspirations, not only because her educational commitment challenged existing prejudices, but because Macaulay had excelled in those fields of literature which many felt were best left to men. 'The very word respect', Wollstonecraft eulogized, 'brings Mrs Macaulay to my remembrance . . . In her style of writing, indeed, no sex appears, for it is like the sense it conveys, strong and clear'.[24] So forceful was Macaulay's denial of the supposition that nature had distinct laws for men and women that her work was itself proof that a word such as 'manly' was no longer the cultural property of one sex alone.

Nor were sympathetic critics unwilling to attribute a similar triumph to Wollstonecraft's writings. In its review of *Rights of Woman*, the *Monthly Review* agreed that 'how jealous soever WE may be of our *right* to the proud pre-eminence which we have assumed, the women of the present age are daily giving us indisputable proofs that the mind is of no sex' (8 (1792): 198). Although the *Monthly* distanced itself from 'Miss W.'s plan for a REVOLUTION in the female education and manners', they suggested that the increasingly important role played by women such as Wollstonecraft ought to merit a corresponding linguistic innovation so that, 'beside the sexual appellations of man and woman, we had some general term to denote the species, like $A\nu\theta\rho\omega\pi o\varsigma$ and *Homo* in the Greek and Roman languages. The want of such a general term is a material defect in our language' (209). If adjectives such as 'manly' had been linked to one of the sexes because of historical patterns of behaviour, then changes in these patterns ought to manifest themselves in a new vocabulary which would abolish rather than perpetuate assumptions about sexual distinction.

Much as she might have agreed with the *Monthly*'s dream of a gender-free language, Wollstonecraft's characteristic strategy was to engage with socio-linguistic contradictions by assuming the laurels of 'manly' virtue on behalf of her sex. Citing the Enlightenment connection between evil and ignorance, she argued in *A Vindication of the Rights of Men* (1790) that 'to labour to increase human happiness by extirpating error, is a masculine godlike affection'.[25] In the same work she chastised Burke for his commitment to emotional rather than rational argument in *Reflections on the Revolution in France* (1790): 'it would be something like cowardice to fight with a man who had not exercised the weapons with which his opponent chose to combat, and irksome to refute sentence after sentence in which the latent spirit of tyranny appeared'.[26] It was almost unfair to bring the force of reason against someone who had not chosen that weapon himself. A person could only fight like a man if she were facing an antagonist who was himself prepared to act like a man. Fair or not, Wollstonecraft insisted that she was compelled to adopt a manly writing style consistent with her own respect for the cause of liberty:

You see I do not condescend to cull my words to avoid the invidious phrase, nor shall I be prevented from giving a manly definition of it, by the flimsy ridicule which a lively fancy has interwoven with the present acceptation of the term. Reverencing the rights of humanity, I shall dare to assert them; not intimidated by the horse laugh that you have raised, or waiting till time has wiped away the compassionate tears which you have elaborately laboured to excite.[27]

Unimpressed with Wollstonecraft's denunciation of Burke's 'horse-laugh', the *Gentleman's Magazine* indulged in another slightly more nervous one at her expense. In their review, the *Gentleman's* expressed their considerable bewilderment at the determination of women writers to wander into the inappropriate literary terrain of politics:

> The *rights of men* asserted by a fair lady! The age of chivalry cannot be over or the sexes have changed their ground. Miss Williams is half afraid of *shivering lances*; but Mrs Wollstonecraft enters the lists armed *cap-à-pie;* – as the ladies some years ago took the field at Warley Common. We should be sorry to raise a horse-laugh against a fair lady; but we were always taught to suppose that the *rights of women* were the proper theme of the female sex; and that, while the Romans governed the world, the women governed the Romans. (61 (1791): 151)

With Wollstonecraft mobilizing the rhetoric of combat on behalf of both the rights of men and Burke's more personal target, Richard Price, gentlemen were left with no one to save. On the contrary, they were themselves being either rescued or challenged by 'manly' women. Chivalry was not dead, it had simply been reversed. And this reversal, far from allowing women such as Wollstonecraft to encounter men such as Burke in any man-to-man style, made it unclear what it meant to be male. An overindulgence by women in romantic literature may have been perceived as threatening to social stability, but it none the less reinforced the corrective role of male authority. But when women adopted this corrective role themselves, it was difficult for men to see how patriarchal authority could be recuperated except with a horse-laugh.

In a sense, the *Gentleman's* was acknowledging a concern that women could contribute to this sexual revolution more by writing about the fate of men – a shorthand for politics generally – than if they simply restricted themselves to writing, however polemically, about the fate of women. But Wollstonecraft was to have the last laugh. *A Vindication of the Rights of Woman* appeared two years later. Dedicated to one of the architects of French educational policy, it was less a departure from the political debate than a relocation of that debate in terms of gender. It brought the two revolutions, which intersected in women writers' determination to participate in the defence of the rights of man, into greater focus than ever – too great, perhaps, for the *Gentleman's Magazine*, which never troubled to review Wollstonecraft's literary offerings again.

Wollstonecraft's arguments in *A Vindication of the Rights of Woman* (1792) were in many ways a reassertion of Macaulay's position that women had equal potential to develop a rational sense of moral integrity. 'As a sex', Wollstonecraft allowed, women might well be 'habitually indolent', but this was because of the influence of 'a false system of education, gathered from books written on this subject by men who, considering females rather as women than human creatures, have been more anxious to make them alluring mistresses than affectionate wives and rational mothers'.[28] Corrupted by this literary tradition, which was characterized most perfectly, both agreed, by the works of Rousseau, but also by British writers such as Chesterfield and Fordyce, women had been enticed by the false promise of an apparently privileged place within the patriarchal order.[29] The inevitable result was that the 'overstretched sensibility naturally relaxes the other powers of the mind, and prevents intellect from attaining that sovereignty which it ought to attain'.[30]

It was, moreover, a self-perpetuating situation. 'Confined to trifling employments', women were 'necessarily dependent on the novelist for . . . amusement', despite the fact that in novels, they inevitably encountered narratives which reinforced the dependent role of women all over again. It was not novels, however, but those superior 'works which exercise the understanding and regulate the imagination' that Wollstonecraft had in mind when she reflected sarcastically on the woman who, because 'her understanding had not been led from female duties by literature, nor her innocence debauched by knowledge', succeeded in being 'quite feminine, according to the masculine acceptation of the word' – useful only in exercising personal vanity and in over-indulging her family.[31] In contrast with such a creature, Wollstonecraft argued that real virtue presupposed the moral autonomy that was normally associated with the capacity for rational enquiry. As Nancy Johnson has suggested, the social contract theory championed by Enlightenment reformers was premised on the idea that the individual was 'a free, rational agent qualified to enter into a binding agreement'. Rousseau insisted on this on behalf of men; she was merely extending it to women.[32] The strategic power of this shift lay in the fact that, however radical its ideas about gender, these translational energies were rooted in thoroughly conventional middle-class biases in favour of industriousness in opposition to the corrupting effects of luxury and fashion.

Anticipating one of the most powerful arguments against her suggestions, Wollstonecraft insisted that her enthusiasm for the idea of masculine women had nothing to do with those women who strove to emulate the least desirable aspects of male life:

> I am aware of an obvious inference: – from every quarter have I heard exclamations against masculine women; but where are they to be found? If by this appellation men mean to inveigh against their ardour in hunting, shooting, and gaming, I shall most cordially join the cry; but if it be against the imitation of manly virtues, or, more properly speaking, the attainment of those talents and virtues, the exercise of which ennobles the human character, and which raise females in the scale of animal being, when they are comprehensively termed mankind; – all those who view them with a philosophic eye must, I should think, wish with me, that they every day may grow more and more masculine.[33]

Truly masculine women were inspired by the possibility of participating in the diffusion of knowledge throughout society; these other, so-called masculine women were primarily interested in mimicking those sorts of male behaviour which this diffusion would help to reform.[34]

Not everyone believed in the viability of this distinction. Maria Edgeworth's novel *Belinda* (1801) parodied the same sort of masculine woman that Wollstonecraft was careful to distance herself from, in the ridiculous figure of Harriet Freke, 'a self-serving, "Amazonian" transvestite'.[35] Freke confuses liberty with personal licentiousness by embracing masculinity as fashion – wearing trousers, hunting, participating in a duel, and shaking hands with alarming ferocity. But crucially, she also speaks the same political language as Wollstonecraft: against slavery, and in favour of 'la liberté' and 'the Rights of Women' (274). To give the point further emphasis, the chapter which features the most critical treatment of Freke is itself entitled 'Rights of Woman' (268). However carefully Wollstonecraft may have distinguished between positive and negative forms of female masculinity, Freke's contradictions suggest that for Edgeworth, these different models were two sides of the same transgressive coin.

In his collection of essays entitled *The Observer,* which the *Analytical Review* praised for its 'gentleman-like ease and scholar-like point' (9 (1791): 137), Richard Cumberland had also ridiculed 'the many Amazonian figures I encounter in slouched hats, greatcoats and half-boots', who seemed to think that men chose their wives on the same basis as they did their hunting and drinking companions (III, 329). Wollstonecraft distanced herself from these

'Amazonian figures' as well, in favour of an emphasis on reason. But like Edgeworth, Cumberland rejected Wollstonecraft's distinction between different forms of female masculinity. Arguing directly against Wollstonecraft's position, Edgeworth and Cumberland both suggested, though in opposite ways, that these various forms of female masculinity were ultimately characterized by an inability to recognize the true importance of literature. Where Harriet Freke rejected books as a bore that 'only spoil the originality of genius' (*Belinda*, 268), Cumberland insisted that these sorts of women were all too interested in literature, but for all of the wrong reasons. For Cumberland, women turned to literature not because they were inspired by a love of knowledge, but because they were ill-equipped to attract the attentions of men:

A lady, who has quick talents, ready memory, an ambition to shine in conversation, a passion for reading and who is withal of a certain age or person to despair of conquering with her eyes, will be apt to send her understanding into the field, and it is well if she does not make a ridiculous figure before her literary campaign is over. (IV, 311)

These literary women, Cumberland continued, were so ridiculous that one would wish to have nothing to do with them, to leave them in peace, except that they insisted on spreading their bias against femininity, which was also a bias against men, to younger women who might still be satisfied with traditional ideas about the proper role of a lady:

If the old stock of our female pedants were not so busy in recruiting their ranks with young novitiates, whose understandings they distort by their training, we would let them rust out and spend their short annuity of nonsense without annoying them, but whilst they will be seducing credulous and inconsiderate girls into their circle, and transforming youth and beauty into unnatural and monstrous shapes, it becomes the duty of every knight-errant in morality to sally forth to the rescue of these hag-ridden and distressed damsels. (ibid.)

Cumberland hastened to add that he was aware of the good impression that English women had made within the literary sphere. Female authors were a welcome presence, so long as they did not allow 'their talents and acquirements ... to overshadow and keep out of sight those feminine and proper requisites, which are fitted to the domestic sphere and are indispensable qualifications for the tender and engaging duties of wife and mother'

(312). This might seem to place women authors at something of a disadvantage, but, he added, the reverse was actually the case. Those women who were honest enough with themselves to want to behave as women were also the most likely to succeed as authors. '[I]t is characteristic of superior merit', he explained, that 'amongst the many instances of ladies now living, who have figured as authors or artists, there are very few, who are not as conspicuous for the natural grace of character as for talents' (312). Far from transcending the idea of sexual difference, literary genius tended to emerge most strongly in those women who were honest enough to admit their unique character *as* women.

What these other would-be authors, whom Cumberland dismissed as 'prattlers and pretenders', failed to understand was that it was not only easier for women to succeed as women than as men, but that as women, they had an inherent advantage over men (312). Men, he explained, because they were required to maintain an air of authority in their public lives, preferred to be conquered in their private moments by the irresistible force of feminine softness. Women didn't need to rely on 'the triumphs of their understanding' because 'their conquests are to be effected by softer approaches, by a genuine delicacy of thought, by a simplicity and modesty of soul, which stamp a grace upon every thing they act or utter' (311). The same dynamic underlay the *Gentleman's* comment that 'while the Romans governed the world, the women governed the Romans' (61 (1791): 151). Women would do better to realize that they conquered through weakness rather than by competing in those fields of literary endeavour which were best left to men.

Not all men shared Cumberland's hostility. James Lackington insisted that although he was far from wishing to confound sexual distinctions altogether, he had 'never seen any solid reason advanced, why ladies should not polish their understandings, and render themselves fit companions for men of sense'. Furthermore, Lackington continued, it was increasingly a reality that, whatever one thought about it, women were participating in the diffusion of learning:

Ladies now in general read, not only novels, although many of that class are excellent productions, and tend to polish both the heart and head; but they also read the best books in the English language, and many read the best authors in various languages; and there are some thousands of ladies, who frequent my shop, that know as well what books to choose, and are as well acquainted with works of taste and genius, as any gentleman in the kingdom, notwithstanding they sneer against novel readers.[36]

It was perhaps in light of this 'sneer against novel readers' that Mary Hays insisted, in her preface to *Memoirs of Emma Courtney* (1796), that 'To the feeling and the thinking few, this production of an active mind, in a season of impression, rather than of leisure, is presented' (5). Her novel was not written as a romantic diversion, nor was it intended to be read as one. Quite the contrary, it was intended to further the growth of serious reading and the diffusion of knowledge that Lackington had attributed to the 'ladies' of the kingdom. However melodramatic its tone, and however deprived of the leisure of reflection she may have been during its creation, *Emma Courtney* was intended to be read as a means of instruction rather than as a distraction.

In her *Letters and Essays, Moral and Miscellaneous*, Hays argued that it 'is time for degraded woman to assert her right to reason, in this general diffusion of light and knowledge' (84). Rejecting 'the absurd notion, that nature has given judgement to man, and to women imagination' (120), she insisted that women were just as capable as men of benefiting from and contributing to the 'present universal diffusion of literature' (188). In the opening pages she quoted George Dyer's opinion that because they were doubly oppressed on the basis of class and gender, women authors such as 'Macaulay, Wollstonecraft, Barbauld, Jebb, Williams, and Smith' were all the more ready to seize the mantle of reform (11). For Hays, as for Barbauld in *An Address to the Opposers of the Repeal of the Corporation and Test Acts*, the margins were less about victimization than a social space in which existing assumptions could be radically and productively reimagined. Inspired rather than dismayed by their disadvantages, and aware of the complex ways in which these disadvantages inhered in literature as a diverse field of cultural production, women were wielding their pens, not merely as proof of their rational capabilities, but in order to demand this recognition for their sex in general. Nor was this transformation to be confined to a select group of famous authors. These women may have played the major role in the task of exposing entrenched ideas about sexual difference as prejudice, but, partly as a result of their literary efforts, all women, however obscurely, recognized these inequities:

chained and blindfolded as they most certainly are, with respect to their own rights; – they know, – they feel conscious – of capability of greater degrees of perfection, than they are permitted to arrive at. Yes they see – there is not an individual among them, who does not at times see, – and feel too with keenest anguish, – that mind, as has been finely said, is of no sex. (104)

If the familiar reformist teleology of historical progress manifested itself in Francis Place's more particular emphasis on the improvement of the lower orders, it emerges in Hays' text as a form of innate knowledge, always present but forcing itself into women's consciousness as an increasingly acute awareness of their alienated condition within patriarchal relations. For advocates of the idea that women should not only have an Enlightenment, but that they should decide the nature of their Enlightenment for themselves, these were fighting words. Whatever the oppressive force of custom, Hays implied that at some level all women understood the nature of their predicament. Writing, because it was more available than other forms of political involvement, and because of the strength of an already existing female literary tradition, was one practice in which these claims could most effectively be promoted.[37]

Hays repeated her argument that 'mind . . . is of no sex; therefore it is not in the power of education or art to unsex it', in *An Appeal to the Men of Great Britain on Behalf of Women* (1798) (187). Echoing Wollstonecraft, she cautioned that there were positive and negative types of manly women. The latter, far from hybridizing ideas about the relationship between sexual difference and manly virtue, only reinforced the distinction by reducing female masculinity to an outlandish fashion:

who can deny this we have been speaking of, to be a masculine attainment, and likely to produce, – masculine ideas, masculine attitudes, – and upon the whole masculine boldness of manner? If any one doubts, he has only to walk the streets of our great cities, where, if he has courage to face the amazons of the present day, he will see enough to satisfy his doubts. There will he meet some, with helmets of firm and compact texture, surmounted with military plume. Here others with leather caps edged with furs. Lo! yonder comes one with headpiece altogether of hairy materials, most likely the spoils of some grimalkin, the diseased idol, of some diseased old lady of quality, who killed it with kindness and french cookery. (188)

For Hays, as for Wollstonecraft, Edgeworth, and Cumberland, the misguided indulgence of these Amazonian women in masculine fashion was a form of licentiousness rather than liberty. Like Wollstonecraft though, Hays insisted that these debased women reinforced the opposition, not between the two sexes, but between moral and immoral or (masculine and effeminate) behaviour – a standard that ought, Hays implied, to apply equally to both sexes. Truly masculine women, far from typifying any kind of excess, demonstrated the same degree of virtuous self-command as did men who merited the same description:

If therefore we are to understand by a masculine woman, one who emulates those virtues and accomplishments, which as common to human nature, are common to no sex; the attempt is natural, amiable, and highly honourable to that woman, under whatever name her conduct may be disguised or censured. For even virtue and truth, may be misnamed, disguised, and censured; but they cannot change their natures, in compliance with the tyranny of fashion and prejudice. (173–4)

Regardless of social stereotypes about sexual difference, the moral worth of 'masculine virtue' was unaltered by the sex of the individual.

Hays acknowledged, however, that when men were honest, 'they allege, that when women are educated too much upon an equality with them, it renders them – presuming and conceited; – useless in their families; – masculine, and consequently disgusting in their manners' (177–8). Faced with this disgust, Hays accepted the compromise position that although the mind was of no sex, cultural habits might justify slight differences of behaviour between the two sexes where it was possible for women to comply 'without materially injuring themselves' (174). She was willing to do so, however, only because these concessions were bound to be minor, for 'such vain distinctions vanish before the superior light of reason and religion' (ibid.). This recourse to reason as a force that would minimize the importance of sexual difference was paradoxical, of course, since reason was itself already gendered in contemporary discourse. To obey the dictates of custom would be to abandon women's claim upon reason in any strong sense of the word. But this was unnecessary, Hays implied, since true reason, however it had been appropriated by patriarchal tradition, stood gloriously aloof from the prejudices of any age.

THE FEMALE QUIXOTES OF THE NEW PHILOSOPHY

Hays's optimism was partially a reflection of the more general confidence of Enlightenment reformers that history, because it was driven by a progressivist logic, was on their side. By the time of *An Appeal to the Men of Great Britain*, however, it had become impossible to ignore the hostile reaction which these arguments had generated. Published in 1798 but written earlier in the decade at a time when the public 'was at leisure and seemed disposed, to encourage the endeavours of individuals to instruct, or amuse', Hays acknowledged that 'times and circumstances are now so different, that some apology is necessary for obtruding it on the public; after having kept it back at a moment, when it might have been better received' (1–2). Rather than denouncing the mounting hostility to reformist politics, Hays worked hard to placate any negative sense which her 'little work' might generate about her own masculine nature:

Know, however, that I come not in the garb of an Amazon, to dispute the field right or wrong; but rather in the humble attire of a petitioner, willing to submit the cause, to him who is both judge and jury. Not as a fury flinging the torch of discord and revenge amongst the daughters of Eve; but as a friend and companion bearing a little taper to lead them to the paths of truth, of virtue, and of liberty. (v)

Unlike Wollstonecraft in *A Vindication of the Rights of Men* (1792), Hays was not attempting to reverse the chivalric order. Rather than asserting her rights on the basis of the equality of her sex, Hays seemed to imply that she was only asking favours; instead of manning literary barricades, she was simply offering a tiny candle which might illuminate the paths of moral improvement. The substance of her arguments remained more radical than these comments suggest, but they none the less reflect the impact of this growing spirit of reaction on the limits of literary expression.[38]

However conciliatory her tone, Hays's *Appeal* was overshadowed by Richard Polwhele's *The Unsex'd Females*, which appeared in the same year. Whereas Hays had insisted that women could not be unsexed by being educated in the same way as men, Polwhele made the opposite point. His title, moreover, alluded to Lady Macbeth's invocation of the spirits before the murder of Duncan. These latter-day masculine women, he implied, wielded pens rather than daggers, but they were equally determined to unsex themselves in the perpetration of unnatural acts. For Polwhele, masculinity most definitely did not offer women the same promise of self-government as it did to men. On the contrary, it suggested a predilection for excess that was all too characteristic of '[t]he Amazonian band – the female Quixotes of the new philosophy' (6). Like Cumberland, Polwhele suggested that for this 'female band despising NATURE'S law', masculinity, even where it was supposedly connected with reason, was merely a new and exaggerated form of fashion (ibid.).

In a footnote, Polwhele suggested that in a previous age when 'a female author was esteemed a Phenomenon in Literature', she was given a favourable reception on the basis of her sex (16). As degrading as he admitted this to be, he none the less insisted that it was better than the current situation in which, because women writers were forced to rely on merit, femininity had been all but sacrificed. In such a situation, both sides were worse off. Women could no longer rely on the favour of their (male) judges, and these judges could no longer look forward to being 'charmed into complacence by the blushes of modest apprehension' (ibid.). Polwhele was not short on individual culprits, but his favourite target was Wollstonecraft, 'whom no decorum checks' (13), and who was friend of neither 'the quick flutter, nor the coy reserve' of conventional femininity (15). Wollstonecraft may have championed the idea that mind has no sex, but Polwhele reminded readers that 'she died a death that strongly marked the distinction of the sexes, by pointing out the destiny of women, and the diseases to which they are liable' (30). Sexual difference could be repressed, but it would return all the more forcefully for having been denied.

Just as the distinct nature of the sexes had reappeared in Wollstonecraft's uniquely female death, so too, Polwhele argued, could evidence of it be discovered precisely where Wollstonecraft had insisted that 'no sex' could be located: in the 'numerous femalities' which characterized Macaulay's *History of England* (37). In marked contrast with George Dyer's canon of politicized women authors, Polwhele's poem concluded with an extended celebration, with biographical footnotes, of a *feminine* canon in which the narrator, none other than Hannah More, hurries her literary sisters away from the sight of Wollstonecraft's corpse:

'O come (a voice seraphic seems to say)
Fly from that pale form – come sisters! come away.
Come, from those livid limbs withdraw your gaze,
Those limbs which Virtue views in mute amaze;
Nor deem, that Genius lends a veil, to hide
The dire apostate, the fell suicide.'   (28–35)

Like Cumberland's, and like Hannah More's, Polwhele's republic of letters had room for all women, but only as long as they understood the importance of behaving as women. Wollstonecraft's death, which is conflated in the poem with her failed suicide attempts, was offered by critics such as Polwhele as certain proof of the excesses that were inherent in her ideal of women's potential for 'manly virtue'.

The backlash against women such as Macaulay, Wollstonecraft, and Hays manifested itself not only in conservative journals such as the *British Critic* and the *Gentleman's*, but in formerly sympathetic journals such as the *Monthly Review* as well.[39] In a review of Maria Edgeworth's *Letters for Literary Ladies*, the *Monthly* rejected the idea which, it said, 'has, of late, been strongly felt by some high-spirited females', that 'women are not only capable of being made rational companions, but ought to be educated for an equal share with the men in all the labours and honours of literary and political life' (21 (1796): 25). It reprinted with evident approval Edgeworth's opinion that

such a degree of intellectual cultivation is desirable for women, as shall enable them to converse with their husbands as equals, and to live with them as friends ... and that it is of more importance to give a young woman a habit of industry and attention, and to form her mind to the judicious and elegant exercise of judgement and taste, than to make her an eminent mistress of any single science or art. (24–5)

As More had suggested, the goal of women's education ought to remain a leisure activity rather than a professional pursuit. To become the mistress of a specialized field of literature was to be guilty of engaging in an illicit love that diverted the focus of one's attention from one's husband. Philosophy, because of its appeal to reason rather than feeling, and because of the amount of intellectual labour which any reasonable acquaintance with it demanded, was seen to be one of the clearest examples of those areas of literary endeavour which women were best to avoid. In their review of Margaret Bryan's *Letters on Natural Philosophy*, the *Monthly Review* politely but firmly shut this door on the fair sex:

To Mrs Bryan we wish to be polite, and our jealousies are not hitherto excited; yet we shall guard our peculiar provinces with care and watchful suspicion. Their borders may be visited for curiosity and amusement, but against a formal inroad and invasion of female Philosophers we shall take arms. In our code, we have written that Politics, Greek, and Analytics, are generally forbidden to the ladies: too much study will spoil their engaging faces and their fascinating manners. (51 (1806): 382)

Their encounters with literature ought to refine women's femininity by enlivening their personality, making them more informed and therefore more agreeable partners for their husbands. But this did not make the value of 'engaging faces' and 'fascinating manners' any less important. Insofar as studious concentration on any one subject, especially so demanding a subject as philosophy, might damage these feminine resources, such encounters were best left to men, who, because they were to be judged on the basis of their minds rather than their faces, were under no such restraints.

Nor is it wholly true to say that these anxieties constituted a departure from uniformly liberal attitudes in the reformist press earlier in the decade. The combined force of a growing political backlash, which was intensified by Godwin's revelation of the details of Wollstonecraft's life and death in his *Memoirs*, added fuel to the condemnation of 'masculine' women in the second half of the decade. These developments seemed to confirm what conservative critics had always insisted: that female virtue was inconsistent with 'manly' aspirations, which were themselves best viewed as part of the political excesses of the age. But many reformist authors had also had long-standing anxieties about the links between sexual difference, literary production, and masculine virtue as a potentially ungendered category of thought. As Claire Connolly argues with reference to Maria Edgeworth, women writers in the eighteenth century had always been forced to negotiate 'the gap between [their] faith in the Enlightenment promise of progress, and [their] awareness of Enlightenment fear and distrust of women'.[40]

In their 1794 review of a translation of J. L. Ewald's *Letters to Emma, Concerning the Kantian Philosophy*, the *Monthly* worried about the strange phenomenon of Kant's popularity with women read-

ers. Averse both to Kant's obscurity and to his scepticism, it struck
the *Monthly* as odd that 'it has engaged the attention of the ladies,
many of whom are zealous adherents to it'. Whether women were
'properly employed in attending to these seemingly abstruse subjects' was beyond anything the *Monthly* was prepared to discuss,
except to note that although the trend was proof that mind was
of no sex, it also proved that women could not simply be reduced
to mind (14 (1794): 542). Whereas Hays allowed that sexual distinctions decreed by custom ought to be observed where they did
not materially injure women's exercise of reason, the *Monthly*
argued precisely the opposite: that women's capacity for reason
ought to be indulged so long as it did not impinge upon the hier-
archically structured relationship between the sexes.

Worse than women's insistence on dressing themselves up in
men's intellectual clothing was the problem, as Edgeworth, Cumberland, Wollstonecraft, and Hays had acknowledged, that for
some masculine women, the fun amounted to nothing more than
a new type of fancy dress. An Edinburgh correspondent to the
Gentleman's, having asserted that '[s]oftness, delicacy, benevolence,
piety, and, I may add, timidity (the guardian of virtue), are the
natural characteristics of women', announced his 'sincere regret'
to 'observe, among the ladies of the present day, a tendency to
masculine manners which is highly disgusting' (65 (1795): 103).
His concern was not simply with the wrinkled brow and ruined
manner of the lady philosopher. Worse than this was the fact that
women were aping men's military valour. The escalating war with
France might inspire virtuous behaviour in men, but it inflamed
women with the worst sorts of desires:

A more unpleasant sight can scarcely be seen than that of a woman
imitating the dress of our sex; and it is infinitely worse when they so far
forget themselves as to imitate that of a soldier . . . Yes, Mr Urban, it is
a fact that, in this town, since the corps of volunteers (who are men of
the highest respectability, and most of them of independent fortunes)
were embodied, the military furore has actually so far seized on several
young and beautiful females as to make them submit to be drilled and
exercised (privately of course) by a common serjeant. Can any thing be
more unworthy, or, I may add, more indelicate, than for ladies with their
petticoats kitted, to submit to be taught the movements of a soldier by
a Highland-man without breeches? (103–4)

Like the lower orders, women could not be trusted to understand
the difference between ideas and actions. A taste for 'masculine

... notions' led to 'a tendency to masculine manners' – submitting to be drilled in private by a Highlander without breeches. More dangerous than the implied promiscuity was the implicit disruption of the defining borders of gendered identity, for if men were no longer wearing the breeches, perhaps it was because women had started wearing them, figuratively and literally, both in public and in private, even going so far as to dress it up in the name of virtue. Anticipating Leigh Hunt's aversion to masculine women, the Edinburgh correspondent insisted that the only reaction could be 'disgust' (103). This sort of woman 'appears to be an unnatural and monstrous being, and, instead of love and the softer passions, she excites only contempt' – and what he intimated was still worse for these supposedly independent women, 'neglect' (ibid.). The supposedly immoral and misplaced desire for an inappropriate form of female agency is contained in the letter, as it was in Hunt's theatre review and Edgeworth's *Belinda*, by the correspondent's re-identification of the masculine woman as spectacle – a grotesque apparition pathetically unaware of the dramatic context within which her efforts were inscribed.

The situation conforms to Stallybrass and White's distinction between a relatively safe form of the grotesque (those women denounced as Amazonian, for whom masculinity was a new fashion), and that more insidious type (manly virtue in women) which insinuates itself within and confuses the boundaries between high and low, rational and emotional, masculine and feminine. As such, it was inevitably marked by a kind of slippage. These Amazonians, because they made no claim to virtue, were more threatening to the social order than the relatively harmless efforts of women philosophers, but they were also a much easier problem to deal with because it was, after all, entirely characteristic of women to violate the decree which nature had stamped out for them. Women were only behaving like women, in other words, when they indulged a weakness for fashion that made them want to behave like men. This paradox, that femininity constituted two opposite things, was lodged squarely at the heart of patriarchal authority. Poovey argues that 'even modesty perpetuates the paradoxical formulation of female sexuality. For a modest demeanour served not only to assure the world that a woman's appetites were under control; it also indicated that female sexuality was still assertive enough to *require* control'.[41] If the claims made by feminist authors undermined the distinctions that made manly identity possible, these distinctions could be re-established through arguments which stressed that what manly women were *really* after was not men's books but their breeches – which meant that these women were all the more urgently in need of the gentle corrective of male attention.

A MEMORABLE GRAVE

Tracing these lines of connection in the opposite direction suggests that the reaction to radical feminists such as Macaulay, Wollstonecraft, and Hays had as much to do with already existing worries about what it meant to be a man as with concerns about the behaviour of women. At the heart of anxieties about what seemed to many to be the fact that, as a result of the privatizing effects of commercial culture, the manly virtue of previous eras had given way to a degrading effeminacy in manners and conduct, was the suspicion that men had ceased to behave as men ought to do.[42] The wise but romantically wounded 'stranger' who makes an appearance near the end of the first volume of Robert Bage's novel, *Man As He Is*, offered an exemplary version of this gendered account of decline: ' "We have, said he, corrected many faults, and we have brought many into more general existence. The manly manners of our more immediate ancestors, we have exchanged for the manners of women" ' (I, 272). This idea was frequently applied to the age generally, but as a correspondent to the *Gentleman's* complained, it was particularly evident within the literary republic:

The publication of any ancient English historian, with illustrations, would not at present pay for the printing. Nobody reads such books. The study is too masculine for our trifling times; and all fly at the flowers of science, and neglect the fruits. (58 (1788): 126)

Literature, because of its potential for diffusing the sorts of knowledge which ought to foster a capacity for reason, was a potential antidote to this collective cultural effeminacy. But riven with party strife, claimed by increasing numbers of unrecognizable and ill-qualified contenders, and produced in such extreme quantities that it could never be assimilated, it was only adding to these ills. Those literary men who remained opposed to the effeminacy of their age were hampered by the fact that, because literature was increasingly implicated in this malaise, they could not exert the sort of moral leadership which was widely attributed to earlier authors such as Steele and Addison. Quite to the contrary, by the end of the century popular literature had become 'a major fashion business'.[43]

If this equation of literature's faults with a feminine rather than a masculine identity implied that male authors had become unwilling cultural cross-dressers, unavoidably implicated in the effeminacy of an age in which literature, far from helping to restore public virtue, had itself become part of the moral rot, those other cross-dressers, manly women, became a predictable target of these anxieties. They were both curse and cure: their presence exacerbated a wider identity crisis about the masculinity of literature generally, but representations of such women as transgressive also helped to contain anxieties by offering a potential explanation for these problems – a strategy which was especially available because the image of corrupted femininity already provided an established way of speaking about instabilities rooted in the uncertain fluctuations of a credit-driven commercial society.

For many intellectuals, this urgent sense of cultural decline – which heightened the attractiveness of both the image of an impossibly pure femininity which blissfully transcended contemporary social ills and of a debased femininity which provided a means of conceptualizing those ills – found its focus in the excesses of the French Revolution.[44] As Mitzi Myers puts it, 'the English grew Victorian as the French turned republican'.[45] For Burke, the Revolution, because it was a rebellion against nature, was most poignantly a violation against nature's most perfect embodiment, Marie-Antoinette, whose bed was 'pierced with an hundred strokes of bayonets and poniards', and who 'had but time to fly almost naked ... to seek refuge at the feet of a king and husband, not secure of his own life for a moment'.[46] Burke's fascination was not limited to Marie-Antoinette. His sense of the connection between femininity and violation manifested itself equally in his account of the exertions of those women who, having already rebelled against their femininity, were most eager to participate in revolutionary violence – 'the furies from hell, in the abused shape of the vilest of women'.[47] By 1796, Burke was portraying France 'as in a state of complete sexual mayhem: prostitutes revered as goddesses, marriage reduced to the "vilest concubinage," the whole spiced with the sauce of parricide and cannibalism'.[48]

For John Robison, the clearest proof of the excesses of the revolution was similarly that 'the women have . . . taken the complexion of the men, and have even gone beyond them'. Reflecting that it 'is in nature, it is the very constitution of man, that woman, and every thing connected with woman, must appear as the ornament of life', Robison recorded a ceremony which announced the simultaneous corruption of both religious worship and feminine modesty in none other than Notre Dame cathedral, where the differences between the sacred and the profane had once been so respected:

In their present state of national moderation (as they call it) and security, see Madame Tallien come into the public theatre, accompanied by other *beautiful* women, (I was about to have misnamed them Ladies) laying aside all modesty, and presenting themselves to the public view, with bared limbs, *à la Sauvage*, as the alluring objects of desire . . . 'We do not', said the high priest, 'call you to the worship of inanimate idols. Behold a master-piece of nature, (lifting up the veil which concealed the naked charms of the beautiful Madms. Barbier): This sacred image should inflame all hearts'. And it did so; the people shouted out, 'No more altars, no more priests, no God, but the God of Nature'.[49]

Only in so misguided a climate as revolutionary France could people mistake this display of female nudity, which was nothing more than the violation of that feminine modesty decreed by nature, for nature itself.[50] The ultimate proof of this was that these more-than-manly women, so blinded by zeal that they could forget their domestic attachments, were 'denouncing their husbands, and . . . their sons, as bad citizens and traitors'. Not satisfied even with this, in order to 'express their sentiments of civism and abhorrence of royalty, they threw away the character of their sex, and bit the amputated limbs of their murdered countrymen'.[51]

Thomas Gould's pamphlet, *A Vindication of the Right Honourable Edmund Burke's Reflections on the Revolution in France, in Answer to All His Opponents*, was structured by a similarly split image of femininity in which the French Revolution was rendered intelligible by news of a corresponding revolution in female manners:

I believe the Revolution in France is the only one that has happened in the world, in which the fishwomen have taken a very leading part . . . I have myself seen, on the Boulevards of Paris, a woman of fashion, youth, and beauty, forced to the unwholesome embrace of one of the female legislators. It is well known that no trifling sums have been given to these ladies of the Halle, to purchase an exemption from their amorous frolics. The ladies of our fishmarket here, are, I believe, without any disparagement to this sober, gentle, decent, orderly part of the community, the last objects that could provoke the embrace of a man of taste or fashion: they are, however, much superior to their amiable sisters at Paris. (79–80)

Gould's account fuses together several different senses of violation. These fishwomen were, by their very appearance and manners, a rebellion against all that femininity ought to be, and no man of taste or fashion could find them attractive. This could ordinarily be reconciled with their menial social station, but in the topsy-turvy world of revolutionary France they had gained a position of ascendency over those women who, because of their 'fashion, youth, and beauty', were in no way their natural subordinates. This inverted situation threatened not only the feminine modesty of these younger and more beautiful women, but their heterosexuality itself. Feminine modesty ought to manifest itself, most people agreed, in the restraint of women's desire for men, but implicit in this was the assumption that it ought to manifest itself even more fundamentally in the fact that the desire which these women had to restrain was for men rather than women. In threatening this, the fishwomen, who had already rebelled against their own sexual nature, were attempting to unsex these younger and more beautiful women – an argument that coincides with Cumberland's warning about the fate of 'hag-ridden and distressed damsels' who were being encouraged to rethink their ideas about femininity.[52] Not only this, but Gould had witnessed these scenes for himself, and, by implication, had been unable to stop them. Faced with these women who were more manly than men had any right to be, Gould had himself been reduced to playing less than a man's role of sheltering women from the pressures of the world.

None of this had very much to do with those literary advocates of female rights in Britain, except that the burden of these anxieties was often directed against them. As Simpson puts it, '[w]hile the merest hint of an interest in theory and system was enough to cast any writer as a Jacobin, the threat was all the greater if the writer or heroine happened to be a woman'.[53] Gould implicitly

linked Wollstonecraft's uneven style, which he cited as evidence
of 'no small portion of female inconstancy', to the social excesses
of the fishwomen of Paris. Wollstonecraft's insistence that 'a blind
respect for the law is no part of my creed' was proof, he argued,
of her own willing participation in 'the true Amazonian spirit'.[54]
Her desire to be manly amounted to rebellion against her natural
femininity, and by extension, against that most endearing characteristic of femininity – her heterosexuality. By asking other women
to denounce their own femininity (or, at least, a patriarchal idea
of femininity), Wollstonecraft was involving herself in the same
sorts of threatening encounters as had been initiated by these
'female legislators' who rebelled against nature in terms of their
appearance and manner, their claims on civic power, and most of
all, in their seduction of women who had not yet renounced feminine purity.

For Gould, as for Polwhele, Wollstonecraft was the most notorious of these English Amazonians, but she was not alone. Turning
his attention to a pamphlet entitled *Observations on the Reflections of
the Right Honourable Edmund Burke, on the Revolution of France, in a
Letter to the Right Honourable the Earl of Stanhope*, 'the production of
a lady, well known in the literary world' (he correctly guessed
Macaulay), Gould admonished women's mistaken determination
'to *convince*' when it remained the case that 'to *captivate* was the
peculiar province of the sex, and that its appeals to the *heart* were
always successful'.[55] Like Cumberland and Polwhele, Gould argued
that women erred when they tried to reason with men, not because
men were unwilling to be persuaded, but because they were more
likely to be charmed by feminine softness: 'we yield to what we
know we are unable to resist. When this *natural* and *delightful* pecul-
iarity, is superseded by an *affection* of manliness, the female character loses all its charm, it loses all its lustre: our former *vanquishers*
become our equals'. It was not surprising, he suggested, that a
woman who had chosen so indelicate a subject as politics should
be equally mistaken in her choice of appeal: reason over passion.
For his part though, Gould generously allowed that although he
could not say that he had been '*convinced*', he was prepared to
admit that '[s]he has *captivated* me long since [with] a certain *je ne
sais quoi*, that few men of any soul are able to resist'.[56] In doing so,
he reasserted the primary importance of sexual difference that
writers such as Wollstonecraft and Macaulay had been attempting

to displace in favour of an unsexed distinction between moral and immoral behaviour.

More than either Hays's *Appeal* or Polwhele's *The Unsex'd Females*, it was perhaps another 1798 publication, Charles Lloyd's novel *Edmund Oliver*, which most clearly demonstrated the psychic interplay between these connected anxieties about political unrest, cultural effeminacy, and masculine women. The novel charted the moral collapse and rejuvenation of the idealistic Edmund Oliver, ruined by his love for Gertrude Sinclair (linked in the novel's footnotes to Mary Hays), but redeemed by the kindly attentions of Charles Maurice. Gertrude, Maurice writes to his wife (who in her own supplementary role to her husband's more active moral endeavours embodies a conservative ideal of femininity), is the sort of woman to whom idealistic men are most vulnerable: 'her soul is without doubt lofty and aspiring. An impetuosity of feeling, and a fiery daringness of spirit, seem her chief characteristics' (163). Like the sort of 'grave, manly, noble' woman that Macaulay hoped to produce through her educational efforts, Gertrude's eye is directed 'singly to the distant horizon of human perfection' (36), driven by a faith in the dignity of 'grand and general principles, which, unaccommodated to rank or station, respect all human beings alike' (35). Far from achieving anything, though, Gertrude dies an early death which, like Polwhele's verdict on Wollstonecraft, seems to reflect the destructive consequences of her own excessive desires on behalf of the human race.

Order restored, the Maurices, Edmund and his bride, Edith, and a third couple retire from the dehumanizing scenes of social upheaval to an idealized communal situation reminiscent of Coleridge's and Southey's pantisocratic vision. During the days, the men work cultivating the land; in the evenings the couples join together to cultivate their minds. Edmund and his wife have one additional task: overseeing the development of Gertrude's daughter. Although the child is not his own, his connection to her is all that remains of Edmund's disastrous relationship with the younger Gertrude's mother, whose memory can no longer be mentioned except as a cautionary tale:

Edmund and Edith superintend the education of the infant Gertrude: but the name of the mother is always avoided, except when we would subdue the restlessness of an untamed will – and if at any time, desires incompatible with this mortal existence agitate our bosoms, we retire from society to muse awhile on her memorable grave! (294)

The older Gertrude is everywhere present as an absence, a 'memorable grave' which continues to structure the group's social identity, a name which, far from being forgotten, is always avoided. Her memory must, from time to time, be retrieved, though only so that the dangerous temptations which it has come to represent can be more thoroughly erased.

This endless act of mourning, continually returning to the memory of a loss that must always be rekindled by the side of a grave, constituted a further discursive shift that redefined the distinction between masculine and feminine potential. If certain notions of masculinity had been appropriated by radical critics such as Macaulay, Wollstonecraft, and Hays, the discursive struggle could also work in the opposite direction. The moral optimism connected with the earlier desire for social change, which had become problematically associated with masculinity, could be siphoned off, gathered into a broadened and morally compromised version of femininity that was identified with the misguided ambitions of those unstable women who dared to forget the importance of sexual difference. Such a scenario ensured the availability of a redeemed masculinity which, because it had been freed from suspicions of involvement in any sort of cultural excess, could be celebrated as a renewed source of moral authority capable of containing these dangerous feminine transgressions.

In the fallout from the social and political upheavals of the decade, the image of manly women, inspired by lofty principles and determined to lay claim to the literary prerogatives of men, remained alive more as a taboo than a reformist ideal, a spectre of disruptive energy whose ongoing denial would become a paradoxical guarantee of social order. So long as her name could be avoided, or, in times of crisis, remembered in order that the dangers which she represented might be exorcised, the distinctions between high and low, polite and vulgar, rational and emotional, manly and feminine could be recuperated. Leigh Hunt's reaction to Lady Macbeth more than a decade later bore witness to the fact that this exorcism could never be complete. Nor did women's attempts to renegotiate the connections between ideas about literature, cultural propriety, and gender identity cease. They were, however, forced by the spirit of reaction to adopt a more conciliatory tone, as critics responded to an age which no longer seemed capable of distinguishing between liberty and licentiousness by stressing that the republic of letters was one sphere in which the distinct identities of men and women were to be firmly recognized.

CHAPTER FIVE

Oriental literature

It cannot but prove advantageous to those rich and submissive regions, that their foreign masters should be led to entertain a respect for their institutions, and that the desire of knowledge should now occupy, in their minds, part of that attention which was hitherto devoted only to the acquisition of wealth; – and so copious are the stores of science and literature there opened, that there is little doubt of their continuing to afford treasure to the philosophical inquirer, at least as long as treasures of a different kind will be drawn by the conqueror.

Monthly Review, April 1794

THROUGH THE LOOKING-GLASS

So far I have been exploring changing ideas about literature in terms of shifting networks of cultural representations within national and European contexts. It is important to note, though, that the Enlightenment preoccupation with literature as a means for diffusing the light of reason through the darkness of ignorance – what Mary Wollstonecraft called 'the centrifugal rays of knowledge and science now stealing through the empire' – was profoundly entangled with Britain's escalating imperial presence.[1] By 'empire' Wollstonecraft may well have been referring to the British Isles – she isn't clear – but for those who believed that knowledge, properly diffused, would have an inevitably liberating effect, this process was not to be limited to a single nation or continent. In light of this, Wollstonecraft's unspecific reference is revealing: the processes of colonialism were both an internal and a global preoccupation, premised on the same oppositions between civilized and backward states of existence, and keyed to the same developmental model of linear progression.

Chris Bayly suggests that the focus of internal colonialism was agricultural improvement, or as Arthur Young never tired of explaining, the reclamation of the 'wastes which disgrace this country'.[2] But many commentators agreed that the global dimension, even more than the domestic, would reflect glory back onto whatever nation was willing to play a role in fostering the progress of these rays of learning into the darkest corners of the earth. This was felt to be true because of the moral importance of furthering the spread of education, and in more tangible terms, because this global dimension also referred to a second function of print culture, the assimilation of new forms of knowledge from countries 'hitherto so little explored by the telescope of European curiosity' (*MR*, 19 (1796): 519). Because the centrifugal force of knowledge coincided with a pattern of territorial expansion, it was accompanied by the accumulation in Europe of texts and artifacts from other cultures, a process that was subsumed under the banner of the progress of civilization and situated within the disinterested confines of knowledge.

The task of exploring the influence of imperialism on contemporary ideas about literature is not merely supplemental to the challenge of understanding its status within national cultures. It is instead a matter of highlighting a supplementary logic at work in the absorption of subaltern literary traditions within a supposedly pre-political or non-partisan sphere which none the less required that they be resituated within Western epistemological frameworks in order to constitute knowledge. This two-handed process of incorporation and translation/negation ensured that non-Europeans, like women and the lower orders, would serve as the dark lining on the back of a mirror in which the polite classes would continue to see their own civilized reflection. To say that these exclusions could be repressed is not, however, to say that they could be kept from haunting the narratives of imperial identity. Nigel Leask has argued that '[t]he anxieties and transports of Romanticism . . . are as much the product of geopolitics as of metaphysics, and an ideological analysis which stops short at metropolitan social relations is only telling half the story'.[3] I want to suggest that this was equally true, in what we now describe as the Romantic period, of the Enlightenment ideal of the republic of letters, whose story was as indebted to the global context of its development as it was to those European intellectual traditions with which it tended to be identified.

These anxieties manifested themselves not only within particular literary texts, but in changing ideas about the nature of literature itself. The contradictions implicit in the civilizing mission of imperialism both required and resisted the reassuringly disinterested claims of the literary republic. As that most eloquent of postcolonial stutterers, Salman Rushdie's Whiskey Sisodia put it, '[t]he trouble with the Engenglish is that their hiss history happened overseas, so they do do don't know what it means'.[4] For an imperial force, the possibility of national self-definition presupposes access to an objective or rational understanding of subordinate cultures which is – as it always was – predicated on a perceived separation between power and knowledge. But this separation is itself a manifestation of power relations which can never properly reveal themselves without disrupting the legitimizing appeal of objectivity. This chapter is an attempt to explore the extent to which Engenglish ideas about the universality of literature helped to ensure these various oversights. Or to reverse the formula, I want to step through the looking-glass of civilized self-representation by considering the ways that elisions which underpinned universalist ideas about literature were invoked not merely despite, but actively in response to, the manifest and multiple asymmetries of power that characterized imperialist politics.

Recent work such as Gauri Viswanathan's *Masks of Conquest* and Harish Trivadi's *Colonial Transactions* have drawn considerable attention to the historical consequences of the project of exporting British cultural traditions as a means of internalizing the processes of imperial domination within the split-subjectivity of colonial natives by creating an indigenous elite who were English in taste, but not in race.[5] I want to make what is in some ways the same point about the interconnection of ideas about literature, nationalism, and empire by stressing that before the inclusion of English studies in subaltern educational programs in the 1830s, the cultural dimension of imperial conquest was marked by a widespread valorization of the opposite process of developing a more thorough knowledge of Oriental literature. The pre-eminent Orientalist Sir William Jones observed that these forms of literature constituted 'several topicks entirely new in the republick of letters'.[6] 'A new source of speculation has, of late years, been gradually unfolding itself to the learned of Europe, from the treasures of Oriental knowledge', the *British Critic* agreed. 'Scarcely does a year, or indeed a month, pass away, without having occasion to congratulate both the scholar and the moralist, on their receiving from our brethren dispersed over the wide peninsula of India, sufficient exercise for their best and noblest faculties' (4 (1794): 413). If the ongoing consequences of Eurocentric cultural assumptions continue to shape our own critical endeavours, it may be worth remembering that they manifested themselves not only in the construction of programmes of English Studies throughout the world, but in the earlier identification of Europe generally, and England more specifically, as the true home of non-European literary traditions.

So perfectly did the project of fostering a more tolerant atmosphere in British India coincide with national self-interest that many commentators implicitly agreed that territorial appropriation was morally acceptable as long as Britain displayed a proper concern for her subject communities, the greatest proof of which was the interest British authors displayed in Oriental literature. Critics from a range of positions across the political spectrum celebrated 'the talents of our countrymen inhabiting a distant quarter of the globe, employing themselves sedulously and honourably in extending the credit and establishing the reputation of BRITONS in new and unexplored regions of Science and Literature'.[7] As the same collection of essays and translations, entitled *Dissertations and Miscellaneous Pieces Relating to the History and Antiquities, the Arts, Sciences, and Literature, of Asia*, pointed out, the restriction of other cultures from the benefits of European learning amounted to extreme selfishness rather than respect for cultural difference:

It is a consideration which cannot but afford the utmost pleasure to a reflecting mind, that the Arts and Sciences, which are rapidly advancing towards a state of perfection in EUROPE, are not confined to that quarter of the globe. In the East, where Learning seemed to be extinguished, and Civilization nearly lost, amidst the contention of avarice and despotism, a spirit of enquiry has gone forth, which, aided by the ardour of Philosophy, promises to dissipate the gloom of ignorance, and to spread the advantages of knowledge through a region where its effects may be expected to be most favourable to the general interests of society. (i–ii)

By maintaining its imperial administration, Britain was both expanding the borders of the republic of letters as a universal body of knowledge, and bestowing the blessings of that knowledge on an increasingly widely defined populace. In his *Grammar of the Bengal Language* (1778), Nathaniel Halhed agreed that 'the credit of the nation is interested in marking the progress of her conquests by a liberal communication of Arts and Sciences, rather than by the effusion of blood: and policy requires that her new subjects should as well feel the benefits, as the necessity of submission' (xxv). Instead of constituting a priority which could reasonably be expected to supplant the lust for dominion and riches, the advantages which accrued within the world of learning were better described as a surplus which redeemed more selfish impulses. 'Though we may not always be able to approve the motives which have prompted nations and individuals to explore unknown seas', the *Monthly Review* allowed in its account of James Burney's *A Chronological History of the Discoveries in the South Sea, or Pacific Ocean*, 'we are soon induced to forego this preliminary objection, in contemplating the beneficial consequences which have resulted from their enterprize' (42 (1803): 414).

I am not trying to offer a general summation of British ideas about the virtues of imperialism. Far from being monolithic, late eighteenth-century perceptions about the moral worth of empire were marked by a profound heterogeneity which frequently tightened into polemical disagreements. 'Every man of observation must be satisfied', John Bruce argued in his *An Historical View of Plans for the Government of East India and the Regulation of Trade with the West Indies* (1793), 'that the opinions of the Public are far from being in unison, as to the system which ought to be adopted for the future government of British India, or for the regulation of our Asiatic commerce' (4). The ethical debates about imperialism, quickened in the previous decades by the enormous geographic gains from the Seven Years War, the loss of the American colonies, the notorious and seemingly endless trial of Warren Hastings, the publicity of the anti-slavery movement (and related movements such as the *anti-saccharites*, who advocated the purchase of slave-free sugar), and the debates about the merits of renewing the monopoly of the East India Company were too complex to yield any general account of Britain's growing sense of empire.[8]

It was precisely because opinions about the efficacy of empire *were* so divided that the ideal of literature as a public sphere possessed such an important legitimating appeal. On the one hand, the troubling violence of imperial *conquest* could be atoned for by stressing those beneficial literary consequences which helped to ensure the supposedly gentle operation of imperial adminis-trations. On the other hand, the equally disturbing excesses of imperial *commerce* could be contained by an alternative emphasis on the morally improving nature of cultural acquisitions which could never be reduced to self-interest. To be an imperial power was to enforce the lesson that the appreciation (and the possession of material examples) of culture – other nations' or one's own – was above the possibility of selfishness.

On the surface, these emphases on the redemptive power of literature had little to do with contemporary debates about the role of Christianity in British India. But to the extent that they functioned as an attempt to forestall pressures for a missionary presence by establishing an alternative moral dimension to the operations of empire, these arguments for the ethical importance of literature as a means of gathering (rather than exporting) knowledge must be read as a significant element of the more overtly religious debates of the period. To the extent that they could be hailed as a means of avoiding pressures for a Christianiz-ing aspect to the administration of British India, these arguments were precisely about the role of religion, and all the more so when it did not need to be mentioned.

Imperial administrators tended to discourage a direct mission-ary presence for several reasons. The most important of these was the fear that attempts to convert the native populations to Chris-tianity would aggravate anti-British sentiments. Lord Wellesley might have insisted that the function of Fort William College, which he founded in Calcutta in 1800, was to 'enlighten the Oriental world, to give science, religion, and pure morals to Asia, and to confirm in it the British power and dominion', but the Company chaplain was debarred from engaging directly in missionary operations.[9] Instead, the imperial administration tended to adopt the more passive strategy (consistent with the belief that British liberty could best be encouraged by adhering to local 'prejudices') of maintaining an Anglican hierarchy and cathedral in the hope of swaying the native population through an indirect appeal to their supposed reverence for 'ceremonial pomp'.[10]

In its review of Francis Wrangham's *A Dissertation on the best*

Means of civilizing the Subjects of the British Empire in India, and of diffusing the Light of the Christian Religion through the Eastern World, the *Monthly Review* rejected Wrangham's argument for 'the advancement of true religion in Hindostan' through 'the destruction of the predominancy of the Hindoo priesthood, and the establishment of a Christian Cast or tribe', as an attitude which reflected 'more zeal than discretion' (48: (1805): 109–10). Wrangham's case was based on the familiar logic that subaltern communities ought to be compensated for the 'numerous instances of mercantile and military abuse' which had 'desolated her streets with famine, and drenched her fields with blood' by making them the beneficiaries of an enlightened British presence (ibid.). The *Monthly*, however, remained sceptical about Wrangham's belief that 'the divine genius of the Gospel will confer emancipation on millions' (ibid.). It argued that European contact with other peoples had 'reflected so little credit on the religion which they professed, that antipathy against rather than veneration for the Christian Religion must have been excited in the bosoms of the natives'. 'Is it likely', the *Monthly* asked, 'that the work of proselytism will succeed in our hands; or that a few missionaries, however active and conscientious, will be able to counteract the impression made on the inhabitants of the East by our general system of conduct?' (ibid.).

For many, the answer to this question was a definite 'yes'. Dissenting churches could shed their radical stigma at home by volunteering to play an enthusiastic role in the colonies. Christians from a variety of backgrounds decried the hypocrisy inherent in the fact that missionaries were denied the same 'passage to India' that was routinely granted to commercial adventurers. In a series of essays which appeared in the *Eclectic Review*, the Baptist minister John Foster denounced the efforts of those who 'presumed no less than to attempt to intercept the best light of Heaven from shining into the souls of the wretched heathens committed to their legislative care' (2 (1813): 246). Rejecting the scepticism that 'a few missionaries, however active', could make any positive difference in such an enormous and complex situation, he mocked the view that it 'is intolerance to fifty millions of idolaters, that a few Christian instructors should be allowed to tell them that they are guilty and deluded beings, that there is a Redeemer of sinful mortals, that the true God has revealed himself, that idolatry is absurd and wicked, and that women should not be burnt, nor children exposed' (1 (1808): 121).

The stronger these pressures to create a space for religious activism became, the greater was the attraction of literature to the colonial administration, both as a means of redressing the abuses of imperial power and as a way of redeeming native communities from their currently degenerate condition. To be speaking in these ways about literature was *not* to be talking about religion – an evasion which suggests that invocations of the Enlightenment discourse of improvement were, in this geopolitical context at least, haunted by the potentially disruptive spectre of the Christian goal of conversion.

TERRA INCOGNITA

As knowledge became equated with liberty in an age that was, for many people, unrivalled in both its intellectual and imperial advances, the rhetorical and strategic connections between learning and colonizing became increasingly established. Dreams of a national and a universal literature grew up together as entwined manifestations of the Enlightenment compulsion to organize, map out, and administer different types of resources, an expansionary drive that was often figured metaphorically in the colonizing urge to explore or cultivate the unknown. In his essay 'The Art of Criticism' (1791), D'Israeli described the revival of learning in pioneering terms:

The Learned of the Sixteenth Century made new efforts, not only to clear the uncultivated lands of the Republic of Letters, which had remained unexplored by their predecessors, but also to improve those they had inherited. They prided themselves in the freest discussions; they rummaged every library, to bring to light unnoticed Manuscripts. (169)

If an appeal to the disinterested sphere of learning could help to legitimate the more complicated issue of territorial acquisition, then the reverse was equally true: rhetorical appeals to the spirit of imperial expansion highlighted the heroic nature of the scholarly endeavours of authors. In his *Essay to Facilitate the Reading of Persian Manuscripts*, William Ouseley described himself as a 'Literary Pioneer', assisting the European novice by offering him an introduction to the Persian language that was designed 'to remove, in some measure, the thorns and brambles that opposed his entrance to the smiling garden of Oriental Literature' (xxx). The *Monthly Review* affirmed, in its review of *Asiatick Researches*, that '[t]o England it belongs to reap the distinction of clearing this fertile and boundless field' (45 (1804): 305). Whether it was old libraries or foreign languages and cultures (or the libraries of foreign cultures), the point remained basically the same: to be a civilized nation, which amounted to being aware of the value of literature, was to enjoy the prerogative, if not the duty, of retrieving literary resources from whatever wilderness they might be lying in, unrecognized and unappreciated.

So powerful were the parallel attractions of those frontiers which marked the limits of intellectual and geographical mastery that the colonizing metaphor could operate as a free-floating signifier for the expansion of knowledge generally, wholly removed from the particulars of any imperial context. The *Analytical Review* praised the 'spirited animadversions on the "fancied boundary of human knowledge" ' in John Weddel Parsons' *Essays on Education* (1788):

Who indeed can pretend to say that thus far the human intellects shall go, and no farther – here shall the proud waves be stayed – and vainly beat against an insurmountable barrier? He says with spirit, 'Who would with weary steps travel over the beaten path, to what is already known, if he had not in view the undiscovered country, to urge on his hope and ambition?' (II, 475)

In her review of Charles Burney's *A General History of Music*, Wollstonecraft praised Burney in similarly geographic terms for his contribution to the 'advance ... into the *terra incognita* of the human mind' (7 (1790): 210). Burney, explaining how the project had grown beyond his initial estimation, had likened himself to a sailor thrown into a longer voyage than he had expected: 'after I had embarked, the further I sailed, the greater seemed my distance to port'.[11] The lure of horizons, figurative and literal, drove a quest for knowledge that found expression in the language, and coincided with the practice, of escalating territorial expansion.

The influence of these sorts of assumptions was heightened by the strong congruence between the perceived *improving* effects of literature and the *civilizing* imperative underlying the justifications for imperialism. Wollstonecraft's argument, in *An Historical and*

Moral View of the French Revolution (1795), is informed by precisely this association between the ideal of scientific progress and the historical fact of empire:

When the arts flourished in Greece, and literature began to shed it's [sic] blandishments on society, the world was mostly inhabited by barbarians, who waged eternal war with their more polished neighbours ... We have probably derived our great superiority over those (earlier) nations from the discovery of the polar attraction of the needle, the perfection which astronomy and mathematics have attained, and the fortunate invention of printing ... The scientific discoveries have not only led us to new worlds; but, facilitating the communication between different nations, the friction of arts and commerce have given to society the transcendently pleasing polish of urbanity, and thus, by a gradual softening of manners, the complexion of social life has been completely changed.[12]

Print culture is conflated with those scientific developments which facilitated geographic exploration in an over-arching techno-teleological vision of historical progress as the particular province of Western civilization. The 'great superiority' of modern European nations over their ancient predecessors was simultaneously technical and moral: scientific discoveries, including printing, were both a proof of the greater achievements of modern Europe and a means of extending the blessings of those achievements to 'new worlds'. To be able to expand, according to the logic of this argument, was to deserve to do so.[13] M. Meusel's *Guide to the History of Literature* employed the same line of argument in its section on '*The Restoration of the Sciences to the present Time; i.e. from 1500 to 1800*':

The accounts of the former ages seem to regard a totally different class of Beings: but the events which we are at present to contemplate refer immediately to ourselves, and to our actual state of knowledge. – The ... conquest of Constantinople, the discovery of America, that of a passage by the Cape of Good Hope, and, more than all, the invention of the art of printing, had largely contributed to the diffusion of learning and philosophy. (Quoted in *MR* 45 (1804): 529)

Because the linear historical model which assumed the greater cultural worth of contemporary European states over their predecessors could be mapped onto a spatial paradigm of geographic difference, the presence of these colonial powers was widely held to constitute the introduction of a spirit of liberty to regions in which liberty, if it had ever thrived, had been extinguished. It

followed that the liberation of colonial societies did not amount to
their emancipation from European rulers, because those rulers
were already the source of a spirit of tolerance which could not
help but root itself in the soil of non-European cultures.

Reinforced by the swing of focus eastward after the loss of the
American colonies, Orientalists stressed that the pursuit of knowledge was particularly important in the Indian subcontinent which
was the birthplace of European cultural traditions. As the *Asiatic
Annual Register* put it, 'the East' constituted 'the tranquil seat of
literature and commerce, whence Europe was destined to receive
much of her knowledge, and many of her refinements' (1 (1799):
10). One consequence of this sense of historical linearity was a
strategically productive confusion of different forms of destiny.
Because Europe was destined to receive much of its current knowledge from these earlier Oriental traditions, it seemed natural that
the pursuit of intellectual discovery would lead back to the
obscured cultural traditions of Asia itself. Equally natural for
many critics was Britain's destiny to combine these forms of intellectual discovery with a more straightforward colonizing urge.[14]

This was not to be limited to a return to the cradle of civilization
though. On the contrary, the greater the scale of its ambitions,
the more effectively could the colonizing drive be separated from
the particular agency of European powers by an emphasis on the
irresistible progress of learning. Robert Alves's *Sketches of a History
of Literature* (1794), celebrated the westward migration of learning
in a way that acquitted European societies of any particular
responsibility in his argument that

the arts and sciences have taken their rise in the East, and have thence
travelled westward, first to Egypt, and afterwards to Greece and Rome,
that they have generally improved in their progress in proportion to the
nature of the soil and the climate, and the ardour with which they have
been pursued; that neither the warmer nor the colder regions have been
greatly favourable to their culture, the former relaxing, the latter con-
tracting the human faculties; that in the temperate climes of Europe
they have flourished to most advantage; that it is probable they will
thence migrate to the western continent in order to enlighten a new
world; that they will finally spread themselves over the most savage
tribes, and, with their sacred influence, polish and improve the most
uncivilized nations. (12)

Through Alves's recourse to a grand meteorological scenario in
what was, after all, a history of literature, learning is simul-

taneously associated with the temperate European climate and radically distanced from particular interests. The potentially controversial aspects of imperialism are contained by the suggestion that it was, on the one hand, a benevolent and improving force, and on the other, a process that was as inevitable as the weather. Literature, in other words, offered an important metonymic connection through which the conquest of actual communities could be rewritten as the progress of knowledge – the diffusion of learning would by nature expand into those regions which, being either too warm or too cold, had not yet fully benefited from its liberating power.

I have been trying to show how compelling the imaginative connections between literature and empire were on various metaphorical and metonymical levels. The progress of knowledge seemed to coincide with the expansion of the blessings of civilization; the universality of literature as a non-partisan body of knowledge seemed to anticipate and therefore helped to naturalize the global ambitions of imperial powers. I now want to look more directly at the political debates about empire, and the role which these exchanges assigned to literature within the imperial project. In the next section I will suggest that critics stressed that the illiberal realities of violent conquest were redeemed by the development of a body of knowledge about indigenous customs which would help to make imperial administrations more responsive to their subject populations. In the final section, I shift my focus from the satellite to the metropole, and from anxieties about conquest to concerns about the moral effects of commerce. Like worries about conquest, tensions generated by the selfishness of colonial interaction could be contained by an alternative emphasis on a form of cultural accumulation which could be said to be both acquisitive *and* disinterested.

A RIGHT UNDERSTANDING

To say that tensions inherent in the colonial project could be contained through a range of discursive strategies is not, of course, to say that these tensions could be eliminated. The memory of colonial violence could be rewritten as the progress of learning, but its discomforting realities could never be as thoroughly denied as this optimism might suggest. Because the restless pursuit of

Oriental knowledge was inevitably marked by what Sara Suleri has called the 'the idiom of dubiety, or a mode of cultural tale-telling that is neurotically conscious of its own self-censoring apparatus', narratives of empire insisted on the compensatory value of the disinterested work of authors as a supplement which could never quite negate the memory of an originary violence.[15] Charles Hamilton's preface to his translation of *The Hèdaya, Or Guide; A Commentary on the Mussalman Laws* (1791), having taken 'notice of the natural alliance between the diffusion of knowledge and the eradication of prejudice, the prolific source of antipathy, discord, and bloodshed', explicitly connected Britain's role in furthering the progress of learning with the privileges of empire. But it also revealed the nagging doubts that lingered along the edges of these narratives of colonial occupation and cultural redemption:

> To open and to clear the road to science; to provide for its reception in whatever form it may appear, in whatever language it may be conveyed: – these are advantages which in part atone for the guilt of conquest, and in many cases compensate for the evils which the acquisition of dominion too often inflicts.
>
> Perhaps the history of the world does not furnish an example of any nation to whom the opportunity of acquiring this knowledge, or communicating those advantages, has been afforded in so eminent a degree as GREAT-BRITAIN – To the people of this island the accession of a vast empire in the bosom of Asia, inhabited, not by hordes of barbarians, but by men far advanced in all the arts of civilized life, has opened a field of investigation equally curious and instructive. – Such researches must ever be pleasing to the speculative philosopher, who, unbiased by the selfish motives of interest or ambition, delights in perusing the great variegated volume of SOCIETY. (iii)

The competitive element of Britain's territorial expansion, which had been exacerbated by Tippoo Sultan's French allegiances – converting Mysore into a Jacobin outpost, planting a republican 'liberty tree', and donning a cap of liberty – could not easily be reconciled with the redemptive claims of imperial destiny.[16] But this only made the transference of these conflicts into the disinterested world of learning all the more attractive. The passage moves from expressing a penitential hope that these advantages will 'in part atone for the guilt of conquest, and in many cases compensate for the evils which the acquisition of dominion too often inflicts', to a celebration of Britain's unique imperial position, unprecedented in 'the history of the world', before finally situating its focus within the disinterested world of 'the speculative philosopher' to whom these researches 'must ever be pleasing'. The motivations of the philosopher transcended any possible selfishness: his intellectual profit would in turn, through the diffusion of knowledge, become everyone's.

But what Hamilton's transition from a sense of contrition to one of manifest destiny also implies, but never recognizes, is that what 'the history of the world does not furnish an example of' are such widespread instances of 'the guilt of conquest . . . the evils which the acquisition of dominion too often inflicts'.[17] His comments are destabilized both by the juxtaposition of negative and positive images of imperial acquisition, and by the admission that the advantages can only ever '*in part* atone for the guilt of conquest, and *in many cases* compensate for the evils' occasioned by territorial expansion (emphasis added). It is, perhaps, only through a denial of the power relations underlying the acquisition of this knowledge, which is achieved by situating this research within the disinterested world of learning, that the subversive force of these contradictions can be contained. The colonial scene of military struggle is metonymically reduced to a literary text that is to be read rather than conquered – 'a great variegated volume' which has been wiped clean of any trace of blood.

Sir William Jones, whom Said refers to as 'the undisputed founder . . . of Orientalism', advocated a similar role for authors whose work was to aid in the task of governing a conquered people on as liberal a basis as possible.[18] In his *Institutes of Hindu Law*, Jones declared his hope 'that all future provisions, for the administration of justice and government in *India*, will be conformable, as far as the natives are affected by them, to the manners and opinions of the natives themselves'. This, in turn, depended upon the efforts of authors to develop a greater understanding of the 'manners and opinions' of subaltern communities (III, 53). As with Hamilton though, Jones's argument remained wholly collusive with existing structures of authority. 'A variety of causes, which need not be mentioned here', he had explained in the preface to *A Grammar of the Persian Language* (1771), 'gave the English nation a most extensive power in that kingdom' (II, 126). Whatever the nature of these causes which did not need to be mentioned, the result was an ongoing series of administrative difficulties which produced a demand for new forms of learning that would transcend the merely commercial realm, adding new lustre to England's cultural traditions:

The languages of Asia will now, perhaps, be studied with uncommon ardour; they are known to be useful, and will soon be found instructive and entertaining; the valuable manuscripts that enrich our publick libraries will be in a few years elegantly printed; the manners and sentiments of the eastern nations will be perfectly known; and the limits of our knowledge will be no less extended than the bounds of our empire. (127)

Like Hamilton's, Jones's argument moves from a compensatory insistence on the importance of perfecting colonial government to a triumphant emphasis on the study of literature as an end in itself which wholly erases the violent origins of colonial domination which made this possible – the more these contradictions became problematic, the greater the allure of the universality of literature.

   The same line of argument provided conservatives with an effective means of supporting the Pitt ministry's efforts to extend its authority in India by implicitly aligning the government with the good works of authors in opposition to the destructive effects of the Company's military campaigns.[19] In its review of *British India Analyzed,* the *British Critic* admitted that '[a]fter the greatest deductions that can reasonably be made ... great still must have been the sufferings of the Hindoos; degraded, plundered, and often for the purpose of extorting their concealed wealth subjected to various kinds of torture' (4 (1793): 523). Whatever the scale of these cruelties, though, it was of some consolation that as a result of the generous attentions of the British government, research capable of addressing them was already under way:

It has been observed, that in every country, the activity of men's minds and the progress of investigation and knowledge, keep pace with the energy of government. In proportion as the British Government interfered in the internal regulation of British India, we find authors arising to instruct the minds of legislators, and the public, on all the capital points which ought to be studied by statesmen, previously and preparatorily to the formation of a new system of government: the history or political vicissitudes of the people, landed tenures, agriculture, arts, manners, customs, and religion. (524)

The government's response to the Company's acquisition of whole communities whose customs they were largely unaware of could only help to encourage the exertions of authors whose sole reward was 'the conscientiousness of having with success employed their time, for the good of their country and of mankind' (525). By aligning the Enlightenment emphasis on the emancipatory power of knowledge with particular agents in the political struggle for the control of British India, the *British Critic* could simultaneously address the issue of the sufferings caused by imperial expansion, and insist on the proper authority of the Pitt government within these newly acquired regions.[20]

According to these accounts of the redemptive potential of Oriental literature, Britain's inherent predisposition towards liberal forms of government, because it was seen to manifest itself in a tolerance for subaltern customs, involved the colonial administration in two related paradoxes. On the one hand, it meant that in order to diffuse this spirit of liberty, which was inseparable from the effects of learning, the British needed to be educated in the customs of their subjects in order to extend to them the blessings of a progressive civilization. Although the emphasis remained on the emancipatory effects of knowledge, the situation reversed the more straightforward logic inherent in the metaphor of enlightenment: it was the agents of enlightenment who must themselves be educated about the habits of their more ignorant subjects in order to save those subjects from their own ignorance. The focus, in other words, was more on the collection than the diffusion of knowledge, although on a rhetorical level this distributive emphasis (the civilizing impulse) remained the principal legitimation of colonial conquest.

On the other hand, to the extent that the British were able to rule in a manner which demonstrated a respect for local customs, it was also the case that their spirit of liberty had to manifest itself in a respect for customs that were frequently denounced for their illiberality. Masculine virtue, ironically, presupposed a due regard for the effeminate predilections of local peoples, but this policy of non-interference could in no way be based on a respect for the inherent worth of subaltern customs since for many European commentators, 'the Hindus had not the remotest idea of political liberty ... The influence of the climate, conjoined with

the despotism of priestcraft and superstition, unfitted their minds
for the reception of those masculine virtues which dignify our
nature, while they cherished the mean vices of avarice and slavery'
(*AAR* 1 (1799): 8–9). Jones's *Institutes of Hindu Law* was framed
by the larger belief that the policies of the colonial administration
could 'have no beneficial legislative effect . . . unless they were
congenial to the disposition and habits, to the religious prejudices,
and approved immemorial usages of the people, for whom they
were enacted' (III, 53). And yet Jones agreed that

It is a system of despotism and priestcraft . . . filled with strange conceits
in metaphysicks and natural philosophy, with idle superstitions, and with
a scheme of theology most obscurely figurative, and consequently liable
to dangerous misconception; it abounds with minute and childish for-
malities, with ceremonies generally absurd and often ridiculous. (62)

Real tolerance did not translate these sorts of negative judgements into any form of civic practice. Instead, it preserved a spirit
of respect which would expose the limitations of native customs
by contrasting them with a leniency which would be most clearly
evidenced in the study of indigenous literature. To be enlightened
was to recognize the legitimacy of other people's less enlightened
ideas and habits.

   The tension between incorporative and distributive ideas about
knowledge on the one hand, and the paradoxical emphasis on the
importance of tolerating customs which were themselves marked
by a profound spirit of intolerance on the other, were contained
by a distinction which British critics frequently made between the
'true nature' of Hindu culture, which had been erased by waves of
invasions, and the debased reality of their current state. As Said
puts it:

Proper knowledge of the Orient proceeded from a thorough study of the
classical texts, and only after that to an application of those texts to
the modern Orient. Faced with the obvious decrepitude and political
impotence of the modern Oriental, the European Orientalist found it his
duty to rescue some portion of the lost, past classical Oriental grandeur
in order to 'facilitate ameliorations' in the present Orient. What the
European took from the classical Oriental past was a vision (and thousands of facts and artifacts) which only he could employ to the best
advantage. (*Orientalism*, 79)

The efforts of British Orientalists would enable the colonial
administration to synthesize the ideal of tolerance with a respect

for the 'real' nature of local peoples, which, by implication, the British were uniquely capable of understanding. '[F]rom *Sanskrit* literature, which our country has the honour of having unveiled', Jones explained, 'we might still collect some rays of historical truth, though time and a series of revolutions have obscured that light, which we might reasonably have expected from so diligent and ingenious a people' (I, 147). Empowered by the research of Orientalists, Britain's colonial administrators would be able to pursue two different but related forms of synthesis. They would be able to govern in a way that combined a European spirit of liberty with Asiatic customs that were characterized by a spirit of despotism and, at the same time, they would be able to weave a recognition of the current reality of these customs together with a larger sense of the Hindus' true, but forgotten, nature. The *Asiatic Annual Register* offered the hope that after 'seven centuries [of] the most inexorable tyranny recorded in the annals of mankind', Britain's imperial presence would make it possible to believe that 'an ancient and highly cultivated people [might be] restored to the full enjoyment of their religious and civil rights' (1 (1799): xi). The key to these processes was the availability of a body of Oriental literature which British authors were assiduously developing on behalf of a subject population that was thought to be incapable of appreciating these texts.

Structuring all of this was the implicit assumption that, instead of being liberated from the British, the presence of these colonial rulers was itself the surest promise of a new era of liberty. The distantiation of power and knowledge which underpinned Enlightenment ideas about literature was frequently invoked in the context of empire – less to insist that the autonomous influence of learning would fundamentally reshape political authority according to the interests of an informed reading public than in order to stress that because of this separation the selfless pursuit of knowledge and the wilful pursuit of power could coexist without mutual interruption. Nathaniel Halhed insisted that, although it had been officially recognized 'by the most formal act of authority in the establishment of a Supreme Court of Justice', the incorporation of the Kingdom of Bengal within the British Empire none the less required 'the cultivation of a right understanding and of a general medium of intercourse between the Government and its Subjects; between the Natives of Europe who are to rule, and the

Inhabitants of India who are to obey'. Like the Romans who applied themselves to the study of Greek after conquering Greece, Halhed continued, it was important that the English, having become 'the masters of Bengal . . . add its Language to their acquisitions: that they may explain the benevolent principles of that legislation whose decrees they inforce; that they may convince while they command; and be at once the dispensers of Laws and of Science to an extensive nation'.[21] The argument slides from the suggestion that, having conquered a foreign land, the British were morally obligated to develop a working knowledge of local customs through a study of its literature, to emphasizing that the ethical integrity demonstrated by this studious commitment highlighted a moral hierarchy which corresponded to, and implicitly legitimized, the political hierarchy of imperial relations.[22]

The opposition between conquerors and liberators was overshadowed by the alternative distinction between the sort of conquerors whose principal intention was to tyrannize local communities and those benevolent conquerors, such as the British, who had the best interests of their subject peoples at heart. 'Conquests', the *Monthly Review* allowed in a review of Roderick Mackenzie's *A Sketch of the War with Tippoo Sultan,* 'which, still more than those of Alexander, seem likely to confer police, instruction, and civilization on the emancipated helots of oriental despotism, cannot be contemplated with either indifference or aversion by the eye of philanthropy' (19 (1796): 519). British histories of the Indian subcontinent dwelt obsessively on the waves of tyrannical invaders whose brutalities had reduced the Hindus to an enfeebled people whose love of liberty had been extinguished.[23] Having internalized the lessons of their degradations, these histories implied, the Hindus could only be liberated by being reconquered by a more benevolent power. As the *Monthly* repeated in its review of *Essays by the Students of the College of Fort William in Bengal,* '[t]o behold the victor bowing to the institutions, laws, and manners of the conquered people; and labouring to render their dialects familiar to him, in order to avoid offending their prejudices, that he may be better able to learn their complaints, and to redress their grievances; this is a novel sight, and highly gratifying to every lover of humanity' (43 (1804): 191).[24]

If narratives of imperial authority were disturbed by the realities of territorial conquest, this guilt could be overshadowed by an alternative stress on the importance of introducing liberty into an area that had been enslaved by centuries of less enlightened conquerors. Within this scenario, the study of Oriental literature was multiply significant; it highlighted the extent to which the British were conquerors with liberal rather than tyrannical intentions; it allowed administrators access to a body of knowledge about the current practices and assumptions of their native subjects in order to develop a more effective disciplinary regime; and it enabled the British to distinguish between a debased Asiatic culture and those truer forms which manifested themselves solely in Oriental literary traditions that were best understood by the British – a confidence which licensed an otherwise awkward fusion of selfish and supposedly disinterested impulses, in which the complexities of imperial conquest were redeemed through the emancipatory energies of authors.

TREASURED TEXTS

These anxieties about the effects of conquest within the satellite were paralleled by concerns within the metropole that the dynamics of empire would exacerbate the morally enfeebling effects of commerce. If, as many critics believed, commerce had been one of the engines driving Europe's progress from feudal tyranny into an age of unprecedented liberty, then it was natural that it should be the basis of mutually advantageous, extra-European contact. But as we have already seen, commerce was felt by many to be a highly ambiguous force, productive of much good, but also tending to promote an unstable and wholly privatized society marked by alienating networks of fluctuating exchanges which undermined the possibility of exercising public virtue.

These worries were aggravated by concerns about the aberrant nature of imperial commerce. The *British Critic*, in its support of the Pitt government's bid for a more active role in British India, worried that trade with India was dominated by 'mercantile and partly warlike adventurers' who lived there not as members of the community but as conquerors with little interest in the local consequences of their activities (2 (1793): 524).[25] The worst, rather than the most distinguished, elements of British society were rising to the imperial surface. In his arguments at the

Warren Hastings trial, Burke painted a morally outrageous picture of 'the desperate boldness of a few obscure young men':

Young men (boys almost) govern there, without society and without sympathy with the natives. They have no more special habits with the people than if they still resided in England, – nor, indeed, any species of intercourse, but that which is necessary to making a sudden fortune, with a view to a remote settlement. Animated with all the avarice of age and all the impetuosity of youth, they roll in one after another, wave after wave; and there is nothing before the eyes of the natives but an endless, hopeless prospect of new flights of birds of prey and passage, with appetites continually renewing for a food that is continually wasting. (Quoted in Suleri, *Rhetoric*, 32)

The central point, for Burke, was the damage that this endlessly parasitic relationship was wreaking on native communities. But many commentators also worried about the effects this would have on moral standards within the metropole. As with the issue of military conquest, it was precisely this moral vulnerability which heightened the attraction of the increasing presence of Oriental literature as an enriching cultural addition that would contribute to the moral health of the metropole by creating opportunities for reflecting on the history of civilization. Unlike mere financial preoccupations, the study of Asiatic learning was situated within a realm that transcended the very possibility of greed. But rather than supplanting commercial interests, literary endeavours were felt to blend with them, offering both a moral corrective to these excesses and an enduring monument to the grandeur of the British empire. Thomas Maurice argued that '[w]hen British merchants thus endeavour to blend the interests of LITERATURE with those of COMMERCE, they throw a lustre upon the distinguished station which they enjoy; a lustre which wealth alone, however ample or honourably obtained, can never bestow'.[26]

The problem was that ideas about Oriental literature continually threatened to exceed the disinterested limits within which they were supposedly located. Far from operating as a corrective to the acquisitive energies of imperialism, the thirst for knowledge manifested an equally totalizing possessiveness. In its review of Jones's *Design of a Treatise on the Plants of India*, the *British Critic* paraphrased Jones's aspirations for Oriental knowledge in a way that conflated commercial and cultural interests: ' "Give us time," ' it might be said, ' "for our investigations, and we will

transfer to Europe all the sciences, arts, and literature of Asia" '
(1 (1793): 261). 'It is pleasing to reflect', the *Monthly* agreed, 'that
Eastern science is an object of sedulous study by our countrymen;
that we transport, with the treasures, the learning of India' (47
(1805): 316). Rather than redeeming the network of individual
and collective interests which informed the quest for empire by
relocating the focus of those exertions within a more disinterested
context, the pursuit of knowledge, because it could never be separated from the acquisition of texts, echoed these other more
dangerously selfish forms of importation.

The fact that the collection of these forms of knowledge
depended on, and frequently constituted, a form of imperial
exploitation could be contained, however, by an implicit emphasis
on Europe as the location of knowledge, in the absence of which
cultural traditions remained in a kind of wilderness. More important than bringing Oriental texts back to London was the challenge
of bringing them into the light of public notice by removing them
from the opacity of a culture whose identity was lost in a web
of superstition. In their relocation within European intellectual
cultures where their true significance was more capable of being
appreciated, these Oriental texts were, in a sense, only being
returned to their true home.

Apparently unsatisfied with the rate of assimilation of these new
sources of knowledge, whose significance could only be released
into the proper hands – which was to say, the hands of an informed
European – the *British Critic* none the less commended the Orientalists for acting as textual liberators. Far from being restricted
to literary texts, their power extended to the whole range of
Indian culture:

It is no less remarkable than true, that, till within these few years, very
little authentic information has been communicated to Europe concerning the literature, antiquities, and customs of India. The veil of obscurity,
however, which has so long been spread over that immense and interesting portion of the globe, seems now in a fair way of being effectually
removed ... Mr Hastings led the way, by his patronage of Mr Wilkins
and Mr Halhed. Sir William Jones, with that unremitting zeal which
characterizes genius, has since brought to light what has for ages been
concealed. The successful labours of Mr Maurice, already noticed by us,
have produced a systematic arrangement of much curious and important
matter ... The historical disquisition concerning India by Dr Robertson
... has systematized the knowledge of the ancients, has often illumi-

nated what was obscure, and made clear what was doubtful. We wanted however, and we still require, the efforts of individuals, who, penetrating into the interior parts of a beautiful and picturesque region, will give us a faithful representation of ancient monuments and modern manners. Thus the progress of art, the change of manners, and the variation of national character, may be more perspicuously understood, and the stock of universal knowledge extended and improved. (*BC* 1 (1793): 13–14)

What is taken for granted is the sovereign presence of the European gaze from whom the treasures of Indian cultural history had been concealed and by whom – aided by the efforts of those individuals willing to penetrate the interior of this picturesque and beautiful region – this veil of obscurity was being lifted, making what was secret transparent, what was concealed available, and clarifying and organizing what was doubtful in order to extend and improve the stock of universal knowledge. Only in the hands of people who understood the true value of knowledge, and whose awareness of this was equally bound up with a spirit of liberty, could this literary potential be rescued. The text could be saved from itself – just as a people could be saved from themselves – through the providential arrival of a conquering people determined to introduce a note of liberty into a culture that had lost this quality. And this, in turn, could be secured by translating the scene of conquest into a scene of reading – a text which only needed to be studied properly in order to recuperate the Enlightenment confidence in the link between literacy and liberty.

So thoroughly were European rulers identified with liberty, even if the political conditions which ensured the manifestation of that spirit of liberty were initially achieved through conquest, that not only were they capable of putting knowledge to work in ways which undermined Asian despotism and superstition, they even read Asian literature in a manner which set the texts themselves free. *Dissertations and Miscellaneous Pieces* (1793) suggested that for a text to be read by a European was for it to be liberated from imprisonment:

The stores of Oriental Literature being now accessible to those who have ability to make a proper use of them, intelligence *hitherto locked up*, it may be hoped, will delight and inform the enquirers after the History, Antiquities, Arts, Sciences, and Literature of ASIA. (iii–iv; emphasis added)

Sir William Jones, in his *Grammar of the Persian Language*, had argued along similar lines that his work of bringing Oriental texts to the attention of British reading audiences was important because it emancipated the texts from the burden of their own neglect: 'the man of taste will undoubtably *be pleased to unlock the stores of native genius*, and to gather the flowers of unrestrained and luxuriant fancy' (II, 133; emphasis added). The task of fostering an awareness of subaltern customs was felt to have an emancipatory effect because it would allow colonial administrations to adapt themselves to these customs in more tolerant ways. But the intellectual task of relocating Oriental texts within European readerships emancipated the texts themselves. To be resituated within western European languages and readerships was to be converted into knowledge; to remain within a native context was to remain shrouded in ignorance, superstition, secrecy.

European critics often stressed that the Orientalist, in retrieving these forms of knowledge, needed to beware that he did not become infected with those excesses endemic to the culture upon which he was focusing. He must be rational in his enquiry into systems that were fundamentally irrational, not only so that the irrationality might be understood for what it was, but also so that real information might be distilled from it. The *Gentleman's Magazine* blamed Nathaniel Halhed's support for the religious enthusiast Richard Brothers on Halhed's corruption by Oriental literature. 'With all our respect for Mr H's Hindu knowledge', the *Gentleman's* wrote in their review of Halhed's *Testimony of the Authenticity of the Prophecies of Richard Brothers*, 'we fear he has bewildered himself too much in Eastern mysteries to decide the question' (65 (1795): 228). Only when men of letters were careful to respect the realities of cultural difference could non-European literatures be reproduced in a way that did not threaten the moral health of those who came in contact with them. As the *Monthly Review* suggested in its account of the Abbé Rochon's *Voyage à Madagascar*:

A philosophic and scientific traveller to remote and unknown regions, if gifted with curiosity, diligence, and truth, is sure to bring home literary merchandice of great value, if it should likewise be well manufactured; for raw materials, however precious in themselves, require dressing and arrangement; even gold must be refined, and diamonds must be polished. (6 (1791): 555)

More important than simply retrieving these texts was the task of transforming them into precious literary gems. This process of cultural manufacturing depended, however, on the European traveller's constant awareness of the differences between his own values and those of the culture he was exploring. In *Indian Antiquities: or Dissertations of Hindostan* (1793), Thomas Maurice acknowledged the widely shared criticism that, instead of taming the wilderness of Oriental literature, his own style 'abound[ed] too much with those desultory rhetorical flourishes, so common, and often so disgusting, in Asiatic productions' (I, 62).[27]

Critics adapted the metaphor of exploration to reflect the difficulties inherent in this interpretive challenge. Maurice admitted that he was wholly unprepared for such overgrown literary jungles:

> I frankly own to the candid reader that I knew not, at the time, the full extent and magnitude in which I had embarked. At my very entrance into the grand historic field, through the whole ample circuit of which it became necessary for me to range, a field over-run with exotic and luxurient vegetation, such a prospect unfolded itself, as, I confess, at once disheartened and terrified me . . . so deeply were the wild fables of Indian Mythology blended with the authentic annals of regular History. (*Indian Antiquities*, I, 20)

This intellectual wilderness was intimidating, Maurice acknowledged, but at least Orientalists were able to rely on trails blazed by their European colleagues: 'Sir William Jones afforded the clue which has directed my path through this dark and intricate labyrinth' (quoted in *MR* 32 (1800): 54). Like his protégé (and like his Hollywood namesake, Indiana), Jones emphasized that attempts to retrieve the obscured narratives of Oriental culture were as potentially rewarding as they were dangerous:

> To what conclusions these inquiries will lead, I cannot yet clearly discern; but, if they lead to truth, we shall not regret our journey through this dark region of ancient history, in which, while we proceed step by step, and follow every glimmering of certain light, that presents itself, we must beware of those false rays and luminous vapours, which mislead *Asiatick* travellers by an appearance of water, but are found on a near approach to be deserts of sand. (I, 71)

If literary research could be heroicized through a symbolic recourse to the rhetoric of exploration, the epistemological confusion surrounding interpretive work could be similarly valorized as high personal adventure.

The equation of Britain with literary freedom was disrupted by
the fact that these texts languished in similar obscurity in Britain,
either ignored or read as exotic diversions rather than sources of
knowledge. Ouseley remarked in his *Persian Miscellanies; or, an Essay
to Facilitate the Reading of Persian Manuscripts* (1795) that 'the great
mass of Asiatic literature . . . yet remains in manuscript' (x). '[N]o
progress can be made', the *British Critic* agreed in its review of the
Essay,

towards obtaining the treasures, thus lying dormant on the shelves of
our public libraries, till the varied characters in which they are written
shall be more generally understood. It is too much to be lamented, that
the manuscripts in our public collections containing those treasures, are
rather viewed as objects of curiosity, than studied as sources of information; the enlightening of the mind is forgotten amid the splendid
illuminations that adorn the volume. (7 (1796): 1–2)

The transplantation of these Oriental manuscripts to the shelves
of British public libraries was not in itself enough; in order for
their treasures to be fully possessed, they had to be situated within
the proper epistemological framework, encountered not as objects
of curiosity but as sources of information by an enlightened reading public. In other words, they had to stop being read for the
pictures. In *A Grammar of the Persian Language* (1771), Jones had
announced his regret that 'the fine productions of a celebrated
nation should remain in manuscript upon the shelves of our publick libraries, without a single admirer who might open their treasures to his countrymen, and display their beauties to the light' (II,
121). He attributed part of the blame for 'the neglect of the Persian language' in Britain to 'the great scarcity of books, which are
necessary to be read before it can be perfectly learned', but, he
emphasized, the problem had just as much to do with the incorrect
forms of interest demonstrated by an eager reading public: 'the
greater part of them are preserved in the different museums and
libraries of Europe, where they are shewn more as objects of curiosity than as sources of information; and are admired, like the
characters on a Chinese screen, more for their gay colours than
for their meaning' (122).

Complaints about the neglect of Oriental texts within England
implied that the English reading public was characterized by the
same 'false taste' that was routinely attributed to Oriental cultures, a concern that was intensified by wider anxieties about the

state of literature generally. But like the problem of the illiberal nature of the violence that haunted imperial administrations, anxieties about this reduplication of the conditions from which Oriental texts were supposedly being saved could be contained by the suggestion that it was the different ways that both cultures dealt with this situation which highlighted their unique identities. What was for Orientals a sign of cultural decline was more likely to be seen in Britain as a challenge that would inspire the selfless exertions of authors. Maurice suggested that his *Indian Antiquities* was intended to alleviate the difficulties created by the obscurity of Oriental texts: '*in one work, of small expense,* was to be combined the substance of all the most esteemed Persian and Arabian historians . . . productions mouldering upon the shelves of public libraries, or deposited in the inaccessible museums of learned individuals; productions equally high in value and difficult to be procured' (I, 42–3 (1793)).

Underlying the distinction between the rational exertions of British Orientalists and the deceptive and confused nature of both Oriental texts and the cultures in which they languished, was a political argument about the legitimacy of Britain's colonial hegemony. The distinction between truth and superstition, which was so befuddled in Oriental historical records, was homologous to the distinction between liberty and despotism: the right to sovereignty was bound up with a capacity for coherent and rational self-definition.[28] It is in this light that we might read Charles Burney's comment that he had undertaken *A General History of Music* in order 'to fill up, as well as I was able, a chasm in English literature' (I, xi (1776)). The *Annual Register* hailed Bruce's *Travels to Discover the Source of the Nile* as a work that 'fills a great chasm in the history of the universe' ((1790): 167). In contrast to this commitment to collective self-knowledge on behalf of not only the nation but the universe itself, the absence of any indication of rational exertion in a society's literary pursuits implied a corresponding incapacity for civic responsibility. A people so unable to govern their own imaginings, however luxuriant their imaginative potential might be, were characterized by what the *Monthly Review* referred to as the East's '*barbarous effeminacy* [which] excludes the improvements of reason and knowledge' and were, therefore, best governed by other, more rational races (10 (1793): 444–5).[29]

This belief did not, however, eliminate the threat of engulfment posed by the incorporation of native cultures whose apparent absence of any consistent identity was perceived as a monstrous formlessness capable of obscuring Britain's own historical self-consciousness. Jones warned that the '*Indian* territories, which providence has thrown into the arms of *Britain* for their perfection and welfare', contained

a placid and submissive people, who multiply with such increase, even after the ravages of famine, that, in one collectorship out of *twenty-four*, and that by no means the largest or best cultivated ... there have lately been found, by an actual enumeration, a *million* and *three hundred thousand* native inhabitants; whence it should seem, that in all *India* there cannot now be fewer than *thirty millions* of black *British* subjects. (*Collected Works*, I, 150)

By submitting so easily to a form of rule to which the British were themselves constitutionally unable to submit, these foreign subjects threatened to rewrite the authenticating myths of civil society in the alienating terms of self-difference, a condition that was most poignantly evoked by the hybridized spectre of that anomalous group, 'black *British* subjects', whose reproductive excesses were a metonym for a transgressive potential which endangered the coherence of the narratives of empire. Such a confusion, far from diminishing the attractions of Oriental literature, only added to the reassuring potential of that form of social mastery. To know who a people were, even if they were incapable of knowing that themselves, was to establish oneself as their legitimate governor and to exert some kind of controlling influence on a cultural shapelessness which threatened the colonial enterprise.

Whatever the limitations of the Orientalist respect for the autonomy of native customs, it would in a few decades give way to the more strident cultural chauvinism of the 'Anglicist' approach. Arguing that 'a single shelf of a good European library was worth the whole native literature of India and Arabia', Thomas Macaulay insisted that the liberality of the government of British India ought to be measured not in terms of its respect for cultural differences but in its commitment to reorienting the experience of difference according to a hierarchy of cultural values which more accurately reflected the disciplinary needs of the imperial administration.[30] He pointed out that the Orientalist emphasis on accommodating local customs had always been contained within a wider recognition of the superiority of Britain's cultural traditions. However laudable their liberality might have been, he argued, this more relativist view was in fact a mistake, not merely because of the 'absolutely immeasurable' superiority of Britain's cultural traditions, but because Arabic and Hindu traditions could only be understood as a series of delusions, exaggerations, and mistakes: 'History, abounding with kings thirty feet high, and reigns thirty thousand years long – and Geography, made up of seas of treacle and seas of butter'.[31] Governing an empire meant ruling over a population which must be rescued from a depravity that was most forcefully signalled by the worthlessness of its literary traditions. The introduction of English studies, he explained, was the only possible way of redeeming an otherwise culturally bankrupt people.

The prior emphasis on the capacity of Oriental texts to reveal a 'true' native identity re-emerged in what Viswanathan describes as the colonial administration's 'Platonic' emphasis on an English education's power 'to awaken the colonial subjects to a memory of their innate character', placing 'the Indian reader in a position where he renews contact with himself, recovering his true essence and identity from the degradation to which it had become subject through native despotism'.[32] Whereas the earlier emphasis had suggested that by reading Oriental literature the British could know their colonial subjects better than these subjects were capable of knowing themselves, this more aggressively imperialist position insisted that natives were only capable of knowing their 'real' nature as a consequence of reading *British* literature.

Like the Orientalists' emphasis on literature as a medium for the retrieval of knowledge, the introduction of English studies in India was partly a defensive measure intended to forestall pressures for a missionary presence by cultivating a secular evangelism focused on British nationalism. This may have worked in the short term, but its logic of exporting European cultural traditions implicitly legitimated demands for a missionary presence in a way that the relative tolerance of the Orientalists had not. 'As to the native population', the *Quarterly* admitted in its 1830 review of the *Life of Bishop Reginald Heber, Bishop of Calcutta*, 'little progress is likely to be made by direct conversion' (43 (1830): 402). But, it continued, the instruction of the natives in 'English literature' – including reports of 'Shakspeare performed by Gentoos and Mahometans on the shore of the Ganges!' – was better viewed as a prelude than an alternative to instruction in the Christian faith:

> It is altogether a very curious indication of the deep root which English manners and opinions are taking in the minds of the Asiatics; and it may be fairly expected that they will smooth the way for the reception of the religion of England. (ibid.)

The end result of these developments was a growing conviction that 'British rule and Christian power were one and the same', which reinforced a related belief in the classical and therefore universal status of English literature as an expression of this providentialism.[33]

Textual analyses of the role played by literature in these ongoing debates about the nature of empire must not lose sight of the very real differences that existed between the efforts of the Orientalists to preserve a tolerance for native customs, and those more chauvinistic responses which sought to minimize the importance of the sensitivity of the imperial government to local practices. The relative benefits of these alternative approaches remain a subject of debate today. But whatever our own views, in the last decades of the eighteenth century these debates became fixed within the limits of a growing consensus about Britain's imperial status which insisted on the literary republic as a disinterested sphere of learning whose merits partially justified and partially helped to fine-tune the development of emergent geopolitical formations. Fundamental to this process was a strategic and moral confidence that this complex network of private and national interests would be supplemented by an ever-growing body of 'universal' literature.

Romantic revisions

From observing several cold romantic characters I have been led to confine the term romantic to one definition – false, or rather artificial, feelings. Works of genius are read with a prepossession in their favour, and sometimes imitated, because they were fashionable and pretty, and not because they were forcibly felt.

Mary Wollstonecraft, *A Vindication of the Rights of Men*

MEN OF GENIUS

In my Introduction I said that, whether they were sympathetic to the idea or not, most people who thought about it at all considered literature to be the basis of an information revolution with far-reaching political consequences. They may have embraced its promise or denounced its threat, but from Thomas Hardy to William Godwin to John Robison to T. J. Mathias to John Bowles, they identified literature as an 'engine' of change. I emphasized that the reformist argument that these changes would be progressive was a popular but highly contested idea that became increasingly difficult to defend as the political thermometer rose, and that subaltern counterpublics often served as lightning-rods for these anxieties precisely because they reproduced established ideas about the power of print as accurately as they did. I also suggested that some people had begun to insist on an alternative equation of literature with poetry, or more broadly, with 'creative writing', which highlighted the importance of the imagination rather than reason, and which tended to be described in a language that stressed the primacy of feelings rather than of scientific or philosophical debates.[1] I argued that these ideas, which we commonly associate with Romanticism, and which as Jerome McGann argues, continue to structure many of our critical assumptions today, constituted an emergent rather than a dominant discourse. In 1817, Coleridge was still able to write of Wordsworth that 'his fame belongs to another age'.[2]

I want to return to this aspect of the literary culture here, not to complete some totalizing historical study (an encyclopedic account of literature in the period), or even worse, to fulfill some progressivist teleology culminating in the Romantic poets, but to undermine the either/or scenario that implicitly legitimated the Romantic canon as a coherent and historically autonomous literary movement. As with my emphasis on charting the points of both consensus and difference between the reformist lower and middle classes, the radical and conservative elements of the middle class, and radical and conservative feminists, it is important to recognize that the beliefs which identify Romantic writers were shaped by their inscription within the very cultural dynamics that they aspired to emerge out of into the transcendental realm of human (rather than social) experience.

As I said in my introduction, my concern is not to adjudicate on the political character of the Romantics' ideas about poetry and social relations but rather to explore the political complexities that are inherent in our own relation to those writers. Critics such as E. P. Thompson and Nicholas Roe have offered compelling arguments for the continuing reformist integrity of poets such as William Wordsworth and S. T. Coleridge. In 'Disenchantment or Default? A Lay Sermon', Thompson argues that their poetic evolution in the later 1790s was less a rejection of reform than of Godwinian abstraction in favour of a turn 'to something more local, but also more humanly engaged' (36). Roe similarly defends Wordsworth's 'turn from revolutionary politics to marginal life' as an 'imaginative commitment to humanity' that is 'strongly continuous with dissenting and radical theories of human relationship and community'.[3]

Both critics share a sense that Wordsworth's and Coleridge's poetic evolution was shaped by intellectual crisis, but as Thompson argues, critics who focus on the reactionary element of this crisis miss the ongoing spirit of affirmation which is also a part of their writings (36). For Thompson, the problem is not that the Romantic period is foreign to our own experiences, but, on the contrary, that it is too similar: 'It is no good if we see only the recoil, or the doubt: yet so obsessed was a recent generation of critics with similar experiences of disenchantment in their own time, that this has been the tendency'.[1] Writing in 1968, Thompson was ready to consign this conservatism to the past behaviour of 'a recent generation', but Roe, writing twenty-four years later, identifies the same dynamic in 'the particularly coercive attitudes' of 'some new historicist readings ... to texts, contexts and earlier understandings of Romantic imagination' – a disposition that Roe aligns with 'the recent failure of Marxism as a force for world revolution' and the pressures of living in 'a post-revolutionary age, dominated by a "greedy and unsocial selfishness"'.[5]

As I said in my introduction, I am also interested in exploring the political complexities which inhere in our critical relationship to that period. But I want to do so by posing the question of what it would mean to read the Romantics in a different context than the political struggle which tends to frame our encounters with their work. I want to conclude this book by situating Wordsworth's Preface to the 1802 *Lyrical Ballads* within the broader and more complex literary landscape that I have sketched out so far – a move which simultaneously leaves room for other voices and ideas, and complicates our sense of the relation of the Romantics to those other literary energies.

The subjectivist ideas about literature that we now call Romantic are frequently read biographically in terms of an author's consolation for political dejection.[6] This may in itself be accurate, but what is not stressed enough is that writers were responding to crises in print culture as well, and that in both cases they inverted rather than rejected the dominant ideas of their day, reformulating them with an emphasis on private experience rather than the public sphere. If literature had become the place where an individual manifestly *could not* express any idea on any topic, Romantic arguments stressed the power of the poet to give voice to anything of enduring human importance, but in a safely internalized world of individual subjectivity. The supposed inclusivity of the public sphere re-emerged in the emphasis on poetry as the expression of truths which applied to all men, or more accurately, to 'man' abstracted from any specialist knowledge or social context. I shall conclude with a reading of one of the main prose texts that we associate with this argument, but first I want to emphasize the extent to which this shift in focus was itself a response to the combined excesses of the French Revolution *and* the information revolution by way of another brief look at Lloyd's *Edmund Oliver* (1798).

Not only did *Edmund Oliver* teach troubled reformers how to bury the disruptive spectre of the masculine woman who was determined to enjoy her share in the blessings of the Enlightenment, it provided a kind of road map charting the retreat from the public world of literary engagement to the private realm of pastoral insularity. Structured as the salvation of an Enlightenment reformer, the novel functions as a kind of before-and-after advertisement for life beyond the public sphere – both philosophically and biographically, given Lloyd's residence with Coleridge in late 1796 and early 1797.[7] Like Burke, Charles Maurice, who is positioned squarely at the moral centre of the novel, rejected the possibility that 'the constant habit of attack and defence, of intellectual gladiatorship, adopted in literary and argumentative circles' could have anything to do with the promotion of truth (*Edmund Oliver*, 53):

You will hear Edmund, in the circles of London, that the society and frequent intercourse of fellow beings which towns only admit of, are necessary to the growth of mind; to calling forth the activities of the intellect: that men of genius are found in clusters, and that frequent collision is the only mean of eliciting truth. So far am I from admitting this as a fact, that I would exactly reverse the proposition: and insist that no greatness of character, no vastness of conception were ever nursed except in solitude, and seclusion. (52)

Rather than reject the communicative appeal of the public sphere altogether, Lloyd emphasized that persuasion, if it was ever to 'eradicate habits, disentangle the foldings of prejudice, and regenerate the mind', demanded precisely the sort of close personal relationship which advances in print culture had enabled society to transcend: 'we must have gained the confidence of the person we wish to reform; cultivated sympathies with him; and twined ourselves round his heart . . . We must be sentient before we can be rational beings' (127–30). Whatever Godwin's optimism about the ability of 'the collision of mind with mind' to contribute to the general good, Lloyd rewrote the public sphere as a scene of self-indulgent exhibitionism, a dehumanizing force leading to a spirit of irrationality that could only be countered through the intimacy of personal relationships. It may have dressed itself up in the rhetoric of reform, but what most needed to be reformed were its own excesses. At the end of this road leading away from the literary public sphere were the creative ideas and energies of the Romantics, for whom the dream of spiritual regeneration displaced any emphasis on the utility of rational debate about particular issues. The keyword for this new emphasis on subjectivist expression was poetry. Nor, for many of those who held this position, could poetry even be reduced to particular texts, which would be to link it with the objective world of concrete things. Poetry was more a kind of spirit or mode of perception.[8]

There are three main consequences of the cultural dynamics that I have been exploring in this book for interpretations of Romantic poetry. First, it means that Romantic poets were situating themselves not only in comparison with earlier forms of poetry, but with these prior definitions of literature (as knowledge) generally. It suggests that they were responding not simply to the experience of political fragmentation but to crises in print culture as well. Finally, they were often doing so by reshaping existing languages of cultural value in private terms rather than departing from these 'public' languages altogether.

As I suggested in my Introduction, engaging with the issue of professionalism involves shifting our focus away from the question of national agency to an alternative sense of politics as a struggle for different forms of distinction. In this latter case, literature's significance lies in its potential to serve as a powerful form of symbolic capital rather than as an engine of social change. Nor is it a matter of choosing between the two definitions; on the contrary, exploring the meaning of 'literature' in the period requires a bifocal approach that is sensitive to the interpenetration of these alternative political fields. I want to finish by offering a reading of William Wordsworth's Preface to the 1802 *Lyrical Ballads* which situates a familiar Romantic argument within this more nuanced cultural landscape that does not assume in advance the primacy of Romantic values.

WILLIAM WORDSWORTH'S SOCIAL CONTRACT

I want to read Wordsworth's Preface by expanding on David Simpson's comment that Wordsworth's poetry constitutes 'a radical *literature* rather than a *radical* literature' – innovative writing rather than politics by other means.[9] More specifically, I want to suggest that the radicalism of Wordsworth's literary ideas lies not in any break which his work may have made with contemporary assumptions about poetry, though this is what he himself suggests, but in his estimation of the relative significance of poetry in comparison with the more popular idea of literature as the basis of an information revolution whose implications were both exciting and worrying. Wordsworth's arguments for the importance of a more naturalistic form of poetry are frequently seen as a challenge to the reductive effects of too mechanistic an emphasis on reason and to the inadequacies of established ideas about poetry. To an extent this is obviously true, but I want to suggest that Wordsworth inverts rather than rejects the dominant literary preoccupations of his day, and that in doing so, he offers a far more radically revisionary view of literature (one which remains influential) than his more explicit condemnation of ornate poetry would suggest. Whereas professional authors adapted the discourse of classical republicanism to their own bourgeois ends, Wordsworth mimics the language of Enlightenment reform in order to legitimize his own, very different emphasis on the social role of literature as poetry, and what is inseparable from that, on the status of the author as poet.

Like the bourgeois ideal of publicity, Wordsworth bases his estimation of the importance of literature on both its comprehensive scope and its social inclusiveness: 'Poetry is the first and last of all knowledge ... which all men carry about with them' (II, 396). Poetry deals with all subjects, and does so in a way that all men can relate to, simply by being human. This universality has nothing to do with the range of practical subjects with which literature concerns itself, though. Instead, and quite the opposite, poetry unveils a scene of knowledge which is universally binding to the extent that it avoids particular fields of specialized study.

Wordsworth does not simply reproduce the Enlightenment goals of universality and inclusiveness in radically subjectivist terms, however. His description of the nature of good poetry internalizes a familiar political saga within a wholly literary context. For Wordsworth, poetry was itself both the site of 'corruptions' and the means of redressing them (406). These corruptions were the result of the growing preponderance of 'artificial distinctions' (399) in the work of poets who 'indulge in arbitrary and capricious habits of expression' (387). However pleasing these arbitrary devices and artificial distinctions might be to the unenlightened Reader, they satisfy by 'flattering the Reader's self-love' (406) without appealing to 'the nobler powers of the mind' that reside in the exercise of the imagination (404). Like reformist critics who celebrated individual merit over the pageantry of aristocratic privilege, Wordsworth rejects the artificial pomp of unnatural language in favour of an alternative form of prestige that is simultaneously more basic and more dignified. Poetry which eschews the false elevation of poetic diction 'will of itself form a distinction far greater than would at first be imagined' (392). It will be both plainer and more elevated than existing forms of poetry because it will substitute an accurate reflection of the essential dignity of mankind for 'the gaudiness and inane phraseology of many modern writers' (386). The more poetry turns its back on what people mistakenly identify as the trappings of literary distinction, the greater will its distinction ultimately be.

These artificial and arbitrary practices, which amounted to a form of conspicuous display based on unnatural hierarchies, were bad because they appealed to inferior aspects of the human mind, and also because they had created a gap between poetic language and 'the language really spoken by men' (392). 'The Poet' and 'the Reader' ought to be united,[10] Wordsworth suggests, not only because they speak the same language, but because they are bound by what amounts to a contract. As with any contract, it is important that both parties understand exactly what it is they are subscribing to before they enter into a binding agreement. 'It is supposed, that by the act of writing in verse an Author makes a formal engagement that he will gratify certain known habits of association; that he not only thus appraises the Reader that certain classes of ideas and expressions will be found in his book, but that others will be carefully excluded' (385–6).

Wordsworth is quick to assert that he is not offering the Reader his literary arguments in 'the selfish and foolish hope of *reasoning* him into an approbation of these particular Poems', but rather in order that the Reader will know in advance what to expect from them (385). He warns the Reader about his poems because he is well aware that many readers will be convinced 'that I have not fulfilled the terms of an engagement thus voluntarily contracted' (386). Knowing this, he 'request[s] the Reader's permission to

apprise him of a few circumstances relating to their *style*, in order
... that he may not censure me for not having performed what I
never attempted' (389–90). He offers these warnings because he
recognizes that, being out of step with the preferences of his day,
he is in danger of being accused of smuggling in foreign goods
under the name of verse. Readers 'will look round for poetry, and
will be induced to enquire by what species of courtesy these
attempts can be permitted to assume that title' (383). By cau-
tioning the Reader Wordsworth leaves him with no cause for com-
plaint: he has offered his work to the public with an appropriate
consumer warning. No one can object that they didn't know what
they were getting.

At a more fundamental level though, Wordsworth argues that
he is interested in the issue of this contract, not only in the negative sense of pre-empting any objections to his product, but more
positively, because he is trying to salvage the very possibility of
this mutual understanding from an unnecessary demise. Wordsworth may *seem* to be placing the contract between Poet and
Reader in jeopardy by wilfully departing from the poetic norms of
his age, but this is only because these norms already represent a
more profound violation of the terms of this agreement. When
poets depart from the actual spoken language of men, they insti-
tute a kind of despotism, indulging in a literary style that is 'arbitrary, and subject to infinite caprices upon which no calculation
whatever can be made' (398). When this happens, and regardless
of the popularity of these innovations, 'the Reader is utterly at the
mercy of the Poet' (ibid.). There can be no calculation of what is
to be shared between them, and therefore no legitimate way of
establishing a mutually binding agreement. Nothing can be taken
on trust or in good faith. In such a situation, there can be no talk
of a contract. Poetry becomes a kind of tyranny.

In order to rectify this situation, the Poet must re-establish his
sense of mutuality with the Reader. He must 'descend from [the]
supposed height' which the use of artificial devices affords him
'and, in order to excite rational sympathy, he must express himself
as other men express themselves' (398). By acknowledging their
mutuality through his use of the real language of men, the Poet
will resurrect the possibility of some sort of contract between himself and his Reader. When he does not mystify his readers or
forget his responsibility to them, 'he is treading upon safe ground,

and we know what we are to expect from him' (ibid.). What might seem at first to be a merely literary matter is ultimately a matter of justice, of *doing* justice to the Reader, and even more dramatically, of establishing the conditions within which this aspiration for justice becomes possible. It is, in other words, a reformist vision based on an understanding between Poet and Reader which reproduces in the literary domain the social contract theory of eighteenth-century liberalism. Not only must a government, if its authority is to be legitimate, accurately reflect the true interests of its people, it must do so because at some hypothetical originary moment, those people consented to be ruled by this particular form of government.

Wordsworth stakes his claim to the social importance of the Poet on a reformist argument that is analogous to the Enlightenment concept of literature as an engine of change, but he does so by offering a circular vision which celebrates poetry as both the means and the subject of change. Within this argument, literature becomes a *pharmakon*. It is both poison and antidote, the evil which must be uprooted and the cure that is at hand, the site of oppression and the means of liberation. Purged of artificial distinctions and arbitrary innovations on the one hand, and cleansed of 'the vulgarity and meanness of ordinary life' on the other (392), poetry will become an expression of those 'essential passions' and sympathies which bind all men (and, presumably, women) together (386). When poetry accurately reflects the real nature of men, which is to say, when poets write in a way that resembles the way men actually speak, the Poet and the Reader will be united in a more harmonious community based on a shared recognition of the true nature of the language of men, and of the essential passions which this language gives voice to.[11]

The argument draws its force by re-establishing dominant Enlightenment ideas about literature and reform in private rather than public terms. Within the logic of these substitutions, 'language' functions as a kind of metonym for political authority, and human 'nature' as a metonym for rights or interests – depoliticized terms which structure the whole of Wordsworth's redemptive vision. The corruption of language must be addressed in order that Poet and Reader be able to exist on a greater level of parity. They will be able to enter into a contract with one another only when poetic language faithfully reflects the real language used by men. When this is the case, poetry will be the site of a more genuine form of knowledge about man's nature. Like Hannah More's assurance that her educational programmes were designed to teach the lower orders 'principles, not opinions', Wordsworth re-envisions the ideal of universality in a way that neutralizes the threats generated by the appropriation of public sphere arguments by subaltern groups such as women and the working class.[12] Poetry remained universally valid because it dealt with aspects of the human condition that were equally relevant to all, but this in no way legitimated the particular agendas of radical groups.

Writing about Wordsworth's theory in the *Biographia Literaria* (1817), Coleridge mocked the idea that 'the reader is utterly at the mercy of the Poet'. What Wordsworth had in mind, he insisted, was less a description of a poet than of 'a fool or madman: or at best of a vain or ignorant fantast!' Not only was the description of the poet inappropriate, Coleridge continued, the whole idea made no sense as a description of the act of reading. 'How is the reader at the *mercy* of such men', he asked matter-of-factly, 'If he continue to read their nonsense, is it not his own fault?'.[13] The point, of course, is that the description, both of the Poet and of the act of reading, *needed* to be inaccurate in order to reinforce the implicit political parallel that structures Wordsworth's argument. Not to have insisted that such a situation was binding – to have admitted that the reader had other options (such as closing the book) or that this sort of poetry was less than despotism – would have deprived Wordsworth of the discursive power of the language of political reform which underpins his entire argument.

In place of the discourse of rational enquiry Wordsworth substitutes an emphasis on 'pleasure' (a keyword for the utilitarians whose moral calculus the Romantics were so vigorously opposed to) as the defining feature of the communicative process that is initiated by poets. Instead of respecting the sovereignty of reason, the Poet 'writes under one restriction only, namely, the necessity of giving immediate pleasure' (II, 395). Far from diverging with the moral and political concerns that were associated with reformist invocations of reason though, Wordsworth insists that 'the pleasure which I hope to give by the Poems now presented ... is in itself of high importance to our taste and moral feelings' (393). Pleasure is not to be seen in opposition with moral concerns; nor does its centrality to Wordsworth's theory of poetry signify a lack of seriousness of purpose. On the contrary, pleasure fulfils an ethical role more important than reason itself. 'We have no sympathy but what is propagated by pleasure ... We have no knowledge, that is, no general principles drawn from the contemplation of particular facts, but what has been built up by pleasure, and exists in us by pleasure alone' (395).

The danger that haunts Wordsworth's argument is the threat of excess that is implicit in his emphasis on poetry as a form of stimulation that originates with an 'overflow of powerful feelings' (400), and which leads to 'an overbalance of pleasure' (399, 401). If pleasure gets out of hand, if it becomes a new form of excess in itself, then it will lead not to moral rejuvenation, but to the sort of disorder and personal turmoil that was more commonly associated with women novel readers. Poetry, Wordsworth argued, because it tends 'to produce excitement in co-existence with an overbalance of pleasure', will necessarily encourage 'an unusual and irregular state of the mind' (399). When such a situation becomes extreme, it is the equivalent in Wordsworth's psychological focus to political revolution: 'ideas and feelings do not, in that state, succeed each other in accustomed order', which means that 'there is some danger that the excitement may be carried beyond its proper bounds' (399). Like critics who worried that the end result of Enlightenment ideas about literature was the popularity of *Rights of Man* with groups who lacked an educational antidote to Paine's dangerous arguments, Wordsworth worries that his own ideas have the potential to lead to equally dangerous (psychological rather than social) instability.

Aware of these dangers, Wordsworth insists that his mission to teach the reader to feel is carefully balanced against other strategies designed to ensure moderation. By writing in such a way 'that the feeling therein developed gives importance to the action and situation, and not the action and situation to the feeling', Wordsworth aims at teaching the Reader to feel without the aid of 'gross and violent stimulants' (389). But because this situation – however preferable it might be to a dependence on stimulants – could still lead to mental disorder, he further assures his readers that the 'excitement' produced by poetry will be counterbalanced by the effects of metre, which 'cannot but have great efficacy in tempering and restraining the passion by an intertexture of ordinary feeling' (399). Metre will dilute the psychological effect of

poetry because its regularity is calming and because of its 'tendency ... to throw a sort of half-consciousness of unsubstantial
existence over the whole composition' (ibid.).

Poetry, in other words, becomes the equivalent of a safe drug,
capable of weaning people off other more dangerous intoxicants by
offering them a stimulation that is both satisfying and relatively
harmless. Poetry immunizes the Reader against the danger of
excess by exposing him to precisely those situations which are
most likely to lead to excess. It teaches people to feel, but not
to feel too much. Wordsworth thus summons up the dangers of
revolution. He calls the threat of it to mind, dwells on it, highlights
the number of forces that contribute to its potency, but only in
order to unveil a force that is capable of warding it off. Poetry has
the ability to reform society by developing people's sympathetic
capacity, but only if the prevailing standards of poetry are themselves reformed – all of which highlights the importance of
Wordsworth's literary mission.

Wordsworth's argument about the importance of reforming
artificial and elaborate styles of poetry displaces the more secular
ideal of the republic of letters by using the language of this
broader literary perspective within a wholly subjectivist approach.
But rather than confining this revision of traditional ideas about
literature to an implicit level, Wordsworth sizes the Poet up
against the 'Man of science', and against other specialists such as
the Historian and Biographer, in order to assert as clearly as possible the supreme importance of the Poet. It is true, he admits,
that the Poet and the Man of science function in complementary
ways:

Poetry is the breath and finer spirit of all knowledge; it is the
impassioned expression which is in the countenance of all Science ... If
the labours of Men of science should ever create any material revolution,
direct or indirect, in our condition, and in the impressions which we
habitually receive, the Poet ... will be at his side, carrying sensation into
the midst of the objects of the science itself. (396)

Not only does the Poet focus on a form of knowledge which constitutes the very essence of scientific exploration, the Man of science,
if insightful enough, will recognize that pleasure, the central concern of the Poet, is also the guiding principle of those individuals
whose efforts are apparently directed in very different fields of
learning:

We have no knowledge ... but what has been built up by pleasure, and exists in us by pleasure alone. The Man of science, the Chemist and Mathematician, whatever difficulties and disgusts they may have had to struggle with, know and feel this. However painful may be the objects with which the Anatomist's knowledge is connected, he feels that his knowledge is pleasure; and where he has no pleasure he has no knowledge. (395)

Pleasure lies at the heart of all scientific endeavours. The Poet, however, is a kind of scientist whose research is pleasure itself. Because of this, he is not only as important as these Men of science, he turns out to be more important.

Whereas the Poet 'converses with general nature', the Man of science restricts himself to 'conversing with those particular parts of nature which are the object of his studies' (396). The Poet offers a form of knowledge which is simultaneously more general and, because it is grounded in 'daily life', more immediate than the detached concerns of the Man of science, whose work can only ever have an indirect relation to lived experience:

The knowledge both of the Poet and the Man of science is pleasure; but the knowledge of the one cleaves to us as a necessary part of our existence, our natural and unalienable inheritance; the other is a personal and individual acquisition, slow to come to us, and by no habitual and direct sympathy connecting us with our fellow-beings. The Man of science seeks truth as a remote and unknown benefactor; he cherishes and loves it in his solitude: the Poet, singing a song in which all human beings join with him, rejoices in the presence of truth as our visible and hourly companion. (396)

Critics who portray Wordsworth as the prophet of the egotistical sublime, communing with nature and meditating on the continuing power of childhood memories and the importance of the imagination, tend to associate him with a solipsistic version of literature which contrasts sharply with the more cosmopolitan ideal of the public sphere as the site of an interpersonal communicative process. As historical descriptions, these accounts may be relatively accurate, but it is important to recognize that Wordsworth's argument explicitly reverses the contrast, celebrating the sociability of the Poet's song, if not the Poet himself, in contrast with the isolation and detachment of the Man of science. Wordsworth's emphasis that a poet is, above all else, 'a man speaking to men', reproduces one of the central characteristics of Enlightenment ideas about literature as a communicative process (393). But rather than simply asserting this on behalf of the Poet, Wordsworth does so in a way that questions the access of other forms of literature to this social focus. Nor was it simply the 'hard sciences' with which Wordsworth took issue:

The obstacles which stand in the way of the fidelity of the Biographer and Historian, and of their consequent utility, are incalculably greater than those which are to be encountered by the Poet who comprehends the dignity of his art. The Poet writes under one restriction only, namely, the necessity of giving immediate pleasure to a human Being possessed of that information which may be expected from him, not as a lawyer, a physician, a mariner, an astronomer, or a natural philosopher, but as a Man. Except this one restriction, there is no object standing between the Poet and the image of things; between this, and the Biographer and Historian, there are a thousand. (395)

Whatever obstacles might exist, they are compounded by the effects of specialization. The individual who writes as 'a Man' not only produces a form of knowledge which is immediately available to all human beings without requiring them to become specialists in some particular field of learning, he also enjoys the benefit of a more immediate access to his subject matter. To be anything but a Poet – the only type of writer who rises above the division of intellectual labour – is to place a thousand obstacles between yourself and whatever you might choose to write about.

Just what was at stake in Wordsworth's polemical stance becomes a lot clearer if we read the 1802 Preface alongside the first volume of the *Edinburgh Review*, which was launched in the same year. Reviewing Robert Southey's poem, *Thabala, the Destroyer*, Francis Jeffrey widened his critical glance to comment on 'a *sect* of poets, that has established itself in this country within these ten or twelve years' (1 (1802): 63). Gesturing to Wordsworth's Preface, which he described as 'a kind of manifesto, that preceded one of their most flagrant acts of hostility', Jeffrey professed an inability to identify the 'doctrines of this sect', except to describe them as '*dissenters* from the established systems of poetry and criticism' (65). Echoing Wordsworth's opposition to the tyranny of literary conventions, Jeffrey noted that the 'disciples of this school boast much of its originality, and seem to value themselves very highly, for having broken loose from the bondage of ancient authority, and re-asserted the independence of genius'

(63–4). But instead of sharing Wordsworth's confidence, Jeffrey denounced the *'sect'* as the 'most formidable conspiracy that has lately been formed against sound judgement in matters poetical' (64). Turning what he implied was their elevated claims back against them, Jeffrey mocked the gap between their aspirations and their performance. 'That our new poets have abandoned the old models, may certainly be admitted', he allowed, 'but we have not been able to discover that they have yet created any models of their own; and are very much inclined to call in question the worthiness of those to which they have transferred their admiration' (ibid).

The review reversed Wordsworth's adaptation of a reformist vocabulary to a literary scenario by accusing the new poets of the same crimes that the Preface had promised to redress. Rather than ridding poetry of the despotism of its artificialities, these poets were directing their energies into an attempt 'to seduce many into an admiration of the false taste (as it appears to us) in which most of these productions are composed' (ibid). Instead of achieving a simplicity that directed the reader's attention away from the writer's style to the subject matter of the poem, they indulged in 'an affectation of great simplicity and familiarity of language' which had the opposite effect of continually directing the reader's attention to their own inventiveness (ibid). Far from setting the reader free from the tyranny of arbitrary stylistic practices, these literary *'dissenters'* had embarked on a set of innovations which reinforced the problem (ibid).

Their misjudged determination to celebrate the vulgar elements of society had worse consequences than just sullying the grandeur of their poetry. Driven by a 'splenetic and idle discontent with the existing institutions of society', they were predisposed to focus on the 'disorders' of society rather than on 'the wonders and the pleasures which civilization has created' (71). But instead of confronting the 'vice and profligacy of the lower orders' in any responsible way, they tended to depict them as the victims of the 'present vicious constitution of society' (71). Determined to live outside the laws of literary composition themselves, they were all too inclined to sympathise with those who had chosen to live outside of the laws of their society.

Jeffrey's dismissive attitude becomes a bit more understandable when the *Thabala* review is read alongside the other reviews in the volume, the majority of which received the same derisive treatment – what was frequently described as the 'slashing' style favoured by the literary reviews. But it also reflects Jeffrey's sense of the contradictions inherent in the Lake School's 'affectation of simplicity'. Far from rejecting a poetic style that aimed to produce a more 'natural' effect by focusing on the lower orders in a more prosaic writing style, the *Edinburgh* praised these qualities as the chief sources of William Cowper's poetic strength only six months later. It praised Cowper for reversing the 'gradual refinement of taste [which] had, for nearly a century, been weakening the vigour of original genius' by passing 'from the imitation of poets, to the imitation of nature', a shift that was achieved by focusing on 'the ordinary occupations and duties of domestic life, and ... the common scenery of a rustic situation' (2 (1803): 81). Again like Wordsworth, the *Edinburgh* emphasized that this shift in content ought to be doubled by a corresponding shift in language:

He took as wide a range in language, too, as in matter; and shaking off the tawdry incumbrance of that poetical diction which had nearly reduced the art to the skilful collocation of a set of appropriated phrases, he made no scruple to set down in verse every expression that would have been admitted in prose, and to take advantage of all the varieties with which our language could supply him. (81)

The contradiction between the *Edinburgh*'s reaction to the same innovations in the poetry of Cowper and Wordsworth's sect suggests that the latter group's felony lay not in their rustic subject matter or plain language, but in the cultivation of a deliberately eccentric (and therefore unnatural) style which, for Jeffrey, was more egotistical than sublime.

To a degree, this seemed to come down to personality. In contrast to the 'idle discontent' of these literary conspirators, 'the habitual temper of [Cowper's] mind was toleration and indulgence' (80). It would have been difficult to find an author 'so much disposed to show the most liberal and impartial favour to the merit of others in literature, in politics, and in the virtues and accomplishments of social life' (ibid.). In other words, unlike Cowper, the 'new school' of poets were proving to be bad citizens of the republic of letters. Content to limit themselves to each other's company and predisposed to underestimate the worth of all literary endeavours other than their own, they contravened the code of sociability which (at the level of self-representation, at least) characterized the learned community's relations with one another. Wordsworth's dismissal of the importance of the Man of science, the biographer and the historian reflected his more basic failure to appreciate the significance of civility as a mode of affiliation common to the whole of the literary republic.

The irony of Jeffrey's clash with Wordsworth is that, whatever our conclusions today, Jeffrey was by far the more important literary figure of the period. But unlike Wordsworth's commitment to poetry as the unique domain of universal concerns, the *Edinburgh Review* which Jeffrey edited continued to reflect the wide array of interests that had characterized the eighteenth-century republic of letters. Reviews of poetry made up only a small fraction of the journal, whose first volume included reviews of political, historical, scientific, economic, biographical and travel writings, as well as Transactions of the Royal Society of Edinburgh. Like so many Enlightenment thinkers, the *Edinburgh*'s view of literature was based on a sense of both what it included, and the effects that it produced. In its review of Henry Thornton's *An Inquiry into the Nature and Effects of the Paper Credit of Great Britain,* the *Edinburgh* celebrated 'that diffused literature, which multiplies the demand for varied information, and has already liberalised the practitioners in almost every walk of industry' (1 (1802): 173). In both the scope of the books that it chose to review and in its faith in the progressive power of a 'diffused literature', the *Edinburgh* embraced precisely that wider version of print culture that Wordsworth's manifesto set itself against. The 'conspiracy' that Jeffrey detected in the writings of the 'new school' was directed not just against poetic conventions, but against a more fundamental understanding of literature generally.

Paradoxically, Wordsworth's characterization of the Poet as the only writer who addresses those issues which are most basic to us as 'enjoying and suffering beings', celebrates an ideal of the comprehensive scope of imaginative literature which effectively ruptured an already existing, and more generous, version of this same ideal (II, 397). Raymond Williams argues that:

What were seen at the end of the nineteenth century as disparate interests, between which a man must choose and in the act of choice declare himself poet or sociologist, were, normally, at the beginning of the century, seen as interlocking interests: a conclusion about personal feeling became a conclusion about society, and an observation of natural beauty carried a necessary moral reference to the whole and unified life of man. The subsequent dissociation of interests certainly prevents us from seeing the full significance of this remarkable period, but we must add also that the dissociation is itself in part a product of the nature of the Romantic attempt. (*Culture and Society*, 30)

Whereas the ideal of the public sphere was characterized by a sense of the close relationship between the various forms of knowledge which constituted literature, and of the abstract and practical opportunities which this definition generated, Wordsworth insists on disciplinary distinctions in order to celebrate poetry as the unique embodiment of this comprehensive dream. In place of the frequently used phrase 'literature and science', Wordsworth insists on a theory that might be paraphrased as 'literature *or* science'. If the Poet is a safely depoliticized one-man public sphere, communing with himself on the general complexities of the human race and singing a song which all men can relate to simply by being human, poetry becomes, if not the only song, at least the only song worth knowing.

Today there has been a shift in the opposite direction. Theoretical challenges to established literary practices have complicated the rules for the study of literature. When we go into a bookstore, many of us no longer know which section to look in. It may be Politics, or Philosophy, or Gender Studies, or History, or Psychology, or Geography, or even sometimes, but not always that often, Literary Criticism. Underpinning these changes has been a growing refusal to abstract the individual from the social context within which ideas about subjectivity are inevitably defined. As Anthony McIntyre puts it, 'lives happen within a context of a community's sense of self worth and sense of self esteem' (Woollacott). The backlash against these developments tends to denounce them, in strikingly familiar terms, as dangerous innovations, politically driven intrusions from outside the world of literary studies which threaten to contaminate the purity of that world by introducing abstract and inaccessible questions which miss or at least forget the point of 'great literature'. In *The Anatomy of Criticism*, for instance, Northrop Frye warned (in 1957!) that 'the absence of systematic criticism has created a power vacuum and all the other disciplines have moved in' (12). The problem with this objection is that it assumes that there is some stable phenomenon that is immediately recognizable as literature, and that this thing called literature, by its very nature, legitimates a particular range of theoretical approaches. But this forgets that the roots of literature in the modern era have less to do with the celebration of writing as aesthetic expression (and with the appropriate set of critical responses) than with these more theoretically challenging and interdisciplinary approaches.

As Terry Eagleton puts it, '[c]ritics who find such pursuits modish and distastefully new-fangled are, as a matter of cultural history, mistaken. They represent a contemporary version of the most venerable topics of criticism, before it was narrowed and impoverished to the so-called "literary canon" '.[14] The gap between what is recognized as 'literary' and what is merely 'textual' remains in flux, shifting throughout history, and riven with disagreements. Rather than struggling to resolve this problem by establishing some final idea about the relationship between the two (and whether we recognize it or not, 'the literary' is always defined differentially in terms of this relationship), it is perhaps more productive to explore these shifts and tensions in terms of ongoing and inherently political struggles to rethink literature as an productive form of symbolic capital. If one form of the separation of the literary from other more socially grounded concerns is rooted in ideas such as those we find in Wordsworth's Preface, it is important to remember that these ideas were themselves the product of a complex historical crisis of cultural identity and authority. It is possible to agree with aspects of Wordsworth's ideas about poetry without agreeing with his larger claim that poetry must eclipse more secular and interdisciplinary ideas about literature. But we as critics have already internalized the thrust of his argument if we imagine that his main struggle was with the poets of his day, rather than with wider attitudes towards the authority of print culture. Suspending the assumption that we know what literature *is* returns us to the task of exploring the ways different social constituencies formulated and answered the invitation posed by T. J. Mathias 'to consider the nature, variety and extent of the word, Literature'.[15] Sustaining this question enables us to place our own disposition towards particular constructions of literature within theoretical contexts that help to expose our ongoing complicity with many of those arguments from which we would like to think we have finally established a critical distance.

Notes

INTRODUCTION: PROBLEMS NOW AND THEN

1. *Languages of Nature*, ed. and intro. Jordanova, 10. See also Williams's heading under 'Literature' in *Keywords*, 150–4.
2. See, for instance, Greenblatt and Gunn (eds), *Redrawing the Boundaries*.
3. West, *New Cultural Politics*, 19–38.
4. For a discussion of similarities between the reaction against 'theory' in our own age and in the Romantic period, see Simpson, *Romanticism*, 1–17. Klancher suggests what is in many ways the same point viewed from the opposite direction, 'that the productive disarray of early nineteenth-century relations among writers, ideologies, discourses, and social audiences has a more immediate parallel to our own efforts to forge new, sometimes disruptive cultural connections' (*Making of English Reading Audiences*, 173).
5. Klancher, *Making of English Reading Audiences*, 10–11.
6. Darnton, *Kiss of Lamourette*, 152–3.
7. Ibid., 153.
8. Ibid., 152.
9. For a similar approach, see Reiss, *The Meaning of Literature*. Reiss argues 'that we understand our discursive operations and organizations as the creation and establishment of certain historical needs. Literature and its criticism compose one such cultural creation' (9). Although my own analysis often differs from that of Reiss, I share his point that discourses *create*, rather than simply respond to, 'historical needs' by valorizing particular forms of knowledge.
10. 2 June 1851; emphasis added. For the effort of the *Times* to position itself within print culture by stressing its economic and political independence, see Aspinall, *Politics and the Press*, 21; and Gilmartin, *Print Politics*, 45.
11. Kroker, for instance, claims that '[i]n the world of the silicon chip, there are no centres and no margins' (quoted in Cummings, "Virtual English", 15). More sceptical observers have focused on the extent to which these necessarily expensive technological oppor-

tunities, and the sorts of intellectual capital they presuppose, increase rather than surmount the gap between rich and poor, both within and between nations. Menzies has coined the phrase 'Silicon Curtain' after 'Iron Curtain' to convey the more negative effects of global corporate applications of electronic technologies (quoted in Stone, 'President's Report', 6).

12. Siskin, *Work of Writing*, 2.
13. Darnton, *Kiss of Lamourette*, xvii.
14. For a discussion of the problem of periodizing the Enlightenment, see Hulme and Jordanova (eds.) *The Enlightenment*, 2–4. For a more general critique of the issues involved in strategies of periodization, see Jameson, *Political Unconscious*, 27–8.
15. See Collins, *Profession of Letters*, and Roper, *Reviewing Before the Edinburgh*. A discussion of these claims forms the basis of the final section of chapter 2 below.
16. Pratt, *Gleanings in England*, IV, 314.
17. Fraser, 'Rethinking the Public Sphere', 123.
18. Coleridge, *Works*, VI, 36, 37.
19. Fraser, 'Rethinking the Public Sphere', 114.
20. Kramnick, *Republicanism*, 1, 20, 35.
    21. Wordsworth, *Poetical Works*, II, 389 (1802). I am treating the 1790s as a cultural moment. Because historical developments never begin or finish with the abruptness of calendar time, I will occasionally use sources from the late 1780s and early 1800s.
22. Yachnin, 'Politics of Theatrical Mirth', 4.
23. Klancher, *Making of English Reading Audiences*, 160.
24. Habermas, 'Further Reflections', 478–9.
25. Eley, 'Nations, Publics, and Political Cultures', 306.
26. Calhoun, *Habermas and the Public Sphere;* Garnham, 'Media and the Public Sphere'; Robbins, *The Phantom Public Sphere*.
27. Breen, *Women Romantics;* Copley and Whale (eds.), *Beyond Romanticism;* Lonsdale (ed.), *New Oxford Book of Eighteenth-Century Verse*; Mellor and Matlack, *British Literature*; Perkins (ed.), *English Romantic Writers*; Wu (ed.), *Romanticism*.
28. Klancher, 'English Romanticism'; Cole, 'Evading Politics', Young, *White Mythologies*.
29. I am thinking, for instance, of James Chandler's *Wordsworth's Second Nature: A Study of the Poetry and Politics* (Chicago University Press, 1994); Marjorie Levinson's *Wordsworth's Great Period Poems; Four Essays* (Cambridge University Press, 1986); David Simpson's *Wordsworth's Historical Imagination: The Poetry of Displacement* (New York, Methuen; 1987); and Alan Liu's *Wordsworth: The Sense of History* (Stanford University Press, 1989).
30. Young, *White Mythologies*, 88.
31. For a discussion of the theory of subjectivity implied by this, see Bohls, *Women Travel Writers*, 18–20.

32. Klancher, *Making of English Reading Audiences*, ix.
33. Stewart, 'State of Cultural Theory', 12.
34. See Baldick, *Social Mission;* Eagleton, *Function of Criticism*; Palmer, *Rise of English Studies;* Viswanathan, *Masks of Conquest.*
35. Philp, *Godwin's* Political Justice, 224.

1. THE REPUBLIC OF LETTERS

1. In her account of the republic of letters in France in the eighteenth century, Goodman argues that d'Alembert entertained similar doubts about the role of academies as those stressed by the *Analytical Review*, prior to his decision to promote his vision of social reform from within the French Academy (*Republic of Letters*, 27).
2. D'Israeli, *Curiosities of Literature*, 170 (1791).
3. Colley, *Britons*, 5.
4. O'Connor, *Measures of Ministry*, 59–60 (1794).
5. Todd, *Sign of Angelica*, 235.
6. Butler, *Romantics, Rebels, and Reactionaries*, 16.
7. Erskine, *Speeches*, II, 99 and 139–40 (1792).
8. For a study of the reconceptualization of authority both within the Enlightenment, and in the reaction to it, see Jordanova, 'Authoritarian Response'.
9. Godwin, *Political and Philosophical Writings*, III, 14–15.
10. Goldgar, *Impolite Learning*, 2.
11. Ibid., 239.
12. Goodman, 'Seriousness of Purpose'.
13. For an account of the financial boom in the book trade from 1780 until the crash in 1825, see Collins, *Profession of Letters*.
14. Habermas, *Structural Transformation*, 13, 16, 24, 25.
15. Ibid., 25.
16. Ibid., 29, 48, 50.
17. Hays, *Letters*, 13 (1793).
18. Barbauld, *Address to the Opposers*, 31 (1790).
19. Hays, *Letters*, 77 (1793).
20. Wollstonecraft, *Works*, VI, 16.
21. Macaulay, *Letters*, 11 (1790).
22. For historical accounts of technological and economic changes in the printing industry, see Handover and Plant. For a broad analysis of attitudes in the eighteenth century towards the importance of print culture, see Eisenstein, *Print Culture*; and more broadly still, *Printing Press*.
23. D'Israeli, *Curiosities of Literature*, 168 and 96.
24. For the importance of the postal system to the growth of the book trade, see Aspinall, *Politics and the Press*, 7; Collins, *Profession of Letters*, 37–40; and Vincent, *Literacy and Popular Culture*, 32–49. Aspinall

notes that Cobbett claimed that the speed, safety, cheapness, and regularity with which the Post Office circulated newspapers to all parts of the British Isles was the only feather in Pitt's cap (24). For coffee houses, see *Politics and the Press*, 27–9.

25. Wiles, 'Relish for Reading'.
26. Altick, *English Common Reader*, 60 and 39.
27. Aspinall, *Politics and the Press*; Neuberg, *Penny Histories;* Pedersen, 'Hannah More'.
28. Altick, *English Common Reader*, 17.
29. Thale notes that in London in the 1790s there were 'usually two, but sometimes three or four debating societies successful enough to advertise in the newspapers and to attract paying audiences of between 200 and 600 people', composed chiefly of 'artisans, mechanics, and shopkeepers' ('London Debating Societies', 58–9).
30. Thale, *Selections*, xx. See also chapter three below.
31. Curran, *Women Readers*, 192.
   32. Kramnick argues that '[a]mong these dissenters Joseph Priestley best qualifies as the principal architect of bourgeois radicalism. Radical in politics, laissez-faire theorist in economics, innovator in science and technology, founder of the modern Unitarian movement, Priestley schooled England's new men of business in the series of dissenting academies at which he taught while personally serving as the critical link between virtually all aspects of the progressive and innovative bourgeois nexus' (*Republicanism and Bourgeois Radicalism*, 45).
33. Kramnick, *Republicanism*, 44.
34. Philp, *Godwin's Political Justice*, 37.
35. Day, *Letters of Marius*, 17.
36. McLachlan, *English Education*, 28; Crawford, *Devolving English Literature,* 22; Wiles, 'Relish for Reading', 107–11.
37. Hohendahl, *Institution of Criticism*, 52.
38. Simpson, *Romanticism*, 11.
39. These mixed allegiances manifested themselves in the changing stances of political parties in and out of power. Pitt was himself originally in favour of parliamentary reform. And as Aspinall notes, 'The Liberty of the Press' was one of the classic toasts of Whig banquets, 'yet when they returned to power in 1782, and again in 1806, the Whigs made no attempt to increase that liberty by abolishing or reducing the oppressive stamp duties which Tory governments had imposed' (*Politics and the Press*, 66).
40. Kramnick, *Republicanism*, 19.
41. The attribution of the critique of publicity as bourgeois ideology to the nineteenth century (and to Marx in particular) has become something of a commonplace (Baker, 'Defining the Public Sphere', 187), but this critique was already associated with Burke in the early 1790s. Musselwhite argues that 'the *Reflections* cries out again and

again for the notion of 'ideology' which, alas for Burke, did not come into the language until six years after the *Reflections* were completed' ('Reflections', 159).

42. Burke, *Works*, V, 147. Subsequent page numbers in text.
43. In our own time, Simpson argues, 'the most macrocosmic social, intellectual, and educational calamities are being attributed by conservative commentators to an outbreak of "ideology" appearing in the classrooms as a new consciousness of gender and ethnicity and organized by the deeply bunkered command post known as "theory"' (*Romanticism*, 1).
44. Young, *Example of France*, 3–4.
45. Compare this with Benjamin's 'Angel of history': 'His face is turned toward the past. Where we perceive a chain of events, he sees one single catastrophe which keeps piling wreckage upon wreckage and hurls it in front of his feet. The angel would like to stay, awaken the dead, and make whole what has been smashed. But a storm is blowing from Paradise; it has got caught in his wings with such violence that the angel can no longer close them. This storm irresistibly propels him into the future to which his back is turned, while the pile of debris before him grows skyward. This storm is what we call progress' ('Theses on the Philosophy of History', 257–8).
46. For an example of the use of the term by reformers, see the *Monthly Review*'s comments on Wollstonecraft's *Rights of Woman*: 'Philosophy, which, for so many ages, has amused the indolent recluse with subtle and fruitless speculations, has, at length, stepped forth into the public walks of men, and offers them her friendly aid in correcting those errors which have hitherto retarded their progress toward perfection, and in establishing those principles and rules of action, by which they may be gradually conducted to the summit of human felicity' (8 (1792): 198).
47. Mathias, *Pursuits of Literature*, IV, xxiv (1797).
48. King, *Two Sermons*, I, 6 and 15.
49. Ibid., 25.
50. This sense of the dangerous frivolity of French theorists and of the deluded internationalism of those critics who are infected by their ideas, has not, of course, lost any of its rhetorical appeal. In his analysis of the 'mimicry of the styles and language of French and German critical debates', Craig denounces 'a vacuous internationalism which is destructive . . . of native English culture' ('City of Words', 40).
51. For a further account of these texts as the basis of a conspiracy theory about the radical Enlightenment, see Simpson, *Romanticism*, 88–9.
52. For more on these legislative and judicial initiatives, see Booth, 'The Memory of the Liberty of the Press'. For an account of struggles over the distribution of newspapers and pamphlets, see Aspinall,

Politics and the Press. For the repression of the debating societies, see Thale, 'London Debating Societies'. For an excellent political history of the 1790s which includes many of these issues, see Goodwin, *Friends of Liberty*.

53. Quoted in Favret, *Romantic Correspondence*, 81–2.

54. Blackstone, *Commentaries*, IV, 151 (1769).

55. De Constant, 'Liberty', 206 (1815). It was a lesson that the proto-socialist Thomas Spence had learned much earlier when in 1775 he was expelled from the Philosophical Society after submitting a paper entitled *The Real Rights of Man*, 'not for his opinions, nor for even printing the paper, but for hawking it about like a halfpenny ballad' (*Dictionary of National Biography*, LIII: 338). The *Dictionary of National Biography*'s assessment seems to be based on the opinion of Spence's first biographer, E. Mackenzie, who noted that Spence was expelled 'not for printing it only, but for printing it in the manner of a half-penny broadsheet and having it hawked about the streets' (quoted in Wood, *Radical Satire*, 95).

56. Erskine, *Speeches*, IV, 439.

57. Ibid., I, 173.

58. For an examination of these historical developments, see Claeys, (ed.), *Political Writings*, Introduction.

59. For an account of the Brothers controversy, see Barrell, 'Imagining the King's Death'.

60. For a discussion of the legal status of *Political Justice*, see Philp, *Godwin's Political Justice*, 103–5.

61. Erskine, *Speeches*, II, 202–3.

62. Ibid., 202.

63. Godwin, *Works*, III, 119, 118–19, 118 (1793).

64. For the debate about the practical extent of Godwin's commitment to radical politics, see Philp, *Godwin's Political Justice* and 'Thompson', and Thompson, 'Benevolent Mr Godwin' and *Poverty of Theory*, 372–3.

65. Godwin, *Works*, II, 141.

66. Ibid., 132.

67. *Works*, 11, 130–2 (1795).

68. Mathias, *Pursuits of Literature*, III, 35 (1797).

69. Ibid., 37.

70. Booth, 'Liberty of the Press', 109.

71. Klancher, *Making of English Reading Audiences*, 110.

72. Smith, *Politics of Language*, 59. For a study of these dynamics that focuses on the contested nature of reading audiences, see Klancher, *Making of English Reading Audiences*, 105–11.

73. Richardson, *Literature, Education, and Romance*, 45, 65. In his important study of 'the reading public as a social phenomenon', Altick simi-

larly argues that 'the history of the mass reading audience is, in fact, the history of English democracy seen from a new angle' (*English Common Reader*, 8, 3). Altick estimates that Burke's *Reflections* sold 30,000 copies, Paine's *Rights of Man*, part 1, 50,000 copies, and part 2, as high as 200,000 copies, though Hannah More's *Cheap Repository Tracts*, backed by a thousand pounds' support, sold an incredible 2,000,000 copies (*English Common Reader*, 69–75; Pedersen, 'Hannah More Meets Simple Simon', 84). These figures are probably high. Nor is it clear that all copies distributed were actually sold. But they none the less offer a valuable picture of the expanding size of the audiences these works were able to reach. Altick also notes that Paine's trial for *Rights of Man*, part 2, had the ironic effect of intensifying enthusiasm for it (71).

74. Hardy, *Memoir*, vii.
75. Ibid., 19.
76. Ibid., 24.
77. Gerrald, *Trial*.
78. Thale notes that this article was based on a speech by John Thelwall at Capel Court on 24 October 1793, about 'a tyrannous gamecock, 'King Chanticleer,' which ate all the grain, and kicked and cuffed other fowl, left them starving, and which was beheaded for its despotism' ('London Debating Societies', 67).
79. *Dictionary of National Biography*, XVI, 336; Wood, *Radical Satire*, 138–9.
80. Erskine, *Speeches*, III, 318.
81. Ibid., 80.
82. Ibid., 400.
83. Favret, *Romantic Correspondence*, 48. For a similar study of the relationship between trials and texts in the 1810s, see Gilmartin, *Print Politics*, 139–43.
84. See also Worrall, *Radical Culture*, 47.
85. Erskine, *Speeches*, II, 79 (1792).
86. Erskine, *Speeches*, II, 95–6.
87. Ibid., 47–8.
88. Quoted in Butler, *Burke*, 15.
89. Spence, 'Important Trial', II, 14.
90. Aspinall, *Politics*, 42–65; Thompson, *Making of the English Working Class*, 679.
91. See also Gilmartin, *Print Politics*, 21–2 and Wood, *Radical Satire*, 3–17, 96–133.
92. Thompson, *Making of the English Working Class*, 740.
93. Hazlitt, *Complete Works*, XVII, 325–7.
94. Ibid.
95. Southey, *Essays*, 130.
96. Von Gentz, 'Reflections', 489–93.
97. Mathias, *Pursuits of Literature*, IV, ii.

2 MEN OF LETTERS

1. Bourdieu, *Distinction*, 85.
2. Butler, 'Culture's Medium', 124.
3. Burke, *Works*, V, 153 (1790).
4. Colley, *Britons*, 153.
5. Lest we underestimate the oppositional edge of these meritocratic claims, Thompson emphasizes that the extensive 'predatory oligarchic power' of the upper classes existed throughout virtually the whole of the eighteenth century ('Eighteenth-Century English Society', 143). Colley, noting that half of the peerages bestowed were for reasons other than state service, similarly cautions that 'Old Corruption, that Byzantine mesh of sinecures and pensions, continued to characterize British government machinery until the Reform Act' ('Whose Nation?' 106). Her identification of the Reform Act as a termination date for this arrangement is perhaps overly optimistic.
6. Favret, *Romantic Correspondence*, 125.
7. O'Connor, *Measures of Ministry*, 47–8, emphasis added (1794).
8. Stedman Jones, *Languages of Class*, 2. See Claeys, 'Origins of the Rights of Labour'; Leask, *Politics of Imagination*; Pocock, *Machiavellian Movement* and *Virtue*; and Robbins, *Eighteenth-Century Commonwealth*. Surveying this shift, Kramnick notes that '[l]iberalism has been toppled in recent years and replaced by a new hegemonic ideology, republicanism' (*Republicanism and Bourgeois Radicalism*, 35).
9. See, for instance, Barrell's chapter 'A Republic of Taste', in *Political Theory of Painting*, 1–68. I will be using the phrase 'classical republicanism', which is more consistent with current criticism, except in those cases where the discourse is explicitly attached to the ownership of land, where I use 'civic humanism'.
10. Barrell argues that the 'rehabilitation of self-interest . . . was confirmed by representing it as *industrious*'(*English Literature*, 24). This is undoubtably true, but as I argue in this chapter, the idea of industriousness could also be invoked in order to reinforce modified but still political ideas about the importance of disinterested productivity.
11. Porter, 'The Enlightenment', 5.
12. Quoted in Philp, *Godwin's Political Justice*, 73.
13. Habermas, *Structural Transformation*, 3. Tracing the development of these ideas throughout the eighteenth century, Habermas emphasizes that philosophers such as Jean-Jacques Rousseau (97–9) and Emmanuel Kant (103–7) theorized the concept of the public sphere in ways that maintained this fusion of positions.
14. Davidoff and Hall, *Family Fortunes*, 73.
15. Ibid., 110–11.
16. Butler, 'Culture's Medium', 130.
17. Goldgar, *Impolite Learning*, 3.

18. Barrell, *Political Theory of Painting*, 1.
19. Importantly, Barrell's argument is not ultimately for the irrelevance of civic humanism in the period, but on the contrary, for its continuing strength as a primary theoretical category in debates about art.
20. Kramnick, *Republicanism*, 97–8.
21. Ibid., 127, 166.
22. For a similar discussion of this emphasis on a love of work as the basis for an emergent professionalism, see Siskin, *Work of Writing*, 103–29.
23. D'lsraeli, *Curiosities of Literature*, 60 (1791).
24. Mathias, *Pursuits of Literature*, IV, 122 (1797).
25. Quoted in Tyson, *Joseph Johnson*, xxi.
26. For a reading of *The Prelude* which situates Wordsworth's descriptions of his poetic calling within precisely this professional ideology of a love of labour, see Siskin, *Work of Writing*, 109–18.
27. Barrell, *Political Theory of Painting*, 46. See Fraser 'Rethinking the Public Sphere', Kelly, *Women, Writing and Revolution*; and Pilbeam, *Middle Classes in Europe*.
28. Wollstonecraft, *Works*, V, 16 (1790).
29. Ibid., 58.
30. For the growth of middle-class culture, see Corfield (ed.), *Language* and Corfield, *Power*; Davidoff and Hall, *Family Fortunes*; and Perkin, *Origins of Modern English Society*. Thompson argues, along similar lines, that 'a purposive, cohesive, growing middle class of professional men. . . . did not begin to discover itself (except, perhaps, in London) until the last three decades of the century' ('Eighteenth-Century English Society', 142).
31. For a study of the emergence of the threefold distinction between classes whose worth depended on Land, Capital, and Labour, see Corfield, 'Class'. Corfield emphasizes the extent to which the growing sensitivity to the politics of class identity continued to coexist with entrenched assumptions about the organic unity of the social hierarchy, or the 'Great Chain of Being'. The emergence of the word 'class' was less an index of this growing political awareness than a concept whose interpretation provided an important site within which these debates would eventually be staged.
32. Perkin, *Origins of Modern English Society*, 23.
33. Davidoff and Hall argue that voluntary associations, such as the various philanthropic societies, constituted an important element of the public sphere (*Family Fortunes*, 419–36). Colley suggests that 'to many *nouveau riche* and bourgeois elements in Georgian Britain, patriotic activism felt like an opportunity to assert their parity with, and in some cases, their superiority to, the landed classes' ('Whose Nation?', 110). For a similar argument about the relationship between middle-class benevolence and educational initiatives, see M. G. Jones, *Charity School Movement*.

34. For a typical religious tract encouraging these values amongst the lower orders, see Travell, *Duties of the Poor*. Travell's message reflected one of the most popular themes of the middle class in their relations with their social subordinates: 'You are most of you placed in that humble station, which requires constant labour and activity, for the maintenance of yourselves and your families: the first duty therefore which I shall recommend to you, is *Industry*' (5). For the children of the poor, education was an important means of 'improving their little stock of knowledge', but this was only to be undertaken in the least busy times of the year, and only to an extent that was 'sufficient for their humble stations in life, and to enable them to read and understand the plain parts of their duty' (36).

35. Quoted in Jones, *Charity School Movement*, 74. For More's educational efforts, see *Charity School Movement*. For her pamphlet writing, see *Charity School Movement* and Pedersen, 'Hannah Moore'. The careless spontaneity implied in Jones's suggestion that 'to show the poor that poverty was God's discipline and man's opportunity, she worked among them, and in her leisure poured forth a reckless profusion of tracts for their edification', is belied by Pedersen's account of More's studious perusal and skilful imitation of the chapbook literature which she was attempting to displace (11).

36. Keir, *Account*, 80 (1791).

37. Quoted in Colley, *Britons*, 548.

38. Isaac Kramnick similarly argues that the 'special trait of the middle class was its usefulness, its abhorrence of idleness' (*Republicanism*, 31–2).

39. Newman, *Rise of English Nationalism*, 115; Peardon, *Transition in English Historical Writing*, 294. Pinkerton's views were expressed in a series of twelve letters to the *Gentleman's Magazine* on the state of historical literature. See *GM* 58 (1788): 125–7, 96–8, 284–6, 404–5, 499–501, 591–2, 689, 777–8, 877–8, 967–9, 1056–8, 1149–51.

40. Quoted in Goodman, *Republic of Letters*, 37. For more on the declining role of patronage, see Collins, *The Profession of Letters*, 113.

41. Jones, *Collected Works*, II, 125.

42. Barrell, *English Literature*, 50–79.

43. Given the bemusement of the *Analytical*, it is probably worth noting that Pennant was a celebrated zoologist, antiquarian, and traveller. For more on Pennant, see *The Literary Life of Thomas Pennant Esq. By Himself*. My point here is not to offer an analysis of Pennant's work but to note the class dynamics which characterize the treatment Pennant received from the *Analytical*.

44. Burke, *Works*, V, 207 (1790).

45. Indeed, the two are fused together in Anderson's phrase 'print capital' (*Imagined Communities*, 38–46).

46. Boswell, *Samuel Johnson*, 378.

47. Eagleton, *Function of Criticism*, 34.
48. See also Siskin, *Work of Writing* 109–12.
49. Kernan, *Printing Technology*, 97–102.
50. Butler, *Culture's Medium*, 122; Roper, *Reviewing Before the Edinburgh*.
51. Bourdieu, *Distinction*, 100.
52. Wiles, 'Relish for Reading', 103.
53. Altick, *English Common Reader*, 57.
54. Raven, *Judging New Wealth*, 50–1.
55. Quoted in Collins, *Profession of Letters*, 169.
56. Baker, 'Defining the Public Sphere', 184; Eley, 'Nations', 291; Habermas, *Reflections*, 423.
57. See the account of James Luckcock, a radical Birmingham jeweller, in Davidoff and Hall, 14–18.
58. Colley, *Britons*, 90; Richardson, *Literature*, 55–6. Perkin is in this respect perhaps too strenuous in his separation of the professional and commercial sectors as different classes: 'Professional men had a separate, if sometimes subconscious, social ideal which underlay their versions of the other class ideals. Their ideal society was a functional one based on expertise and selection by merit . . . rather than property, capital, or labour' (*Origins of Modern Society*, 258).
59. For an extensive account of representations of men of commerce in late eighteenth-century novels, see Raven, *Judging New Wealth*.
60. Raven notes that this anti-business bias was often doubled within views about business by comparisons of the 'favoured merchant', who was defined 'in terms of the gentlemanly ideals of benevolence, economy, and a responsible attitude towards wealth', with the 'vulgar trader' who accumulated wealth without ever demonstrating good breeding (*Judging New Wealth*, 13).
61. Claeys, 'Origins'. See also, Claeys, Introduction, *Politics of English Jacobinism*, xxxv–lvi.
62. Wollstonecraft, *Works*, VI, 309, 304.
63. Bourdieu, *Distinction*, 125.
64. Burke, *Works*, V, 97 (1790).
65. Pocock, *Machiavellian Moment*, 464.
66. Cowper, *Letters and Prose*, 281 (1793).
67. See also Kernan, *Printing Technology*, 241–64; Klancher, *Making of English Reading Audiences*, 18–26; Lipking, 'Inventing the Common Reader', 57.
68. Kernan, *Printing Technology*, 246.
69. Jordanova, *Languages of Nature*, 15.
70. Simpson, *Romanticism*, 48.
71. Barrell, *English Literature*, 45.
72. Hays, *Letters*, 29 (1793).
73. For the use of this metaphor in the *Encyclopédie*, see Darnton, *Great Cat Massacre*, 191–209. Darnton emphasizes that Diderot and

D'Alembert adapted the model of the tree of knowledge from earlier authors such as Francis Bacon and Ephraim Chambers.

74. These universalizing ambitions, and the scientific claims on which they are necessarily founded, have not disappeared. They return in a highly sophisticated and insistent form in 'myth criticism' based on Jung's theory of a collective unconscious characterized by universal archetypes. For a significant example of myth as the basis of a totalizing approach to literary criticism, see Frye's commitment to 'a coherent and comprehensive theory of literature, logically and scientifically organized' (*Anatomy of Criticism*, 11). Properly managed, Frye continues, 'criticism progresses toward making the whole of literature intelligible' (12). Frye's 'Polemical Introduction' is riddled with phrases such as 'comprehensive view' (12), 'a central expanding pattern of systematic comprehension' (12), 'the whole of literature' (14), 'a totally intelligible structure of knowledge' (14), 'the assumption of total coherence' (16), and 'a systematic structure of knowledge' (18).

75. Lipking, 'Inventing the Common Reader', 156. Klancher notes a similar use of the metaphor of colonialism in discussions about reading audiences (*Making of English Reading Audiences*, 24–5).

76. Wordsworth, 1805 *Prelude*, II, 208–10. It is worth bearing in mind that Wordsworth was reacting to his own determination to 'trace / The Progress of our Being', as much as anybody else's (II, 238–9). Nor was he exempt from a lifelong preoccupation with the classification of his poetry according to various psychological divisions.

77. Wiles 'Relish for Reading', 105.

78. Quoted in ibid., 106. See also Blakey, *Minerva Press*, Collins, *Profession of Letters*, 98, 113; Smith, *Politics of Language*, 157; and Todd, *Sign of Angelica*, 219–20.

79. My thanks to Emma Major for pointing the passage from the Donaldson letter out to me.

80. See also Irwin, *The English Library*.

81. Kernan, *Printing Technology*, 243.

82. Roper notes that 'the number of new titles printed annually had increased fourfold since the *Monthly* and *Critical* had been founded, and journals which had once dealt with between twenty and thirty books and pamphlets each month were now despatching sixty to seventy, sometimes more, and still falling behind' (*Reviewing Before the Edinburgh*, 37).

83. Holcroft, *Hugh Trevor*, 394 (1797).

84. Hays, *Appeal*, 6 (1798).

85. See Collins, *Profession of Letters*, 95; and Kelly, 'Romantic Fiction', 196–215.

86. Bohls, 'Women Travel Writers', 3; Kelly, 'Romantic Fiction', 207.

87. Todd, *Feminist Literary History*, 112. See also Richardson, *Literature*, 187.

88. Simpson, *Romanticism*, 11.
89. Wollstonecraft, *Works*, VII, 26.
90. Langford, *Polite and Commercial People*, 407. Altick, *English Common Reader*, 63–6; Collins, *Profession of Letters*, 53–7; and Irwin, *The English Library*, 206.
91. Bohls, *Women Travel Writers;* Mills, *Discourses of Difference;* Pratt, *Imperial Eyes*.
92. Mathias, *Pursuit of Literature*, IV, 87 (1797).
93. MacDonald, *Thoughts on Public Duties*, 10 (1795).
94. Focusing on the eighteenth-century book-trade, Raven suggests that this extravagance was in part the result of a shared recognition amongst booksellers that, in an increasingly competitive market, 'a war fought by price reduction would bring most operators to their knees'. Deprived of this option, booksellers concentrated on advertising and sales techniques designed to sell 'highly finished, modish works' (*Judging New Wealth*, 51–2).
95. Macaulay, *Letters on Education*, 13. It is important to recognize that, like fears about the inflated numbers of publications, these concerns about their declining quality were far from novel. For worries about the decay of learning, the dangers of abridgements, the public's taste for 'trash', the decline of patronage and the tyranny of reviewers at the end of the seventeenth century, see Goldgar, *Impolite Learning*.
96. Roper reads this notice as part of a shift by the *Critical Review* from a moderate conservative to a more actively reformist position (*Reviewing Before the Edinburgh*, 176).
97. Klancher, *Making of English Reading Audiences*, 4.
98. For a detailed account of the importance of the reviews within the literary trade see Butler, 'Culture's Medium'; Collins, *The Profession of Letters*, 135–51; Morgan, *Literary Critics*, and Roper, *Reviewing Before the Edinburgh*.
99. Roper, *Reviewing Before the Edinburgh*, 36–7.
100. Butler suggests that 'the impact of the journals was paradoxical, since they were so organized as to underline the compartmentalization of knowledge and its increasing specialization. Though not quite so fragmented as the dictionary and the encyclopaedia, they did not distinguish one field above another or otherwise attempt to group, still less to hierarchize, knowledge' ('Culture's Medium', 122). My own emphasis on the unifying ambition which underpinned the organizational focus of both encyclopaedias and journals suggests that compartmentalization was important as a means of highlighting the internal coherence of these various areas of learning as one unified body of knowledge.
101. Siskin argues that the criticism of the reviews functioned as a way of compensating for the lack of an official professional body for writers (*The Work of Writing*).

102. D'Israeli; *Curiosities*, 95–6 (1791).
103. Pratt, *Gleanings in England*, IV, 314 (1799).
104. Butler, *Romantics*, 15.
105. Parrinder, *Authors and Authority*, 65–6.
106. Klancher, *Making of English Reading Audiences*, ix.
107. Roper rejects this pessimistic assessment, pointing out the unlikeli-
hood that reviews, usually owned by individuals with an interest in
the book trade, would be overwhelmingly negative about the current stock of new books (*Reviewing Before the Edinburgh*, 32). He
argues that these abuses were more characteristic of the 'slashing'
style of criticism favoured by the quarterlies in the early nineteenth
century. This does not, of course, undermine the discursive force
of these self-representations within the period.
108. For the debate about the status of so-called letters to the
editor in the reviews, which were more often essays written in the
epistolary form by members of staff, see Klancher, *Making of English
Reading Audiences*, 21–6.
109. D'Israeli, *Curiosities of Literature*, 32 (1791).
110. Pratt, *Gleanings in England*, IV 308, 311, 314 (1799).
111. In his autobiography, the bookseller Lackington fired his literary
slingshot at 'those GOLIATHS in literature, ycleped *Critics* (with
whom not many little Davids are hardy enough to contend)'
(*Memoirs*, ix).
112. Habermas, *Structural Transformation*, 52. See also Kramnick, *Republicanism*, and Newman, *Rise of English Nationalism*.
113. Parrinder, *Authors and Authority*, 105–8.
114. Shelley, *Frankenstein*, 37.

PREAMBLE: SWINISH MULTITUDES

1. Richardson makes a similar point in his instructive reading of Elizabeth Gaskell's *My Lady Ludlow*, in which Lady Ludlow worries that
educating the lower orders will amount to giving them "edge-tools"
for undermining the class system' (1). For the debate about the
political wisdom of Sunday Schools, see Altick, *English Common Reader*,
67–9; and Jones, *Charity School Movement*.
2. For more on the various consequences of the expansion of the reading public, see Claeys, Introduction, *Political Writings*, xvii–lvi; Collins, 51–72; and Smith, *Politics of Language*. Simpson identifies these
tensions about the limits of 'the people' within Locke's own writing
in 'his explicit claim that 'the vulgar, and mass of mankind' cannot
be expected and should not be encouraged to follow 'the long and
sometimes intricate deductions of reason'" (*Romanticism*, 29). Richardson points out that these anxieties about who ought to constitute
'the people' manifested themselves in the 'infantilization' of women,

the working classes, and colonial subjects (*Literature*, 156). Approaching the same issue from a slightly different angle, Bohls stresses that subordinate groups were identified in terms of their bodies, which, because of the Enlightenment emphasis on reason, was the inferior term within the body/mind opposition (*Women Travel Writers*, 77).

3. Klancher, *Making of English Reading Audiences*, 99.
4. Calhoun, *Habermas*, 37.
5. Eley, 'Nations', 321.
6. Habermas, *Structural Transformation*, 42.
7. Thompson, *Making of the English Working Class*, 12.

3 THE POORER SORT

1. Quoted in Ashfield (ed.), *Romantic Women Poets*, 173–4.
2. Place, *Autobiography*, 175.
3. Hardy, *Memoirs*, 102, 109. For an account of self-taught individuals connected with the LCS, see Thale, Introduction, 'London Debating Societies', xx.
4. Richardson, *Literature, Education and Romanticism*, 241.
5. Hardy, *Memoirs*, viii.
6. Wollstonecraft, *Works*, VI, 241.
7. Lackington, *Memoirs*, 92; Place, *Autobiography*, 109.
8. Place, *Autobiography*, 109.
9. Hardy, *Memoirs*, 4.
10. Lackington, *Memoirs*, iv, xv.
11. Ibid., 130.
12. Ibid., 230. O. Smith points out that Lackington was far from alone in his effort to break down the artificial restrictions which structured the book trade. William Lane's Minerva Press was one such example. John Bell's publication of 104 volumes of poetry, collectively entitled *The Poets of Great Britain complete from Chaucer to Churchill*, at an unusually low price, was countered by a group of forty London booksellers who attempted to undermine the project by publishing a fancier collection, for which Samuel Johnson was employed to write the preface, now known as *Lives of The Poets*.
13. Place, *Autobiography*, 16, 222–3.
14. Wollstonecraft, *Works*, I, 113, 157.
15. Place, *Autobiography*, 127.
16. Thelwall, *Poems*, vi, ix. For a biographical account of Thelwall, see Claeys, Introduction, *Politics of English Jacobinism*; and Thompson, 'Hunting'.
17. Lackington, *Memoirs*, 121–2, 241, 257.
18. Place, *Autobiography*, 82. For a more sceptical reading of Place's *Autobiography*, which emphasizes Place's attempt to rewrite his radical past in more genteel terms, see McCalman, *Radical Underworld*, 8–14.

See also Richardson's reading of Place's autobiography in *Literature, Education, and Romanticism*, which I have discussed above.

19. Place, *Autobiography*, 127–8.
20. Ibid., 128.
21. This argument has found its most familiar theoretical elaboration in our own age in Benjamin's 'Theses on the Philosophy of History', especially in section VII, which argues that because 'all rulers are the heirs of those who conquered before them', the adherents of historicism necessarily empathize with 'the victor'. 'A historical materialist therefore ... regards it as his task to brush history against the grain' (pp. 256–7).
22. Hardy, *Memoirs*, 120.
23. Habermas, 'Further Reflections', 428.
24. Knox quoted in Eagleton, *Function of Criticism*, 35, emphasis added; More quoted in Thompson, *Making of the English Working Class*, 117; Reid, *Rise and Dissolution of the Infidel Classes*, 1 (1800), emphasis added.
25. Erskine, *Speeches*, II, 48.
26. Klancher, *Making of English Reading Audiences*, 29–38.
27. Ibid., 34.
28. For further accounts of *Pig's Meat*, see Gallop, Introduction, *Pig's Meat*; O. Smith, *Politics of Language*, 68–109; Worrall, *Radical Culture*, 23–6. Smith offers a useful comparison of *Pig's Meat* with Eaton's *Politics for the People*. For an account of the Spencean ultra-radical tradition, see McCalman, *Radical, Underworld*.
29. McCalman, *Radical Underworld*. Wood notes that this stylistic diversity was complemented by Spence's 'infiltration of rapidly developing communications networks' – a strategic flexibility that included producing and distributing coins with political mottos on them, publishing children's books, and conducting graffiti campaigns (*Radical Satire*, 64, 85).
30. Klancher, *Making of English Reading Audiences*, 43.
31. Pederson, 'Hannah More', 103–4.
32. Thompson, *Making of the English Working Classes*, 177; Worrall, *Radical Culture*, 19–21.
33. For an historical analysis of the links in the period between millennial prophecy and radical politics, see Mee, *Dangerous Enthusiasm*.
34. For an account of the struggle over the taxation of the press, see Aspinall, *Politics and the Press*, 16–23.
35. For an account of this process of exaggeration within the backlash against the reform movement, see Claeys, Introduction, *Political Writings*, xxxv–xliii.
36. Newman, *Rise of English Nationalism*, 210.
37. Quoted in ibid.

38. Thale, *Selections*, xv.
39. Hardy, *Memoirs*, 8.
40. Ibid., vii, 104.
41. Quoted in ibid., 21.
42. Ibid., xvi, viii. For a general introduction to the LCS, see Thale, Introduction, *Selections*, xv–xxix; and Thompson, *Making of the English Working Class*.
43. Hardy, *Memoirs*, 116.
44. Erskine, *Speeches*, III, 335.
45. Quoted in ibid., 149–50, 182, 177.
46. Hardy, *Memoirs*, 121.
47. Ibid., 99, 106. For an historical argument which suggests the influence of this communicative ideal on the eighteenth-century world of letters, see Habermas, *Structural Transformations*, 43–51.
48. Hardy, *Memoirs*, 114–15.
49. Thompson, *Makling of the English Working Class*, 201; Dinwiddy, 'Conceptions of the Revolution', 547.
50. Thelwall, *Speech*, v. Claeys suggests that the two meetings, held on 26 October and 12 November 1795, 'were probably the largest of [their] kind ever held', attracting more than 150,000 people (Introduction, *Politics of English Jacobinism* xxv). The Two Acts, which proscribed this sort of political meetings, received royal ascent on 18 December.
51. Thelwall, *Speech*, 12.
52. Thelwell, *Peaceful Discussion*, 18.
53. Thelwall's warnings take on greater relevance in light of Thale's description of the repeated and frequently successful efforts of government and loyalist agents to disrupt his public meetings ('London'). See also Thompson, 'Disenchantment or Default?'.
54. Thelwell, *Peaceful Discussion*, 11, 23
55. Ibid., 6.
56. Ibid., 16–17.
57. Thompson, *Making of the English Working Class*, 176.
58. Place, *Autobiography*, 198.
59. Hardy, *Memoir*, 108.
60. Place, *Autobiography*, 131.

4 MASCULINE WOMEN

1. Wollstonecraft, *Works*, V, 193.
2. Pateman, 'Fraternal Social Contract', 110. For an analysis of the tensions generated by Wollstonecraft's endorsement of 'an ideal bourgeois male as the standard against which women are to be measured' (134), see Landes, 129–38.
3. *Reflector*, 1 (1812): 280.

4. Kelly, 'Romantic Fiction', 207; Richardson, *Literature, Education, and Romanticism*, and Todd, *Feminist Literary History*.

5. Miles, *Gothic Writing*.

6. Bohls, *Women Travel Writers*.

7. Favret, *Romantic Correspondence*.

8. Myers, 'Impeccable Governesses', Richardson, *Literature, Education, and Romanticism*, 167–212.

9. Davies, 'Moral Purchase', Ferguson, *Subject to Others*; Midgely, *Women against Slavery*.

10. Major, 'A Sociable Commerce: Femininity, Conversation and Christianity in the Works of Hannah More' (MA thesis, University of York, 1996).

11. Clearly, this is a selective account of critical strategies in our own age; their single most important lesson is of the impossibility of doing justice to these responses to the critical limitations of their age in any summary way.

12. I should acknowledge at the outset that the term 'feminist' is historically anomalous (though no more so than the word 'Romanticism'). With this in mind, I want to use the term as a convenient shorthand for those writers who extended current political issues to the question of gender.

13. See also Guest, 'Dream of a Common Language'.

14. Polwhele, *Unsex'd Females*, 35 (1798).

15. Quoted in Richardson, *Literature, Education, and Romanticism*, 168.

16. Hays, *Appeal*, 114.

17. Kelly, 'Romantic Fiction', 191; Simpson, 'Romanticism', 5.

18. Ryan, 'Gender and Access', 266.

19. Mathias, *Pursuits of Literature*, IV, 2.

20. Todd, *Sign of Angelica*, 199.

21. Landes, *Women and the Public Sphere*, 146. In her discussion of the backlash against women's social and political aspirations during the French Revolution, Landes argues that their crime was not that they became involved in public affairs, but rather that they increasingly did so in order to promote their interests *as* women: 'in 1789 women aren't seen as threatening because they can still be thought of as participants in the larger revolution against class inequalities. Only as they begin to develop a set of independent priorities do they become threatening' (ibid.).

22. Macaulay, *Letters on Education*, 204 (1790).

23. For a broader analysis of cultural attitudes informing dominant eighteenth-century ideas about femininity, see Poovey, *Proper Lady*, 3–47. Poovey explores the ways that the image of the 'proper lady' distorts women writers' texts, but she also focuses on the ways that women writers were able to reinterpret traditional ideas about feminine behaviour in order to accommodate dissenting visions about the role of women.

24. Wollstonecraft, *Works*, V, 174–5 (1792).
25. Ibid., 53.
26. Ibid., 10. O'Connor similarly argued that 'Those who write from their passions, and those who will not receive information through any other channel, wholly unfit themselves to develope or to comprehend the cause of this stupendous Revolution' (*Measures of Ministry*, 5–6). Ironically, Burke shared O'Connor's view, though he identified this irrationality with very different social groups.
27. Wollstonecraft, *Works*, V, 7.
28. Ibid., 199, 73.
29. For a reading of Rousseau's analysis of gender politics, see Landes, *Women and the Public Sphere*, 66–89; and Pateman, 'Fraternal Social Contract', 114.
30. Wollstonecraft, *Works*, V, 130.
31. Ibid., 256, 244.
32. Johnson, 'Rights', 100. My analysis of the connections between Wollstonecraft's insistence on women's rational capacity and contemporary debates about literary production does not engage with the important issue of her effort to mediate between women's capacity for reason and for feeling or sensibility. For this debate, see Kaplan, 'Wild Nights', 31–56; and Poovey, *Proper Lady*, 48–113.
33. Wollstonecraft, *Works*, V, 74.
34. Landes similarly argues that 'Wollstonecraft fears being mistaken by her own readers for a masquerading woman', caught between her aspirations for women and her enthusiam for those social roles that were defined as 'manly' (*Women and the Public Sphere*, 134).
35. Richardson, *Literature, Education, and Romanticism*, 168.
36. Lackington, *Memoirs*, 263–4, 266.
37. For an analysis which sets women's involvement in these debates within the larger historical context of the Bluestockings, see Curran, 'Women Readers'.
38. This backlash was reinforced by what Claeys describes as a wider turn from political and social debate to a moral focus on the 'degenerate, libertine aspects of the "new philosophy" as a means of heralding a "reformation of manners"' ('Introduction', *Political Writings*, 1). Claeys notes that this shift was reinforced by Godwin's publication of *Memoirs of the Author of a Vindication of the Rights of Woman* in 1798.
39. Thale similarly notes, in her study of the London debating societies, that political restrictions on the freedom of political debate were 'accompanied by retrogression of thinking and feeling in other areas', namely in an insistence on traditional gender roles ('London Debating Societies', 73, 75, 83). Noting the shift in the topics specifically relating to Wollstonecraft's writings, Thale concludes that within these reactionary debates about domestic relations, Wollstonecraft 'is no longer a thinker. She is now a fallen woman' (p. 84).

40. Connolly, Introduction, *Letters for Literary Ladies*, xvi.
41. Poovey, *Proper Lady*, 21. For a more extended analysis of the para-doxes of feminine propriety, see Poovey, 15–30.
42. For an account of the very different role the Paris salons afforded women in the French Enlightenment, and of the tensions this gener-ated, see Goodman, *Republic of Letters*, 52–89. In the context of my own study of concerns about the effeminacy of English culture, Rous-seau's fear of salon culture's effects on men is prophetic: 'Unable to make themselves into men, the women make us into women' (quoted in *Republic of Letters*, 54). Goodman emphasizes that Rous-seau's fears about the undue influence of women were related to his larger worries about 'the emasculation of philosophy itself' (p. 62).
43. Raven, *Judging New Wealth*, 63.
44. For an analysis of 'the equation of writing women with demands for female equality and both together with all the excesses of the Terror in France', see also Curran, 'Women Readers', 184. It must be noted, however, that conservative women authors such as More, Sarah Trimmer, and Jane West were virtually always exempted from this equation.
45. Myers, 'Reform or Ruin', 199.
46. Burke, *Works*, V, 141–2. In her reading of Burke's use of Marie-Antoinette in the *Reflections* as a means of formulating and legitimiz-ing a particular political philosophy, Colley emphasizes Burke's par-ticipation in the common assumption that the quality of a civilization could be judged according to its treatment of women (*Britons*, 253). For more on this assumption, see Myers, 'Reform or Ruin'!
47. Burke, *Works*, V, 142. For an account of the march of women to Versailles on October 5–6, 1789, see Landes, 109–12.
48. Simpson, *Romanticism*, 117. Landes argues that these associations of the French Revolution with women's revolution against their own nature were reinforced by the prior perception that 'the Revolution was a revolt against the traditional patriarchy of the father-king' (*Women and the Public Sphere*, 104). See also Poovey, *The Proper Lady*, 30–5. Pateman widens the context of these dynamics still further in her consideration of Freud's opinion that social contract theory was always already premised on an implicit act of patricide: the murder of the primal authoritarian father by sons determined to live as equals ('Fraternal Social Contract', 110–12).
49. Robison, *Proofs of a Conspiracy*, 250, 245, 251–2.
50. Iversen situates an account of this event within her exploration of a wider crisis of representation which characterized the Revolution generally ('Imagining the Republic', 130).
51. Robison, *Proofs of a Conspiracy*, 251.
52. Cumberland, *The Observer*, IV, 311.

53. Simpson, *Romanticism*, 121.
54. Gould, *Vindication*, 6.
55. Ibid., 85–6.
56. Ibid., 98, 97–8.

5 ORIENTAL LITERATURE

1. Wollstonecraft, *Works*, VI, 224 (1795).
2. Quoted in Bayly, *Imperial Meridian*, 122.
3. Leask, *British Romantic Writers*, 12.
4. Rushdie, *Satanic Verses*, 343.
5. See also Bhabha's essay 'Of Mimicry and Man: The Ambivalence of Colonial Discourse', in *Location of Culture*, 85–92.
6. Jones, *Collected Works*, I, 10 (1784).
7. *Dissertations and Miscellaneous Pieces*, IV–V (1793).
8. For the effects of the Seven Years War, the American Revolution, and the anti-slavery movement, see Colley, *Britons*. For the trial of Warren Hastings see Marshall, *Impeachment*; and Musselwhite, 'Trial'.
9. Quoted in *Dictionary of National Biography*, VII, 183.
10. Bayly, *Imperial Meridian*, 142. See also Marshall, *Problems*, 70–3.
11. Burney, *General History of Music*, xii (1776).
12. Wollstonecraft, *Works*, VI, 16.
13. As we have seen in chapter 1, O'Connor agreed that 'The ancients had made some progress in political enquiry; but the invention of the mariner's compass, and the art of printing, have given us such advantages, as are scarcely to be calculated' (*Measures of Ministry*, 20).
14. For European critics' interest in the kinship within 'the Indo-European family of languages' (15), see Majeed, *Ungoverned Imaginings*, 12–16. Majeed interprets the search for a common linguistic source as a unifying desire inspired by the growing heterogeneity of the British empire.
15. Suleri, *Rhetoric*, 3. Musselwhite argues that the 'major development during the latter half of the eighteenth century was the change in the status of the East India Company from being a purely commercial concern to being an organ of imperial power' ('Trial', 79). Marshall suggests that '[a]s a general proposition the majority of the Company's servants agreed that the conquest of Indian provinces was not in the Company's best interests, but they rarely exercised the restraint in their relations with Indian powers which would have enabled them to avoid war and the acquisition of territory after a successful war' (*Problems*, 17).
16. Bayly, *Imperial Meridian*, 114, 173.
17. Majeed notes that the June 1783 Report of the Select Committee of the House of Commons, whose purpose was to investigate the administration of justice in Bengal, 'described the period of British

rule from 1773 to 1782 as one in which 'Disorders and Abuses of every Kind multiplied" (*Ungoverned Imaginings*, 8). Bayly points out that '[a]fter 1790 the pace of British military expansion in India speeded up notably. Between 1789 and 1805 the Company's total strength increased from about 115,000 to 155,000, making it one of the largest European-style standing armies in the world' (*Indian Society*, 85).

18. Said, *Orientalism*, 78.
19. Bayly, *Imperial Meridian*, 119–21. For an account of the ongoing struggle between the British government and the East India Company for the control of British India, see Marshall, *Problems*, 21–51. Bayly emphasizes that many of the strategies adopted by the Pitt government, such as the use of executive overseeing boards capable of subordinating private impulses to the more 'public' maintenance of the imperial administration, were typical of Pitt's state-building policies within Britain which aimed at developing a salaried and more carefully trained civil service in areas such as the newly created customs department (*Imperial Meridian*, 120).
   20. For another example of a pamphlet which stages the argument for reparation in terms of the efforts of the Pitt government to intervene, see Bruce, *An Historical View*.
21. Halhed, *Grammar*, i–ii, ii (1778).
22. Contrary to Halhed's suggestion, Majeed argues that 'the main reason why Jones [wished] to compose a reliable digest of Indian laws. . . was to check the power of pandits in the court' (*Ungoverned Imaginings*, 19). He argues that the emphasis placed by British administrators on a sensitivity to local customs was ultimately an attempt 'to legitimize British rule in an Indian idiom' (22). Musselwhite similarly explains the growing emphasis on the importance of developing an informed understanding of native practices in terms of 'the increasing involvement of the East India Company in Indian affairs, first by strategies of "dual control", then by treaties of alliance, then by control of the revenue supplies and finally by the exercise of direct authority' ('Trial', 81).
23. See the extended historical account in the first volume of the *Annual Asiatic Register* (1799); and Maurice, *Modern History*.
24. In opposition to this view, Bayly suggests that Haileybury College and Wellesley's Fort William College were designed to isolate British civil servants 'from "the climate and the vices of the people of India" and the people's "peculiar depravity" . . . To the men of Wellesley's generation, young civil servants could only be released from dependence on Indians by command of their language' (*Imperial Meridian*, 150).
25. Marshall (*Problems of Empire*) and Musselwhite ('Trial') suggest that these concerns were accentuated by the hostility that was generated

by men who used the wealth they acquired in India to buy parliamentary seats.

26. Maurice, *Modern History*, I, 68.
27. Leask notes that Robert Southey was also 'taken to task by the evangelical John Foster in his review of *Kehama* for endorsing "improbable" fictions and being contaminated by Hindu religion' (review of *Ungoverned Imaginings*, 245).
28. Bayly argues that '[t]he Protestant empire was reinforced by the "governing race" principle which emphasised the fitness of Britons to rule by virtue of their "moral independency" and their understanding of the rule of law' (*Imperial Meridian*, 109).
29. Viswanathan cites as 'the central paradox of British deliberations on the curriculum as prescribed for both England and India' the point that, 'while Englishmen of all ages could enjoy and appreciate exotic tales, romantic narrative, adventure stories, and mythological literature for their charm and even derive instruction from them, their colonial subjects were believed incapable of doing so because they lacked the prior mental and moral cultivation required for literature – especially their own – to have any instructive value for them' (*Masks of Conquest*, 5).
30. Macauley, '1835 Minute', 91 (1835).
31. Ibid., 92–3.
32. Viswanathan, *Masks of Conquest*, 141.
33. Bayly, *Imperial Meridian*, 146. See, for instance, De Quincey's essay, 'How to Write English', 55–64.

CONCLUSION: ROMANTIC REVISIONS

1. Reviews of Hazlitt's *Characters of Shakespeare's Plays* provide some indication of this shift. The *Edinburgh* commented that the 'book ... is written less to tell the reader what Mr. H. *knows* about Shakespeare or his writings, than to explain to them what he *feels* about them – and *why* he feels so – and thinks that all who profess to love poetry should feel likewise' (28 (1817): 472). The *Quarterly* commented that 'Mr. Hazlitt does not undertake to make us understand the poet better, and in truth he is sometimes not very intelligible himself; but he endeavours to persuade us that, without his assistance, we shall be incapable of *feeling* his beauties' (18 (1817–18): 458; emphasis added).
2. Coleridge, *Works*, VII. 2, 158.
3. Roe, *Politics of Nature*, 144, 153, 71.
4. Thompson, 'Disenchantment', 36.
5. Roe, *Politics of Nature*, 4–5, 153.
6. Roe concludes his study of Wordsworth's and Coleridge's radical political commitments from 1793–98 in *The Radical Years*, for instance,

by suggesting that 'it was failure that made Wordsworth a poet' (275). Importantly, Roe's study emphasizes their immersion within a milieu committed to this wider idea of the political role of literature.

7. For a reading of *Edmund Oliver* in terms of Lloyd's relation to Coleridge and his contemporaries, see Allen, 'Charles Lloyd'.

8. Parrinder, 'Authors', 100–2.

9. Simpson, *Romanticism*, 159.

10. Wordsworth capitalizes these words throughout the Preface. I retain the capitals because they reinforce the point that arguments about poetry are also necessarily arguments about the social role or distinction of the poet, which necessarily depend upon the relationship of the poet to a particular interpretation of the reading community. I have also preserved Wordsworth's insistently gendered interpretation of these roles.

11. Although he does not develop an analysis of the ways this Enlightenment subtext authorizes Wordsworth's arguments about poetry in the Preface, Parrinder similarly notes that the 'theory of poetic language that it puts forward seems to promise a complete emancipation of poetry from the tyranny of literature and its conventions' ('Authors' 48).

12. Quoted in Jones, *The Charity School Movement*, 74.

13. Coleridge, *Works*, VII. 2. 81.

14. Eagleton, *Function of Criticism*, 123–4.

15. Mathias, *Pursuits of Literature*, IV, ii.

Bibliography

PRIMARY SOURCES

Alves, Robert. *Sketches of a History of Literature*. Edinburgh, 1794.

Bage, Robert. *Man as He Is*. 3 vols. London, 1792.

Barbauld, Anna. *An Address to the Opposers of the Repeal of the Corporation and Test Acts*. 2nd edn. London, 1790.

Barruel, Abbé. *Memoirs, Illustrating the History of Jacobinism*. Translation from the French. 4 vols. London, 1797.

Blackstone, Sir William. *Commentaries on the Laws of England*. 4 vols. Oxford, 1765–69.

Boswell, James. *The Life of Samuel Johnson*, ed. George Hill, vol. 1. New York, NY: Harper and Brothers, 1904.

Bowles, John. *Letters of the Ghost of Alfred Addressed to the Hon. Thomas Erskine and the Hon. Charles James Fox on the Occasion of the State Trials at the Close of the Year 1794 and the Beginning of the Year 1795*. 2nd edn. London, 1798.

A *Second Letter to the Right Hon. Charles James Fox, upon the Matter of Libel*. London, 1792.

A *Brief Reply to the Observations of Ben. Bousfield, Esq. on Mr. Burke's Pamphlet, Respecting the Revolution in France*. Dublin, 1791.

Bruce, John. *An Historical View of Plans for the Government of East India and the Regulation of Trade with the West Indies, and Outlines of a Plan of Foreign Government, and of Domestic Administration, for the Asiatic Interests of Great Britain*. London, 1793.

Burdon, William. *Various Thoughts on Politics, Morality, and Literature*. Newcastle upon Tyne, 1800.

Burke, Edmund. *The Works of the Right Honourable Edmund Burke*, new edn, vol. 5. London, 1808.

Burney, Charles. *A General History of Music, from the Earliest Ages to the Present Period*. 4 vols. London, 1776.

Coleridge, Samuel Taylor. *The Collected Works of Samuel Taylor Coleridge*, ed. Kathleen Coburn. 14 vols. London: Routledge and Princeton University Press, 1969–93.

Lectures and Notes on Shakespeare and Other English Poets, compiled by T. Ashe. London: George Bell and Sons, 1902.

Considerations on Mr. Paine's Pamphlet, Called the Rights of Man. Edinburgh, 1791.

Cowper, William. *The Letters and Prose of William Cowper*, ed. James King and Charles Ryskamp, vol. 4. Oxford: Clarendon Press, 1984.

Crichton, Alexander. *An Inquiry Into the Nature and Origin of Mental Derangement*. 2 vols. London, 1798.

Cumberland, Richard. *The Observer: Being a Collection of Moral, Literary and Familiar Essays*. 4th edn. 4 vols. London, 1791.

Darwin, Erasmus. *Zoonomia; Or, The Laws of Organic Life*. 2nd edn, vol. 1. London, 1796.

Day, Thomas. *A Letter to Arthur Young Esq. On the Bill Now Depending in Parliament to Prevent the Exportation of Wool*. London, 1788.

  The Letters of Marius: Or, Reflections upon the Peace, the East-India Bill, and the Present Crisis. 3rd edn. London, 1784.

De Constant, B. H. 'On the Liberty of the Press; or an Enquiry How Far Government May Safely Allow the Publication of Political Pamphlets, Essays, and Periodical Works'. *Pamphleteer* 6 (1815): 205–38.

De Quincey, Thomas. *Uncollected Writings*. 2 vols. London, 1892.

A Defence of the Constitution of England against the Libels That Have Been Lately Published on It; Particularly in Paine's Pamphlet on the Rights of Man. n.p., 1791.

D'Israeli, Isaac. *Curiosities of Literature, Consisting of Anecdotes, Characters, Sketches and Observations, Literary, Critical, and Historical*. London, 1791.

Dissertations and Miscellaneous Pieces Relating to the History and Antiquities, the Arts, Sciences, and Literature, of Asia. Dublin, 1793.

Donaldson, John. *Letter to the Right Hon. William Pitt, Shewing How Crimes May be Prevented, and the People Made Happy*. London, 1796.

Drake, Nathan. *Essays, Biographical, Critical, and Historical, Illustrative of the* Tatler, Spectator, *and* Guardian. 3 vols. London, 1805.

Eaton, Daniel Isaac. *The Pernicious Effects of the Art of Printing upon Society, Exposed*. London, 1793.

Edgeworth, Maria. *Maria Edgeworth's Novels*, vol. 1. London, 1893.

Erskine, Thomas. *The Speeches of Thomas Erskine*. Comp. James Ridgway. 2nd edn. 4 vols. London, 1813.

Fenwick, Eliza. *Secresy; or, The Ruin on the Rock*. 1795, ed. Isobel Grundy. Peterborough, ON: Broadview Literary Texts, 1994.

Foster, John. *Critical Essays Contributed to the* Eclectic Review, ed. J. E. Ryland. 2 vols. London, 1868.

Gerrald, Joseph. *The Trial of Joseph Gerrald*. Edinburgh, 1794.

Godwin, William. *Political and Philosophical Writings of William Godwin*, ed. Mark Philp. 7 vols. London: William Pickering, 1993.

  Things as They Are, or The Adventures of Caleb Williams, ed. Maurice Hindle. London: Penguin, 1988.

Gould, Thomas. *A Vindication of the Right Honourable Edmund Burke's Reflections on the Revolution in France, in Answer to All His Opponents*. n.p., 1791.

Green, Thomas. *An Examination of the Leading Principles of the New System of Morals, as That Principle is Stated and Applied in Mr. Godwin's Enquiry Concerning Political Justice.* London, 1798.
  Slight Observations upon Paine's Pamphlet. London: 1791.
Halhed, Nathaniel Brassey. *A Grammar of the Bengal Language.* Bengal, 1778.
Hamilton, Charles, trans. *The Hèdaya, Or Guide; A Commentary on the Mussalman Laws*, vol. 1. London, 1791.
Hardy, Thomas. *Memoir of Thomas Hardy. Written By Himself.* London, 1832.
Hays, Mary. *Appeal to the Men of Great Britain on Behalf of Women.* 1798, ed. Gina Luria. New York: Garland, 1974.
  Letters and Essays, Moral and Miscellaneous. London, 1793.
  Memoirs of Emma Courtney, ed. Eleanor Ty. Oxford University Press, 1996.
Hazlitt, William. *The Complete Works of William Hazlitt*, ed. P. P. Howe. 21 vols. London: Dent, 1930–34.
Hervey, Frederick. *A New Friend on an Old Subject.* London, 1791.
Holcroft, Thomas. *Hugh Trevor*, ed. Seamus Deane. 1794–7; Oxford University Press, 1983.
Johnson, Samuel. *The Yale Edition of the Works of Samuel Johnson*, ed. W. J. Bate and Albrecht B. Strauss, vol. 4. New Haven: Yale University Press, 1969.
Jones, Sir William. *The Collected Works of Sir William Jones.* 6 vols. London, 1799.
Keir, James. *An Account of the Life and Writings of Thomas Day, Esq.* London, 1791.
King, Walter. *Two Sermons Preached at Gray's Inn Capel, on Friday April 19, 1793.* London, 1793.
Lackington, James. *Memoirs of the First Forty-Five Years of the Life of James Lackington.* London, 1792.
Lloyd, Charles. *Edmund Oliver.* 1798. Oxford: Woodstock, 1990.
Macaulay, Catherine. *Letters on Education, with Observations on Religious and Metaphysical Subjects.* London, 1790.
Macaulay, Thomas. '1835 Minute on Education in India'. *Indian Musalmans: Being Three Letters Reprinted from the 'Times'; With an Appendix Containing Lord Macaulay's Minute On Education in India.* Ed. William Nassau Lees. London, 1871.
MacDonald, Thomas. *Thoughts on the Public Duties of Private Life, with Reference to Present Circumstances and Opinions.* London, 1795.
Mason, George. *A British Freeholder's Address to His Countrymen, on Thomas Paine's Rights of Man.* n.p., 1791.
Mathias, T. J. *The Pursuits of Literature, or What You Will: A Satirical Poem in Dialogue.* 3rd edn. London, 1797.
Maurice, Thomas. *Indian Antiquities: or Dissertations of Hindostan.* 7 vols. New Delhi: Concept, 1984.

The Modern History of Hindostan. 2 vols. London, 1802–03.

More, Hannah. *Essays on Various Subjects, Principally Designed for Young Ladies.* 5th edn. London, 1791.

O'Connor, Arthur. *The Measures of Ministry to Prevent a Revolution Are the Certain Means of Bringing It On.* 3rd edn. London, 1794.

Ouseley, William, ed. *The Oriental Collections: Consisting of Original Essays and Dissertations, Translations and Miscellaneous Tracts of Asia.* 3 vols. London, 1797–99.

Persian Miscellanies: An Essay to Facilitate the Reading of Persian Manuscripts. London, 1795.

Paine, Thomas. *Rights of Man*, ed. Henry Collins. Harmondsworth: Penguin, 1969.

Pennant, Thomas. *The Literary Life of Thomas Pennant, Esq.* London, 1793.

Place, Francis. *Autobiography of Francis Place*, ed. Mary Thale. 1824; Cambridge University Press, 1972.

Polwhele, Richard. *The Unsex'd Females: A Poem, Addressed to the Author of* The Pursuits of Literature. London, 1798.

Pratt, Samuel. *Gleanings in England: Descriptive of the Countenance, Mind, and Character of the Country*, vol. 4. London, 1799.

Priestley, Joseph. *An Examination of Dr. Reid's Inquiry into the Human Mind on the Principles of Common Sense.* 2nd edn. London, 1775.

Letter to the Right Honourable William Pitt on the Subject of Toleration and Church Establishment. London, 1787.

The Proper Objects of Education in the Present State of the World. London, 1791.

Reid, William Hamilton. *The Rise and Dissolution of the Infidel Societies in this Metropolis.* London, 1800.

Remarks on Mr. Paine's Pamphlet, Called the Rights of Man. Dublin, 1791.

Robison, John. *Proofs of a Conspiracy against all the Religions and Governments of Europe, Carried On in the Secret Meetings of Free Masons, Illuminati, and Reading Societies.* 5th edn. Dublin, 1798.

Shelley, Mary. *Frankenstein or the Modern Prometheus*, ed. Marilyn Butler. 1818; Oxford University Press, 1993.

Shelley, Percy Bysshe. *The Complete Works of Percy Bysshe Shelley*, ed. Roger Ingpen and Walter E. Peck. Vol. 7. London: Ernest Benn; New York: Gordian Press, 1965.

Southey, Robert. *Essays, Moral and Political.* Vol. 1. Shannon: Irish University Press, 1971.

Spence, Thomas. 'The Important Trial of Thomas Spence'. *Spence and His Political Works.* 1803; Leamington Spa: Courier Press, 1917. 33–75.

TEN MINUTES ADVICE TO THE PEOPLE OF ENGLAND, On the Two Slavery-Bills Intended to Be Brought into Parliament the Present Session. London, 1795.

Thelwall, John. *Peaceful Discussion and Not Tumultuary Violence the Means of Redressing National Grievance.* London, 1795.

Poems Written Chiefly in Retirement, with Memoirs of the Life of the Author. London, 1801.

The Speech of John Thelwall at the Second Meeting of the LCS and Other Friends of Reform, Held Near Copenhagen-House, 12 November, 1795. London, 1795.

Travell, F. T. *The Duties of the Poor, Particularly in the Education of Their Children.* 5th edn. London, 1799.

Von Gentz, Friedrich. 'Reflections on the Liberty of the Press in Great Britain'. *Pamphleteer* 15 (1820): 455–96.

Wollstonecraft, Mary. *The Works of Mary Wollstonecraft*, ed. Janet Todd and Marilyn Butler. 7 vols. London: William Pickering, 1989.

Wordsworth, William. *The Poetical Works of William Wordsworth*, ed. E. de Selincourt and Helen Darbishire, vol. 2. Oxford: Clarendon Press, 1944.

The Prelude, or Growth of a Poet's Mind, ed. Ernest de Selincourt. London: Oxford University Press, 1926.

Young, Arthur. *The Example of France a Warning to Britain.* 3rd edn. London, 1793.

SECONDARY SOURCES

Allen, Richard C. 'Charles Lloyd, Coleridge, and *Edmund Oliver*'. *Studies in Romanticism* 35 (1996): 245–94.

Altick, Richard. *The English Common Reader.* University of Chicago Press, 1957.

Anderson, Benedict. *Imagined Communities: Reflections on the Origin and Spread of Nationalism.* rev. edn. London: Verso, 1991.

Ashfield, Andrew, ed. *Romantic Women Poets, 1770–1838.* Manchester University Press, 1995.

Aspinall, Arthur. *Politics and the Press, 1780–1850.* 1949. Brighton: Harvester, 1973.

Baker, Keith Michael. 'Defining the Public Sphere in Eighteenth-Century France: Variations on a Theme by Habermas'. Calhoun, *Habermas*, 181–211.

Baldick, Chris. *The Social Mission of English Criticism, 1848–1932.* Oxford: Clarendon Press, 1987.

Barrell, John. *English Literature in History: An Equal, Wide Survey.* London: Hutchinson, 1983.

'Imagining the King's Death: The Arrest of Richard Brothers'. *History Workshop Journal* 37 (1994): 1–32.

The Political Theory of Painting from Reynolds to Hazlitt. New Haven: Yale University Press, 1986.

Bayly, C. A. *Imperial Meridian: The British Empire and the World, 1780–1830.* London: Longman, 1989.

Indian Society and the Making of the British Empire. Cambridge University Press, 1988.

Benjamin, Walter. 'Theses on the Philosophy of History'. *Illuminations*, ed. Hannah Arendt, trans. Harry Zhon. New York: Schocken, 1969. 253–64.

Blakey, Dorothy. *The Minerva Press*. London. Printed for the Bibliographical Society of the Oxford University Press, 1939.

Bohls, Elizabeth A. *Women Travel Writers and the Language of Aesthetics, 1716–1818*. Cambridge University Press, 1995.

Booth, Alan. 'The Memory of the Liberty of the Press: The Suppression of Radical Writing in the 1790s'. *Writing and Censorship in Britain*, ed. Paul Hyland and Neil Sammells. London: Routledge, 1992. 107–22.

Bourdieu, Pierre. *Distinction: A Social Critique of the Judgement of Taste*, trans. Richard Nice. Cambridge, MA: Harvard University Press, 1984.

Breen, Jennifer, ed. *Women Romantics Writing in Prose, 1785–1832*. London: Everyman-Dent, 1996.

Butler, Judith. *Gender Trouble: Feminism and the Subversion of Identity*. New York: Routledge, 1990.

Butler, Marilyn. Introduction. *Burke, Paine, Godwin, and the Revolution Controversy*. Cambridge University Press, 1984. 1–17.

    'Culture's Medium: The Role of the Review'. Curran, *Cambridge Companion to British Romanticism*, 120–47.

    Romantics, Rebels, and Reactionaries: English Literature and Its Background, 1760–1830. Oxford University Press, 1982.

Calhoun, Craig. Introduction. *Habermas and the Public Sphere*, ed. and intro. Calhoun. Cambridge, MA: MIT Press, 1992.

Chandler, James. *Wordsworth's Second Nature: A Study of the Poetry and Politics*. University of Chicago Press, 1994.

Christensen, Jerome. *Practicing Enlightenment: Hume and the Formation of a Literary Career*. Madison, WN: University of Wisconsin Press, 1987.

Claeys, Gregory. 'The Origins of the Rights of Labour: Republicanism, Commerce, and the Construction of Modern Social Theory in Britain, 1796–1805'. *Journal of Modern History* 66 (1994): 249–90.

    Introduction. *Political Writings of the 1790s*, ed. and intro. Claeys, vol. 1. London: William Pickering, 1995. xvii–lvi.

    Introduction. *The Politics of English Jacobinism: Writings of John Thelwall*. ed. and intro. Claeys. University Park, PA: Pennsylvania State University Press, 1985.

Colley, Linda. *Britons: Forging the Nation, 1707–1837*. London: Pimlico, 1992.

    'Whose Nation? Class and National Consciousness, 1750–1830'. *Past & Present* 113 (1986): 97–117.

Collins, A. S. *The Profession of Letters, 1780–1832*. London: George Routledge and Sons, 1928.

Connolly, Claire. Introduction. Maria Edgeworth, *Letters For Literary Ladies*, ed. and intro. Connolly. 1795. Everyman: London, 1993.

Copley, Stephen, and John Whale, eds. *Beyond Romanticism: New Approaches to Texts and Contexts, 1780–1832.* London: Routledge, 1992.

Corfield, Penelope. 'Class by Name and Number in Eighteenth-Century Britain'. *History* 72 (1987): 38–61.

ed. *Language, History and Class.* Cambridge: Basil Blackwell, 1991.

Power and the Professions in Britain, 1700–1850. London: Routledge, 1995.

Craig, Cairns. 'City of Words'. *New Statesman* 27 October 1989: 39–40.

Crawford, Robert. *Devolving English Literature.* Oxford: Clarendon Press, 1992.

Cummings, Peter. ' "Virtual English": Multimedia Presentation in Literature Teaching'. *ACCUTE Newsletter* (September 1996): 13–18.

Curran, Stuart, 'Women Readers, Women Writers'. *The Cambridge Companion to British Romanticism.* ed. Curran. Cambridge University Press, 1993.

Darnton, Robert. *The Business of Enlightenment: A Publishing History of the 'Encyclopedie', 1775–1800.* Cambridge, MA: Harvard University Press, 1979.

The Great Cat Massacre, and Other Episodes in French Cultural History. N.Y.: Vintage Books, 1984.

The Kiss of Lamourette: Reflections in Cultural History. N. Y.: W. W. Norton & Co., 1990.

'Sounding the Literary Market Place in Prerevolutionary France'. *Eighteenth-Century Studies* 17 (1984): 477–92.

Davidoff, Leonore, and Catherine Hall. *Family Fortunes: Men and Women of the English Middle Class, 1780–1830.* London: Routledge, 1987.

Davies, Kate. 'A Moral Purchase: Femininity, Commerce and Abolition, 1788–1792. Unpublished paper, 1997.

Dictionary of National Biography, ed. Sidney Lee. 70 Vols. London: Smith, Elder, 1885–1912.

Dinwiddy, John. 'Conceptions of the Revolution in England'. *The Transformation of Political Culture: England and Germany in the Late Eighteenth Century*, ed. Eckhart Hellmuth. Oxford University Press, 1990.

Doyle, Brian. *English and Englishness.* London: Routledge, 1989.

Eagleton, Terry. *The Function of Criticism.* London: Verso, 1984.

Eisenstein, Elizabeth L. *Print Culture and Enlightenment Thought.* Chapel Hill: Hanes Foundation, 1986.

The Printing Press as an Agent of Change: Communications and Cultural Transformations in Modern Europe. 2 vols. Cambridge University Press, 1979.

Eley, Geoff. 'Nations, Publics, and Political Cultures: Placing Habermas in the Nineteenth Century'. Calhoun, *Habermas*, 289–339.

Elshtain, Jean Bethke. *Public Man, Private Woman: Women in Social and Political Thought.* Princeton University Press, 1981.

Favret, Mary. *Romantic Correspondence: Women, Politics, and the Fiction of Letters.* Cambridge University Press, 1994.

Ferguson, Frances. 'Romantic Studies'. Greenblatt and Gunn, *Redrawing the Boundaries*, 100–29.

Ferguson, Moira. *Subject to Others: British Women Writers and Colonial Slavery, 1670–1834.* London: Routledge, 1992.

Fraser, Nancy. 'Rethinking the Public Sphere: A Contribution to the Critique of Actually Existing Democracy'. Calhoun, *Habermas*, 109–42.

Frye, Northrop. *The Anatomy of Criticism: Four Essays*. Princeton University Press, 1957.

Fuss, Diana. *Essentially Speaking: Feminism, Nature and Difference*. New York: Routledge, 1989.

Gallop, G. I. Introduction. *Pig's Meat; or, Lessons for the Swinish Multitude: The Selected Writings of Thomas Spence, Radical and Pioneer Land Reformer*, ed. Gallop. Nottingham: Spokesman, 1982.

Garnham, Nicholas. 'The Media and the Public Sphere'. Calhoun, *Habermas*, 359–76.

Gilmartin, Kevin. *Print Politics: The Press and Radical Opposition in Early Nineteenth-Century England*. Cambridge University Press, 1996.

Goldberg, Brian. ' "Ministry More Palpable": William Wordsworth and the Making of Romantic Professionalism'. *Studies in Romanticism* 36 (1997): 327–47.

Goldgar, Anne. *Impolite Learning: Conduct and Community in the Republic of Letters, 1680–1750.* New Haven: Yale University Press, 1995.

Goodman, Dena. *The Republic of Letters: A Cultural History of the French Enlightenment*. Ithaca: Cornell, 1994.

 'Seriousness of Purpose: Salonnières, Philosophes, and the Shaping of the Eighteenth-Century Salon'. *Proceedings of the Annual Meeting of the Western Society for French History* 15 (1988): 111–18.

Goodwin, Albert. *The Friends of Liberty: The English Democratic Movement in the Age of the French Revolution*. Cambridge, MA: Harvard University Press, 1979.

Greenblatt, Stephen, and Giles Gunn, eds. *Redrawing the Boundaries: The Transformation of English and American Studies*. New York: MLA, 1992.

Guest, Harriet. 'The Dream of a Common Language: Hannah More and Mary Wollstonecraft'. *Textual Practice* 9 (Summer 1995): 303.

Habermas, Jurgen. 'Further Reflections on the Public Sphere'. Calhoun, *Habermas*, 421–79.

 The Structural Transformation of the Public Sphere. Trans. T. Burger and F. Lawrence. Cambridge, MA: MIT Press, 1989.

Handover, P. M. *Printing in London: From 1746 to Modern Times*. Cambridge, MA: Harvard University Press, 1960.

Hohendahl, Peter. *The Institution of Criticism*. Ithaca: Cornell University Press, 1982.

Hulme, Peter, and Ludmilla Jordanova, eds. *The Enlightenment and its Shadows*. London: Routledge, 1990.

Irwin, Raymond. *The English Library*. London: George Allen and Unwin, 1966.

Iversen, Margaret. 'Imagining the Republic: The Sign and Sexual Politics in France'. Hulme and Jordanova, ed., *The Enlightenment*, 123–39.

Johnson, Nancy. 'Rights, Property, and the Law in the English Jacobin Novel'. *Mosaic* 27 (1994): 99–120.

Jones, Gareth Stedman. *Languages of Class*. Cambridge University Press, 1983.

Jones, M. G. *The Charity School Movement*. 1938. London: Frank Cass, 1964.

Jordanova, Ludmilla. 'The Authoritarian Response'. Hulme and Jordanova, eds., *The Enlightenment*, 201–16.

Introduction. *Languages of Nature: Critical Essays on Science and Literature*, ed. and intro. Jordanova. London: Free Association Books, 1986.

Kaplan, Cora. 'Wild Nights: Pleasure/Sexuality/Feminism'. *Sea Changes: Culture and Feminism*. London: Verso, 1986. 31–56.

Kelly, Gary. 'Romantic Fiction'. Curran, *Cambridge Companion to British Romanticism*, 196–215.

Women, Writing, and Revolution, 1790–1827. Oxford: Clarendon Press, 1993.

Kernan, Alvin. *Printing Technology, Letters and Samuel Johnson*. Princeton University Press, 1987.

Klancher, Jon. 'English Romanticism and Cultural Production'. *The New Historicism*. Ed. H. Aram Veeser. New York: Routledge, 1989. 77–88.

The Making of English Reading Audiences, 1790–1832. Madison, WN: University of Wisconsin Press, 1991.

Kramnick, Isaac. *Republicanism and Bourgeois Radicalism: Political Ideology in Late Eighteenth-Century England and America*. Ithaca: Cornell University Press, 1990.

Landes, Joan. *Women and the Public Sphere in the Age of the French Revolution*. Ithaca: Cornell University Press, 1988.

Langford, Paul. *A Polite and Commercial People: England 1727–1783*. Oxford: Clarendon Press, 1989.

Leask, Nigel. *British Romantic Writers and the East: Anxieties of Empire*. Cambridge University Press, 1992.

The Politics of Imagination in Coleridge's Political Thought. London: St. Martin's, 1988.

Review of *Ungoverned Imaginings: James Mill's 'History of British India' and Orientalism*, Javed Majeed. *History Workshop Journal* 36 (1993): 242–49.

Levinson, Marjorie. *Wordsworth's Great Period Poems; Four Essays*. Cambridge University Press, 1986.

Jerome McGann, Marilyn Butler, and Paul Hamilton. *Rethinking Historicism: Readings in Romantic History*. Oxford: Basil Blackwell, 1989.

Lipking, Lawrence. 'Inventing the Common Reader: Samuel Johnson and the Canon'. *Interpretation and Cultural History*, ed. Joan H. Pittock and Andrew Wear. London: Macmillan, 1991. 153–74.

Liu, Alan. *Wordsworth: The Sense of History*. Stanford University Press, 1989.

Lonsdale, Roger, ed. *The New Oxford Book of Eighteenth-Century Verse*. Oxford University Press, 1987.

Majeed, Javed. *Ungoverned Imaginings: James Mill's* The History of British India *and Orientalism*. Oxford: Clarendon Press, 1992.

Marshall, P. J. *The Impeachment of Warren Hastings*. London: Oxford University Press, 1965.

　Problems of Empire: Britain and India, 1757–1813. London: George Allen and Unwin, 1968.

McCalman, Iain. *Radical Underworld: Prophets, Revolutionaries and Pornographers in London, 1795–1840*. Cambridge University Press, 1988.

McGann, Jerome. Introduction. *The New Oxford Book of Romantic Period Verse*. Oxford University Press, 1993.

　The Romantic Ideology: A Critical Investigation. University of Chicago Press, 1983.

McLachlan, H. *English Education Under the Test Acts: Being the History of the Non-Conformist Academies, 1662–1820*. Manchester University Press, 1931.

Mee, Jon. *Dangerous Enthusiasm: William Blake and the Culture of Radicalism in the 1790s*. Oxford: Clarendon Press, 1992.

Mellor, Anne K., ed. *Romanticism and Feminism*. Bloomington: Indiana University Press, 1988.

　and Richard E. Matlack. *British Literature, 1780–1832*. Fort Worth: Harcourt Brace College Publishers, 1996.

Midgely, Claire. *Women Against Slavery: The British Campaigns, 1780–1870*. London: Routledge, 1992.

Miles, Robert. *Gothic Writing, 1750–1820: A Genealogy*. London: Routledge, 1993.

Mills, Sara. *Discourses of Difference: An Analysis of Women's Travel Writing and Colonialism*. London: Routledge, 1991.

Morgan, Peter F. *Literary Critics and Reviewers in Early Nineteenth-Century Britain*. London: Crook Helm, 1983.

Musselwhite, David. 'Reflections on Burke's *Reflections*'. Hulme and Jordanova, *The Enlightenment*, 142–62.

　'The Trial of Warren Hastings'. *Literature, Politics and Theory: Papers from the Essex Conference 1976–84*, ed. Francis Barker, Peter Hulme, Margaret Iversen, and Diana Loxley. London: Methuen, 1987.

Myers, Mitzi. 'Impeccable Governesses, Rational Dames, and Moral Mothers: Mary Wollstonecraft and the Female Tradition in Georgian Children's Books'. *Children's Literature* 14 (1986).

　'Reform or Ruin: 'A Revolution in Female Manners.'' *Studies in Eighteenth-Century Culture* 11 (1982): 199–216.

Neuburg, Victor. *The Penny Histories: A Study of Chapbooks for Young Readers over Two Centuries*. London: Oxford University Press, 1988.

Popular Literature: A History and Guide. Harmondsworth: Penguin, 1977.

Newman, Gerald. *The Rise of English Nationalism: A Cultural History, 1740–1830*. New York: St Martin's, 1987.

Palmer, D. J. *The Rise of English Studies*. London: Oxford University Press, 1965.

Parrinder, Patrick. *Authors and Authority: English and American Criticism, 1750–1990*. London: MacMillan, 1991.

Pateman, Carole. 'The Fraternal Social Contract'. *Civil Society and the State: New European Perspectives*, ed. John Keane. London: Verso, 1988. 101–28.

Peardon, Thomas. *The Transition in English Historical Writing, 1769–1830*. New York: Columbia University Press, 1933.

Pedersen, Susan. 'Hannah More Meets Simple Simon: Tracts, Chapbooks, and Popular Culture in Late Eighteenth-Century England'. *Journal of British Studies* 25 (1986): 84–113.

Perkin, Harold. *The Origins of Modern English Society, 1780–1880*. London: Routledge, 1969.

Perkins, David, ed. *English Romantic Writers*. New York: Harcourt Brace, 1994.

Philp, Mark. *Godwin's Political Justice*. London: Duckworth, 1986.
  'Thompson, Godwin, and the French Revolution'. *History Workshop Journal* 39 (1995): 89–101.

Pilbeam, Pamela M. *The Middle Classes in Europe 1789–1914*. Basingstoke: MacMillan, 1970.

Plant, Marjorie. *The English Book Trade: An Economic History of the Making and Sale of Books*. 2nd edn. London: Allen and Unwin, 1965.

Pocock, J. G. A. *The Machiavellian Moment: Florentine Political Thought and the Atlantic Republican Tradition*. Princeton University Press, 1975.
  Virtue, Commerce, and History: Essays on Political Thought and History, Chiefly in the Eighteenth Century. Cambridge University Press, 1985.

Poovey, Mary. *The Proper Lady and the Woman Writer: Ideology as Style in the Works of Mary Wollstonecraft, Mary Shelley, and Jane Austen*. University of Chicago Press, 1984.

Porter, Roy. 'The Enlightenment in England'. *The Enlightenment in National Context*, ed. Roy Porter and M. Teich. Cambridge University Press, 1981.

Pratt, Mary Louise. *Imperial Eyes: Travel Writing and Transculturation*. N.Y.: Routledge, 1992.

Reiss, Timothy J. *The Meaning of Literature*. Ithaca: Cornell University Press, 1992.

Richardson, Alan. *Literature, Education, and Romanticism: Reading as Social Practice, 1780–1832*. Cambridge University Press, 1994.

Robbins, Bruce. Introduction. *The Phantom Public Sphere*, ed. Robbins. Minneapolis: University of Minnesota Press, 1993.

Robbins, Caroline. *The Eighteenth-Century Commonwealthman*. 1959. New York: Athenaeum, 1988.

Roe, Nicholas. *The Politics of Nature: Wordsworth and Some Contemporaries*. London: Macmillan, 1992.

    Wordsworth and Coleridge: The Radical Years. Oxford: Clarendon Press, 1988.

Roper, Derek. *Reviewing Before the Edinburgh, 1788–1802*. London: Methuen, 1978.

Rushdie, Salman. *The Satanic Verses*. New York: Viking, 1988.

Ryan, Mary P. 'Gender and Access: Women's Politics in Nineteenth-Century America'. Calhoun, *Habermas*, 259–88.

Said, Edward. *Orientalism*. London: Penguin, 1978.

Simpson, David. 'Romanticism, Criticism, and Theory'. Curran, *Cambridge Companion to British Romanticism*, 1–24.

    Romanticism, Nationalism, and the Revolt Against Theory. University of Chicago Press, 1993.

    Wordsworth's Historical Imagination: The Poetry of Displacement. New York, NY: Methuen, 1987.

Siskin, Clifford. *The Work of Writing: Literature and Social Change in Britain, 1700–1830*. Baltimore: Johns Hopkins University Press, 1998.

Smith, Olivia. *The Politics of Language, 1791–1819*. Oxford: Clarendon Press, 1984.

Stallybrass, Peter, and Allon White. *The Politics and Poetics of Transgression*. London: Methuen, 1986.

Stewart, Susan. 'The State of Cultural Theory and the Future of Literary Form'. *Profession* (1993): 12–15.

Stone, L. 'Literacy and Education in England, 1640–1900.' *Past and Present* 42 (1969): 69–139.

Stone, Marjorie. 'President's Report: The Widening Gyre'. *ACCUTE Newsletter* (September 1996): 2–8.

Suleri, Sara. *The Rhetoric of English India*. University of Chicago Press, 1992.

Thale, Mary. 'London Debating Societies in the 1790s'. *Historical Journal* 32.1 (1989): 57–86.

    Introduction. *Selections from the Papers of the London Corresponding Society, 1792–1799*. Cambridge University Press, 1983. vii–xxix.

Thompson, E. P. 'Benevolent Mr. Godwin'. *London Review of Books*. 8 July 1993. 14–15.

    'Disenchantment or Default? A Lay Sermon': *The Romantics: England in a Revolutionary Age*. New York: The New Press, 1997, 33–74.

    'Eighteenth-Century English Society: Class Struggle Without Class?' *Journal of Social History* 3.2 (1978): 133–65.

    'Hunting the Jacobin Fox'. *The Romantics*.

    The Making of the English Working Class. London: Penguin, 1980.

    The Poverty of Theory. London: Merlin Press, 1978.

Todd, Janet. *Feminist Literary History*. New York: Routledge, 1988.

    The Sign of Angelica: Women, Writing and Fiction, 1660–1800. London: Virago, 1989.

Trivadi, Harish. *Colonial Transactions: English Literature and India*. Manchester University Press, 1993.

Tyson, Gerald, P. *Joseph Johnson: A Liberal Publisher*. University of Iowa Press, 1979.

Vincent, David. *Literacy and Popular Culture: England 1750–1914*. Cambridge University Press, 1989.

Viswanathan, Gauri. *Masks of Conquest: Literary Study and British Rule in India*. New York: Columbia University Press, 1989.

West, Cornell. 'The New Cultural Politics of Difference'. *Out There: Marginalization and Contemporary Cultures*, ed. Russell Ferguson, Martha Gever, Trin T. Minh-ha, and Cornell West. Cambridge, MA: MIT Press, 1990. 19–38.

Wiles, Roy McKeen. 'The Relish for Reading in Provincial England Two Centuries Ago'. *The Widening Circle: Essays on the Circulation of Literature in Eighteenth-Century Europe*, ed. Paul J. Korshin. Philadelphia: University of Pennsylvania Press, 1976. 87–115.

Williams, Raymond. *Culture and Society, 1780–1950*. New York: Harper, 1958.

   Keywords: A Vocabulary of Culture and Society. Fontana: Crook Helm, 1976.

   Foreword. Jordanova, *Languages of Nature* 10–14.

Wood, Marcus. *Radical Satire and Print Culture, 1790–1822*. Oxford: Clarendon Press, 1994.

Woollacott, Martin. 'A Ceasefire – But No Surrender'. *Guardian*. 3 September 1994, *Outlook*.

Worrall, David. *Radical Culture: Discourse, Resistance, and Surveillance, 1790–1820*. Detroit: Wayne State University Press, 1992.

Wu, Duncan, ed. *Romanticism: An Anthology*. Oxford: Blackwell, 1994.

Yachnin, Paul. 'The Politics of Theatrical Mirth: *A Midsummer Night's Dream*, *A Mad World My Masters*, and *Measure for Measure*'. *Shakespeare Quarterly* 43.1 (1992): 51–66.

Young, Robert. *White Mythologies: Writing History and the West*. London: Routledge, 1990.

Index

CAMBRIDGE STUDIES IN ROMANTICISM

GENERAL EDITORS
MARILYN BUTLER, *University of Oxford*
JAMES CHANDLER, *University of Chicago*

CPSIA information can be obtained
at www.ICGtesting.com
Printed in the USA
LVOW12s1617150717
541465LV00003B/172/P